CASE STUDIES IN PSYCHOTHERAPY

CASE STUDIES IN PSYCHOTHERAPY

THIRD EDITION

Editors

Danny Wedding

Raymond J. Corsini

THOMSON

BROOKS/COLE

Australia • Canada • Mexico • Singapore • Spain

United Kingdom • United States

Edited by Janet Tilden
Production supervision by Kim Vander Steen
Designed by Jeanne Calabrese Design
Composition by Point West, Inc.
Printed and bound by Sheridan Books

Cover image © Robert Kristofik

ISBN: 0-87581-437-9

Library of Congress Catalog Card Number: 00 134166

Wadsworth/Thomson Learning
10 Davis Drive
Belmont CA 94002-3098
USA

For information about our products, contact us:
Thomson Learning Academic Resource Center
1-800-423-0563
http://www.wadsworth.com

For permission to use material from this text, contact us by
Web: http://www.thomsonrights.com
Fax: 1-800-730-2215
Phone: 1-800-730-2214

Printed in the United States of America
15 14 13 12 11 10 9 8 7

DAVID H. BARLOW

AARON T. BECK

L. BRYCE BOYER

ALBERT ELLIS

ARNOLD A. LAZARUS

MICHAEL MANIACCI

HAROLD H. MOSAK

PEGGY PAPP

FREDERICK S. PERLS

CARL R. ROGERS

DEANE H. SHAPIRO, JR.

BARBARA S. SULLIVAN

IRVIN D. YALOM

CONTENTS

FOREWORD   IX

PREFACE   XII

1 **Psychoanalysis**

WORKING WITH A BORDERLINE PATIENT / *L. Bryce Boyer*   3

2 **Adlerian Psychotherapy**

THE CASE OF ROGER / *Harold H. Mosak and Michael Maniacci*   23

3 **Analytical Psychotherapy**

CHRISTINA / *Barbara S. Sullivan*   49

4 **Person-Centered Therapy**

THE CASE OF MRS. OAK / *Carl R. Rogers*   57

5 **Rational Emotive Behavior Therapy**

A TWENTY-THREE-YEAR-OLD WOMAN GUILTY ABOUT NOT
FOLLOWING HER PARENTS' RULES / *Albert Ellis*   81

6 **Behavior Therapy**

COVERT SENSITIZATION FOR PARAPHILIA / *David H. Barlow*   107

7 **Cognitive Therapy**

AN INTERVIEW WITH A DEPRESSED AND
SUICIDAL PATIENT / *Aaron T. Beck*   119

8 **Existential Psychotherapy**

FAT LADY / *Irwin D. Yalom*   137

9 **Gestalt Therapy**

THE CASE OF JANE / *Frederick S. Perls*   163

10 Multimodal Therapy

THE CASE OF GEORGE/*Arnold A. Lazarus*   183

11 Family Therapy

THE DAUGHTER WHO SAID NO/*Peggy Papp*   195

12 Asian Psychotherapies

MEDITATION AND PSYCHOTHERAPY:
A CASE STUDY/*Deane H. Shapiro, Jr.*   225

INDEX   243

FOREWORD

Observing an expert perform a skills-based task has always been the most effective way for an apprentice to learn a complex procedure. For this reason, studying the work of master craftsmen (and women) has always been at the heart of the apprenticeship system. This method of training is more effective when it has been preceded by instruction that allows novices to place their observations into a meaningful conceptual context. This book, which presents case studies conducted and written by experts in specific therapeutic modalities, corresponds to the apprenticeship aspect of a training program. The primary text, *Current Psychotherapies*, parallels these case studies chapter by chapter. Although a reading of that text is not necessary for a fruitful reading of these case studies, it can heighten understanding of what the therapists are doing by presenting the theoretical and applied underpinnings of their systems.

As the editors have stated in introducing "The Case of Jane" by Fritz Perls, a system of psychotherapy is an extension of its author. It is a "way of being" as well as a "way of doing." Those of us who train clinicians understand that trainees should not slavishly emulate techniques of one or another psychotherapist. To become a reincarnation of an eminent therapist is the unrealizable dream of the neophyte and adulator. Who among us can realistically dream of becoming another "Fritz?" And even if we could, would it be desirable?

All clinicians personalize the systems that they have studied and chosen to use. Their therapy reflects their personal life histories, the scripts, values, attitudes, and dispositions that form (mostly at a tacit or implicit level) the weft of that elusive fabric we call the psyche. None of us can entirely escape the conditions that have made us who we are, and our experiences inevitably get enmeshed in the treatment plan and the procedures that we use with our clients. For this reason, the therapist, as a person, becomes the primary instrument of therapy. The techniques become secondary.

Most of you who will read these case studies are motivated by an interest in improving your clinical skills. A first reading will excite a sense of profound admiration for the clinicians who worked the marvels of "therapeutic outcome" described in the studies. Their virtuosity should not discourage you from aspiring to their level of expertise. One must keep in mind that these cases are not examples of their least accomplished performances. The editors chose them precisely because they are instructive of the highly evolved clinical skills these therapists possessed at an advanced point in their careers. Although these clients challenged their resources to the utmost, they were clients who were apt, and suitable, for the treatments these therapists were prepared to provide.

Becoming a skilled clinician is like becoming skilled at any other complex human activity. It is the work of the "long-distance runner." It is building a repertoire of techniques and broad strategies that fit a consistent theoretical paradigm, honing various clinical skills, and learning to recognize the appropriate moments to use them. It is the work of fashioning coherent treatment plans for particular individuals who will be facing us filled with hope and anxiety. It is becoming a therapeutic personality—the privileged instrument of every successful therapy—polished by the inevitable stresses, frustrations, and failures of life—and of our profession, for not every therapeutic relationship turns out as we had hoped it would.

The case study can teach the reader a good deal more than how to treat one individual who has a particular constellation of problems, by using one particular therapeutic modality. Take the first case, for example. Boyer works with a borderline patient and, consistent with his approach, does a transference analysis. But we learn more than what the therapist did with a severely troubled middle-aged woman. The author presents us with a cameo portrait of a woman who was raised in a wealthy but pathological environment. We learn of the peculiar educational and childrearing experiences that shaped her early childhood and youth; there are lessons of developmental psychology that emerge in the account, as we witness the slow deformation of the healthy child into a psychotic adult; there is a social psychology implicit in her interactions with an exploitative world and the implicit racial overtones of her sexual acting out; and there is the abnormal psychology, with the personological features and habits that turned into masque-like simulacra of human traits and passions. It has all the characteristics of *film noir*.

This book raises questions that go far beyond psychotherapy as it is strictly construed. The concerns and the personages that are depicted in these cases implicitly evoke issues of cultural anthropology, social psychology, hermeneutics, psychopedagogy, developmental psychology, and cognitive science. For example, profound philosophical and epistemological questions are raised by Yalom's account of "The Fat Lady." One glimpses here the *Yin* and *Yang* of therapist and client, as the shuttle of their mutual transference plays out on a therapeutic loom that enmeshes both of them—and leaves *both of them* changed.

Psychotherapeutics has borrowed the terms *etic* and *emic* from cultural anthropology. The former, etic, characterizes a nomothetic or universal approach to framing theories of personality development; the latter refers to principles that are more culture-sensitive and culture bound. An emic approach refrains from generalizing principles beyond the group in which they have been found to be valid. In the limiting case, it treats each individual as possessing his or her own "culture." The first case study of this book reflects the etic—the nomotheticism of psychoanalysis. The last case study of this book reflects the emic—a more or less cross-cultural orientation to conceptualizing clients' problems and solutions. Inclusion of the last case reflects the editors' recognition of the richness that non-Occidental philosophies and approaches to healing can bring to the Western therapist.

It is wise to remember at this point that this conceptualization of the culture-specificity of any therapy is not a true dichotomy. Like any other psychological, anthropological, or sociological variable, culture-specificity lies on a continuum. All the case studies in this book can be placed somewhere on that continuum.

Readers of this book will no doubt experience an approach-avoidance dilemma with several, if not most, of the therapies described here, for there are drawbacks and benefits for each system. The editors make no apology for that and expect both the practitioner and the trainee to struggle with the issue of choice. The decisions you make about therapy will be quite personal. Some prefer a predominantly intra-psychic approach to therapy; others a more contextual, social engineering approach. Some like the freedom of a time-unlimited model; others a time-limited, even very brief, model. Some will prefer didactic and directive methods; others will be inclined to the Socratic, client-centered approaches. Some will veer to etiological and history-focused exploration; others will prefer teleological, motivational, or even exclusively present-focused perspectives. Some will prefer a reductionistic model; others a holistic model that involves exercise, nutrition, physical fitness, medical exams, and heavy social penetration of clients' ambient worlds. Some of you will prefer the highly cognitive; others the principally affect-centered. You will find examples of all of these among the twelve case studies of this volume.

The following case studies will be rich ore to exploit, but in mining them you will inevitably transform them. These studies are like rushing streams, of which the Greek philosopher Heraclitus spoke, into which you can dip your foot (or even plunge). You cannot, however, do the same thing twice; not because the case history will change, but because *you* will have changed at a second reading. Be that as it may, you have a banquet table set before you. The chapters were a pleasurable and useful read for me. I have no doubt they will also be for you.

Frank Dumont

PREFACE

Psychotherapy is a difficult calling. Its practice requires creativity as well as intelligence, ingenuity as well as training, and hard work as well as good intentions. It is easy to do badly, but exceedingly difficult to do well. Its ranks include both charlatans and grand masters. Psychotherapy involves skills that are almost never completely mastered, and it provides opportunities for, and indeed demands, life-long learning.

Unfortunately, the very features that make psychotherapy so fascinating also make it difficult to teach or explain. Those of us who presume to instruct others in this arcane craft realize that modeling is our most powerful tool—it is often more heuristic to *show* students what we do rather than *tell* them what we do. But all of us realize the limits of our own training: there are myriad clients with multiple problems, and their needs are protean.

One way to deal with the limits of our own experience and training is to expose students to role models through case histories such as those collected in this volume. Each case is written by an experienced psychotherapist, and each parallels a chapter in the sixth edition of the companion volume, *Current Psychotherapies*. More than half a million students have used *Current Psychotherapies* to learn about the theoretical underpinnings and fundamental methods of a dozen or so therapeutic systems. The cases in the current volume were carefully selected to expand and supplement the information in the parent text.

The serious student of psychotherapy can benefit greatly by reading *Case Studies in Psychotherapy* in tandem with the core chapters in *Current Psychotherapies*. We're convinced students who make this investment will appreciate more fully both the beauty and the art of psychotherapy.

Danny Wedding
weddingd@mimh.edu

Raymond J. Corsini
70313.1542@compuserve.com

Editors' Introduction

The work of L. Bryce Boyer with a borderline patient is the best example of contemporary psychoanalysis that we could locate after reviewing dozens of published case histories. This case demonstrates protracted treatment (over eight hundred sessions spanning seven and one-half years) and illustrates how a skilled therapist manages problems such as personal vacations, sexual misbehavior in the therapy hour, and suicide attempts. We believe Dr. Boyer does a particularly good job of analyzing transference and countertransference.

This case history raises important issues, not the least of which is whether or not we as a society can afford to offer expensive treatment by highly skilled practitioners to patients with severe mental health problems. Psychoanalysis of the type illustrated here is perhaps the most expensive of therapies, and the gains won by this woman were achieved at considerable personal and financial cost.

It may be useful for students to imagine how they would handle the therapeutic challenges presented by this most difficult patient and to contrast this treatment with that provided by Dr. Boyer. Most people working in the mental health field will eventually encounter a borderline patient like the one described in the following case.

WORKING WITH A BORDERLINE PATIENT

L. Bryce Boyer

Fifty-three years old when first seen, Mrs. X was a twice-divorced Caucasian, friendless, living alone and almost totally impulse-dominated. She looked and dressed like a teenage boy. She had been a chronic alcoholic for some twenty years and had been hospitalized repeatedly with a diagnosis of schizophrenia. She had been jailed many times, and while in the "drunk tank" had masturbated openly, smeared feces and screamed endlessly. She had lived dangerously, having on various occasions provoked sexual assault by gangs of black men in ghettos. In the last twenty years she had had many forms of psychiatric care (excluding shock therapies), but without effect. She had lived for about a year in a colony designed for faith healing, led by a guru. There appeared to be but two redeeming features when she was first seen: (a) She had concluded that her problems were based on unconscious conflicts and wanted an orthodox analysis. (Various respected analysts had refused her.) (b) Having been told by the most recent therapist of her psychotic son that her interactions with him kept him sick, she wanted very much to stop contributing to his illness.

Her forebears were wealthy aristocrats and included Protestant religious figures. The males all graduated from prestigious universities, and the

Reprinted by permission of the author. Dr. L. Bryce Boyer and *The Psychoanalytic Quarterly.* "Working with a Borderline Patient" originally appeared in *The Psychoanalytic Quarterly* Volume 46, 1977, pp. 389–420.

females, products of noted finishing schools, were patrons of the arts. Her parents treated those who were not their social peers as subhumans. Her bond salesman father's chronic alcoholism resulted in the loss of his and his wife's fortunes during the patient's late childhood. From then on her nuclear family lived on the largesse of relatives.

Her mother was highly self-centered and throughout the patient's childhood and adolescence remained in bed during the daytime for weeks on end, depressed, hypochondriacal, and unapproachable. She vacillated between two ego states. In one, she lay with her aching head covered by cold cloths, moaning and complaining about mistreatment by all, but particularly her husband. In the other, she lay in reveries, reading romantic novels. Much later in treatment the patient remembered that when her mother was in such a dreamy state, she permitted the child to lie with her and perhaps to fondle her mother's genitals, manually and with her face. The mother's withdrawals seemingly could be interrupted only by the temper tantrums of two of the sisters when parties were being planned for social lions or when she was planning to take the grand tour alone. She often left unannounced for her annual European jaunts but sometimes she would confide in the docile Mrs. X that she was leaving and swear her to secrecy, assigning her the task of tending the other children, who voiced their objections dramatically when they knew of their mother's impending departure.

The patient was the second of four sisters, born three years apart. All were reared by a senile woman who had been the mother's nursemaid. The oldest remains a frequently hospitalized alcoholic spinster. The younger two are vain, childless divorcees who live on generous alimony and who continue to have a succession of young lovers. All five females were contemptuous of the father, whom the mother divorced after the patient was married. Thereafter, the mother gave up her depression, hypochondriasis, and withdrawal and became a spirited woman. She had platonic affairs with young male authors whom she sponsored. The father married a warm woman, became abstinent, and returned to work. After many years, he regressed to serious depression and committed suicide by throwing himself in front of a train. This was one year before the patient first saw me. She had had no contact with him since his remarriage and thought of him only with contempt. When she heard of his death and burial, she felt totally detached. At the beginning of therapy, she indiscriminately idealized her mother and devalued her father.

When she was less than three years old, an incident occurred on board an ocean liner. Something happened in a stateroom which frightened the child so that she fled crying to her mother, who was having breakfast with the ship's captain. Her mother ignored her anguish, but a black waiter comforted her, holding her and giving her a cube of sugar. The patient explained to me that she felt the outcome of her treatment hinged on the recall of that memory and on my capacity to accept what she had to tell me without disgust, anger or anxiety.

Before attending school she was an avid reader of fairy tales, and in her first year she did well. But during the second, she became incapable of learning. She read unwillingly and with great difficulty and was unable to learn the simplest mathematics. She never passed a single test during her grammar or finishing school years. This was unimportant to her parents; they taught her that her obligation to the family was to be charming, to exploit her beauty and wit, and to get a rich doctor as a husband who would support the family.

During the second year of schooling she became sexually involved with a swarthy chauffeur who wore black gloves, but she did not reveal their frightening activities, believing that risking death was somehow in the service of her sisters' getting parental love.

During her latency period, she was exceedingly docile and well-behaved. She had a severe obsessive-compulsive neurosis and believed that her family's lives depended on her thought and actions. She was a religious martyr who projected onto her parents the wish that she die so that her sisters would be the recipients of all her parents' love. In this way the sisters would become less disturbed.

When she was eleven she was sent away from home for the first time to attend a finishing school. She soon lost her previous nighttime terrors of attack by something vague and unvisualized, and gave up her endless nocturnal rituals. While there, she became enamored of a popular girl who seemed perfect, although she knew of her hypocrisies and manipulations. She was content to be one of an adoring coterie of this popular girl so long as the girl's attentions were equally divided among her worshippers. When the patient was sixteen, however, her idol became enamored of another girl and the patient went into a catatonic-like state. She was sent home from school, and for the next five years she remained passive, felt mechanical, and went through the motions of living.

She never had any boyfriends and was awkward at parties. She wistfully reveled in her mother's attractiveness as a hostess and vaguely wished that she would someday be her mother's social equal.

While she was in her teens, her father, an outcast at home, spent much time boating. The patient, in her role of family protector, willingly went with him, taking the helm while he got drunk in the cabin. She believed her parents wanted her dead and that she should be killed. She went with her father not only to look after him but to make it easy for him to murder her for the good of her sisters.

When her older sister was able to get a rich medical student to propose marriage, the patient was galvanized into activity and got him to choose her instead. Once married, she was sexually passive and anesthetic. On their honeymoon her husband became so infuriated by her sexual passivity that he sought to murder her, being thwarted only by chance. She felt no resentment and never told anyone, thinking his act had been further evidence of the validity of her being destined to be the savior-martyr.

She lived with his parents in one city while he continued medical school in another. He sent her occasional letters in which he depicted his affairs with sensual women. She was vaguely disappointed. His senile father, a retired minister, considered her passivity to be the result of her having been possessed and sought to exorcise her by giving her enemas while she was nude in the bathtub. This was condoned by her mother and her husband. She felt neither anger nor excitement. She wondered at times if he were getting some sexual or sadistic pleasure from his actions and fantasized seducing him or committing suicide in order to humiliate him by exposing him—all for the good of others.

Following his graduation, her husband joined the military and they moved to another part of the country, whence he was shipped abroad. She was utterly without friends or acquaintances. His letters were rare and included accounts of his affairs with uninhibited women. She bore him a defective daughter and could not believe she was a mother. She feared touching the baby, leaving her care to maids. She felt the baby's defect to be her fault which was somehow associated with her actions with the chauffeur. She began to drink in secret. On leave, her husband impregnated her and she bore another daughter who again she could not believe was hers and whom she could not touch. She began to frequent bars and to pick up men to whose sexual demands of any nature she would submit, always with total subsequent amnesia. She learned of her actions by having them told to her by the children's nurses. Then she bore a defective son who became an autistic. She was totally helpless in the face of his unbridled hyperactivity and feces-smearing. He was hospitalized after about a year and remained so until his early adolescence, rarely acknowledging her existence in any way. Her husband divorced her, her daughters were sent away to institutions, and she lived alone.

For twelve years and periodically later her life was occupied with bar activities and sexual encounters for which she continued to have amnesia. She would pick up black men and submit to their manifold sexual abuses. She passively assented and at times encouraged them to take her money and jewelry. One of her many therapists suggested that she would feel less worthless if she were to prepare herself for some occupation and stop living on what amounted to charity. She managed to complete a practical nursing course and then worked in various psychiatric hospitals where she felt she was of some use because she could understandingly care for psychotic and senile patients. She was fired from a number of such positions for being absent and for appearing on the job while intoxicated or hung over.

In one of the hospitals where she worked, she met a male patient who was her physical counterpart, even to the color of her hair and eyes. They were so alike she wore his clothes. He was addicted to various drugs, including alcohol, and totally dependent on his family and welfare. She soon began to live with him. She adored him as she had her mother and the girlfriend of teenage years. She knew of his many faults but totally idealized him. She felt complete and rapturous with him and at times believed they were psychological and even physical continua. They were married, and the idyllic fusion persisted. Periodically, they bought whiskey and went to bed where they remained for days, engaging in polymorphous sexuality to the point of exhaustion, occasionally lying in their excreta. While she never had an orgasm, she felt complete. Such episodes were especially pleasant to her when she was menstruating and she and her partner were smeared with blood, which she sometimes enjoyed eating. After some nine years of marriage, he divorced her for reasons which she never understood, particularly since she supported him financially. Then she became a mechanical person once again and resumed her pursuit of men in bars.

A year before treatment began, she obtained an undemanding job as a file clerk where her superiors tolerated her lateness and incompetency. She lived on her meager salary and placed no value on material possessions. She believed that she had never had a hostile wish and that throughout her life she had invariably sought to help others.

COURSE OF TREATMENT

Over the years, I have gradually come to accept for treatment almost solely patients whose activities are apt to influence the lives of others, such as educators, physicians, and professionals who work in the mental health field. Yet it did not occur to me to refuse her request to try psychoanalytic treatment. I found appealing her determination to undergo for predominantly altruistic purposes a procedure which she well knew would be painful. And I felt comfortable with her.

She was seen at what she knew to be reduced rates three times weekly on the couch for about five years, payments being made from a small endowment from a deceased family friend. After a trial six-month interruption she resumed treatment on the couch twice a week for two more years, making a total of over eight hundred interviews in seven and a half years.

Before analysis is undertaken with such patients, I tell them that our work is to be cooperative and of an experimental nature and that we cannot expect to set a time limit; that they are to make a sincere effort to relate aloud whatever comes to their minds during the interviews and to report their emotional states and physical sensations; that I do not send statements and expect to be paid what is owed on the last interview of the month; that they will be charged for cancellations unless their scheduled interviews are filled by another patient; and that I am away frequently for short periods and one long period during the course of each year and will inform them of the expected dates of absence as soon as I know of them. When an occasional patient inquires what is to be expected of me, I state that I shall keep the scheduled interviews and be on time; that I do not give advice unless I deem it necessary; that I see my role as seeking to understand as much as I can about the patients and will tell them what I have learned when I consider them ready. I explain that I expect to be wrong at times and that the final validation will depend on the patient's responses and memories. For these patients I have found such specific conditions offer needed ego and superego support.

As is common with patients with borderline personality disorders, during the first two structured interviews, Mrs. X's productions were but slightly tinged with primary process thinking. However, there was a periodic affective disparity which confused me; I was undecided whether it constituted *la belle indifférence* or schizophrenic dissociation.

During her third interview she eagerly lay on the couch, her speech promptly became heavily influenced by primary process thinking and she was at times incoherent. Her verbal productions were highly symbolic and her language was often unusually vulgar. She made tangential references to fairy tales, fusing elements of *Beauty and the Beast, Cinderella, Hansel and Gretel* and *Snow White,* and told a story which involved a good witch who transported children through a magical opening into a paradise in which the protagonists fused and became perpetually indistinguishable and parasitic, needing no others for their constant bliss. She also alluded to a white elephant and a spider.

She did not seem frightened by her productions or her style of presentation. There was some embarrassment about her foul language but her principal reaction was one of mild curiosity as to why she talked so strangely. My own reaction to her behavior was one of mild surprise at the degree of such prompt regression, of empathy with her embarrassment, and of detached intellectual curiosity.

I felt at ease with this patient. As a result of idiosyncratic childhood experiences, I have long comprehended unconscious meanings of primary process thinking and have been able to use its contents in synthetic manners. I have also devoted many years to the study of folklore and know most of the psychoanalytic literature dealing with the fairy tales to which she referred, as well as that dealing with the spider. I believed that I understood from her behavior and verbal productions that her conflicts pertained especially to attempts to master early primal scene traumata and fusions with aspects of various people, oral and anal sadism, and intense sibling rivalry. I thought that the actual, affect-laden recovery of primal scene memories would be crucial in her treatment and assumed that her vulgarity indicated that they had occurred in connection with the period of cleanliness training or had become attached to experiences which occurred then. I attributed some of her easy regression to a toxic alcoholic brain syndrome and was dubious about the oft-repeated diagnosis of schizophrenia.

I had the uncanny feeling that she had talked to me in a distorted childish language as though I were an actual loved figured from her early life. Retrospectively, I regret not having validated my hunch. Had I done so, I might have been aware that she had globally identified me with the only person of her childhood whom she could trust (her maternal grandfather); and my added comprehension would both have made her progress in treatment less mystifying to me and perhaps precluded a near-disaster.

In the fourth interview she came to the office drunk, although I had the impression that she was less intoxicated than she seemed. Her lips were painted black and there were white streaks on her face. She was dressed in garish, revealing clothes which exposed filthy underpants. She screamed and cursed and threatened to attack me with outstretched claws. I felt as though I were observing a puppet show. There was an obscure reference to my being a vampire. She threw harmless objects, aimed to narrowly miss me so that I felt unthreatened. She then picked up a heavy sone ashtray and menaced me with it. I felt no anxiety, but sat still and remained silent and observant. When she found me unafraid, she cried and threw herself on the couch, spread her legs apart and partially bared her tiny breasts. When I remained passive and silent, she sat at my feet, hugged my legs and eventually touched my penis. She seemed surprised that it was not erect. I then removed her hand and said it was unnecessary for her to express her conflicts physically and advised her to tell me her problems with words. She reacted with rage and tried to claw my face. It was easy to fend her off; I effortlessly held her at arm's length. If she had chosen to do so, she could have easily kicked my genitals as she threatened to do. Her strange behavior and dress seemed to be designed to test the level of my tolerance of what she felt would be anxiety-provoking or disgusting. I viewed her allusion to me as a vampire as indicative of splitting and projective identification.

I have come to understand the operational functions of projective identification in rather simple terms. I believe that which is projected remains to a degree unrepressed and that the patient maintains some level of continuing to feel what he seeks to project onto the therapist, thereby continuing to be preconsciously aware of what he imagines the analyst to experience. Patients' initial aim when they project hostile wishes onto the therapist is to control their potency by defending themselves from the imagined hostility of the therapist and controlling the latter's actions. The therapist is used as a repository for projected internalized objects and attitudes which make patients feel uncomfortable, and they believe they have succeeded in locating them within the analyst. Patients fear that their hostile wishes or thoughts may result in the destruction of the therapist or retributive damage to themselves. Once they believe that such hostility is a part of the analyst, they watch the analyst's behavior. Over time, effective interpretations, combined with patients' observations that the projection's alleged presence within the therapist has not proved deleterious, enable the patients to reintroject them gradually in detoxified form and to integrate them into their evolving personalities. Some patients fear that their love is destructive and project it onto the therapist for safekeeping; similarly, with treatment these patients come to view love as not dangerous.

Discussants have often wondered about my relative lack of fear of attack by psychotic patients. Empirically, I have never been actually attacked, although I have been frightened at times. In my own past, one of my important love objects suffered from a borderline personality disorder and periodically regressed into acute paranoid psychotic episodes. That person was impulsive and violent; and as a young child, I learned to judge the degree of physical danger and to stay away from potentially murderous attacks.

In the fifth interview, Mrs. X remembered none of what had happened. When I told her what she had done, she was aghast. She vowed spontaneously not to come drunk to the office again. Most of the interviews of the first year, however, took place with her either mildly intoxicated or hung over.

For several months many interviews included periods of incoherency which were at times grossly vulgar and talk which was obviously symbolic of early primal scene observations. Periodically, I inquired whether her interview behavior was designed to test my level of tolerance, to determine whether she could disgust or anger me or make me uncomfortable. Such queries usually resulted in a temporary cessation of her blatant vulgarities and "crazy" talk.

At times she ascribed her speech content or immodest behavior to my will, and from the outset I used such material to help her learn about her splitting mechanisms and projective tendencies and their defensive uses. An example follows.

The physical set-up of my consultation room is such that a shared waiting room has a sliding door which separates it from a tiny hallway that has three other doors, one opening into my office, one into my private lavatory and one to an exit. Mrs. X had the first interview of the day, and it occurred at an hour when I had to unlock the office building. I generally arrived early enough for other activities before seeing her. She customarily arrived for her interview just on time, making enough noise so that she could be heard entering the waiting room, although the sliding door was shut. One morning when I emerged from the lavatory some ten minutes before she was expected, I noted that the sliding door was ajar, but I assumed I must have left it so. At the time her appointment was to begin, she buzzed to announce her presence. Since I had not heard her before the buzz, I suspected some acting out had transpired. During the first few minutes of her hour, her talk dealt manifestly with hostility-laden events in her office on the previous day and included the interjection "Oh, shit" and the phrase "He pissed me off." I then assumed that she had been repeating spying activities of her childhood pertaining to adults' uses of the toilet, but that she did not choose to direct my inquiries to the past. Instead, I asked how long she had been in the waiting room before she buzzed, and I obtained some previously withheld information. It had been her wont to arrive some minutes before I opened the building and to park where she could watch me unseen. On that particular morning, she had noiselessly followed me into the building, entered the waiting room, opened the sliding door and eventually heard the toilet flush.

Discussion of her behavior and its motivations on that day occupied several interviews and the analysis of some dreams. It developed that she had contradictory views of me. In one, I was a sadistic voyeur who had become a psychoanalyst in order to spy on the "dirty" activities and thoughts of my patients, to titillate myself and to learn how to frustrate patients by determining precisely what they wanted of me, so that I could torture them by refusing to accede to their desires. I "got my jollies" by means of subtly exhibitionistic behavior which excited in my patients those wants that I frustrated. At the same time, I had had a traumatic childhood and had undergone much suffering because of exhibitionistic and frustrating parents and wanted, as a psychoanalyst, to relieve my patients of their misery. It was as if I were two people. I was at times totally hateful, bad and hurtful and at other times solely loving, good and helpful, and my alternating personalities determined my totally unpredictable behavior. It was my will that she observe my every act so that she could become exactly like me and arrive at social and professional success, but it was also my will that she should not embarrass me by letting me know that she had read my mind and was following instructions.

When I indicated to her how she had ascribed to me precisely the qualities which she had previously described as her own, she was impressed, and for a time she could more clearly contemplate her self-view as all good and all bad and her projective tendencies. It was then possible to review the events in the office on the day that preceded her acting out and to delineate ways in which her behavior with me and her ascriptions to me had been in the service of defense against anxiety and guilt over behavior and wishes related to people in her work setting. She had acted toward me as she felt her co-workers had acted toward her. I suggested that she had sought to master a feeling of helplessness through identification with the aggressor, and I postulated that this behavior constituted a lifelong pattern. I did not have sufficient cathected data to make a more specific statement.

At times she was flirtatious in her dress and actions and sought to entertain and amuse me, imitating, as it developed, her mother's party behavior and obeying her parental injunctions about how to "hook" a rich doctor. At the same time she had fused sensations of urinary or fecal urgency and, despite a hysterectomy some years before treatment began, felt blood on her legs and expressed the wish to smear me with it. Sometimes there was vaginal itching. Occasionally, she spread her legs and began to undress, meantime rubbing her pubis. When I asked her about her thoughts and feelings, it became apparent she was unaware of her actions. On a few occasions, she wondered whether I felt lonely and wanted my face in her crotch. When I commented that she seemed to believe she had put part of herself into me, she recalled what she believed to have been early childhood and latency experiences of lying with her mother and palpating her mother's genitals with her hands and face; she remembered the feeling of pubic hair on her nose and cheeks. In her sober interviews, she was often largely withdrawn and "headachy" or had other somatic complaints, which we came to understand as her imitating one part of her mother's periodic daytime bed behavior. I also focused on her primitive wish to fuse with me as a representative of her mother.

For many months she picked up men at bars and submitted to their sexual demands. When I tried to show her that these men were father figures, she regularly corrected me, making me aware that they represented the phallic and nurturant mother with whom she sought to fuse. However, she gradually became cognizant that her conscious contempt for her father covered rage at him, and with amazement she slowly recovered memories of boating with him. During one session she misinterpreted a noise to mean I was masturbating behind her. I remarked that perhaps there had been a time when she had seen her father masturbate. Over a period of weeks, she recovered the memory of her actions with the chauffeur, which included his placing her hands on his erection, while he wore black gloves. Then she gradually recalled with much embarrassment that during adolescence on the boating excursions with her father, she had watched him masturbate in the cabin; she slowly became aware of her anger that he had preferred masturbation to using her sexually.

In the interviews that followed, material continued that involved nighttime dreams and overt or covert themes of mutilations, murders, and desertion. There was obvious blurring of ego boundaries. My interpretations, as always, were transferential and as genetic as I deemed advisable and aimed at reinforcing previous interpretations of the defensive use of splitting. She gradually became aware that she had much anger which she had denied and uncritically projected onto policemen and other establishment figures. Now she began to be more critical of her automatic devaluation of them as parental representatives. Later she would be able to comprehend a pattern of projection of aggression and reintrojection of aggressively determined self- and object images and the subsequent use of splitting operations.

In this early period, I delayed focusing on the fusion of anal, vaginal and urethral sensations, judging that data pertaining to this evidence of lack of structuralization of drives would be remembered at a later time when interpretations would be more meaningful. I believed that the content of her primary process thinking during the third interview had already heralded the fact that primal scene traumata were partial organizers of her particular ego structure. Periodic interpretations of her wish to fuse with me were gradually understood and elaborated by her. For example, she often responded that she wished to be taken into one or another of my orifices, even including my pores, and to circulate in my blood, to lodge in my brain and govern all my activities, while secretly spying on my actions to learn from them how I handled those elements which she had projected onto me. Only much later, after she had reintrojected detoxified versions of those projections, did she see this fantasy as self-destructive. She then strove to clarify actual differences between us.

About five months after Mrs. X was first seen, she learned that I had an interest in anthropology and asked to borrow a magazine from the waiting room which included an article on stone-age humans. She had lost her capacity to read easily and with comprehension after the first grade; and I suggested that she wanted permission to learn to read understandingly again and to develop herself as a person rather than to follow the assigned role of dumb-blond doctor-seducer. She promptly enrolled in high school, then college, and slowly developed the capacity to read and write with comprehension. During the following years she received only A's in her extension division college courses.

After she had been in treatment for about six months, I left for a period of six weeks. She had known of my planned absence from the beginning of her sessions and I had thought her anxiety about the separation had been well understood before I left, since we had dealt extensively with her reactions to her mother's European jaunts. However, immediately after my departure, she attempted suicide by taking an overdose of pills, which I had not known she possessed. She was rescued, so far as could be determined, by chance. It was noted in her hospital chart that she had mentioned her mother's father. During my absence she had no remembered thought about me until the day before her scheduled appointment; and when she appeared for her interview, she seemed surprised that I was alive. She had not died, therefore I must have. When she entered the room, she looked everywhere for something but when I inquired what she was trying to find, she declined to tell me. Much later, I found out that she had sought a white elephant.

She had hoped that her death would result in my professional destruction. She now viewed her father's drunkenness and affairs as ways of risking death in the hope that he would thereby get even with her mother for her contemptuousness. She also recalled the Oriental custom of committing suicide on the doorstep of the wronged person.

Soon after my return, poignant memories of her early relationship with her mother's father emerged. Apparently, her relationship with that loving man was the only consistently dependable one of her childhood. It formed the basis of the element of basic trust which enabled her to develop psychologically as far as she did. He had held her on his lap, listened to her seriously, and was always considerate of her needs. One time, when she was envious of one of her sisters' having received a soft, stuffed animal as a present, she told her grandfather that she wanted a similar toy which she could care for as though it were a baby. He responded by telling her the story of an orphan baby elephant in India which was adopted by a boy whom it loved and always obeyed, no doubt a variant of Kipling's "Toomai of the Elephants." He promised to get her a white elephant for

Christmas. She believed he meant a living animal rather than a toy. In fact, he gave her another white stuffed toy, but she retained the belief that he would eventually give her the living pachyderm. When she was almost seven years old, he died; but she had the set idea that when she got a white elephant someday, she would also find her grandfather and once again have a dependable, loving relationship with a kindly person who did not misuse her.

She had apparently entered a satisfactory early latency period adjustment, but the death of her grandfather caused her to lose her capacity to learn and to use fantasy constructions in an adaptive manner. She had not been taken to his funeral where she might have viewed his corpse and thus been confronted with the reality of his demise. Her loss of the capacity to learn had been based on her wish to deny having learned of his death; she would never again learn anything if she had to accept this learning.

I shall now turn to an example of how my coming to understand my emotional response enabled me to change an impasse into a beneficial step. When her son as a young child had come home from the hospital for brief periods, she had taken men home with her and in a drunken state performed fellatio and submitted to sodomy before him. She had no memory of her actions, but would be informed by the nurses. Sometimes, when she was unwittingly angry with me, she would return to her shameful feelings on being told by the nurses what she had done. I gradually noted that I began to respond to such recitations by irritation and sleepiness; and I found myself being subtly punitive toward her. For some weeks there was a therapeutic stalemate, during which her acting out increased and our rapport all but disappeared. I regretted having accepted her for treatment and wondered why I had done so. I fell into a brief trance-like state during an interview with her and when I became fully alert again, had repressed the content of my reverie. That night I had a dream which reminded me of my own past. I had learned in prior periods of personal analysis that I had become an analyst with an unconscious motivation of curing the important but psychologically disordered and dangerous love object to whom I have alluded previously. Analysis of my dream made me aware of another reason: I had sought to protect a younger sibling from the love object. I then knew that I had accepted Mrs. X in treatment to effect changes not only in her but in her psychotic son. Then I became aware that I had identified myself with her abused child and was expressing my anger by withdrawal and by refusing to recognize her, as she had previously reported her son to have done. Such knowledge permitted me to regain my objectivity. Finally, I could interpret her wish to provoke me to abuse her. She responded by remembering dreams and hypnopompic fantasies in which she was forced to watch women being raped anally or having huge phalluses shoved into their mouths. Three years later I was able to interpret her behavior as an attempt to master her terror and her feelings of dissolution when she had watched the sexual activities of her parents.

Soon she began to experience choking sensations during the interviews. Analysis of dreams showed her use of the body-phallus equation and her wish that I would force her to reintroject both good and bad aspects of herself, which she had projected onto me. Affect-laden memories of her experiences with the chauffeur appeared. Following her grandfather's death, she had turned to the black-gloved man (whom she partly confused with the Negro who had comforted her during the shipboard experience) in an effort to regain a loving relationship with a man who would take her on his lap, as her father refused to do. He had forced his phallus into her mouth, causing her to choke. She had concealed their activities, rationalizing that she was supposed to die through choking in her effort to provide her sisters with their parents' finite love. She also now remembered nightly efforts to determine whether her parents were alive by checking to make sure they were breathing while they were asleep. The choking conversion symptom disappeared.

She now recalled with emotion nightly rituals during her latency period. Her family's house was very old. While electrical contrivances had been installed in her third-story bedroom, there remained a gas jet. At night it was permissible to have illumination from the jet but the lights were not to be used. She was terrified that a vague, never visualized something would attack her from the dark. She feared even more that leaking gas would poison her. She engaged in endless prayers for her own salvation and for the other members of the family. She engaged in counting rituals which were supposed to influence God to save them. She used the rituals to stay awake, believing that she was safe from attack so long as she remained alert. She had a collection of dolls and stuffed animals which covered most of her bed, and she tenderly put them to sleep with caresses and cooings. She endlessly repeated, "Now I lay me down to sleep, I pray the Lord my soul to keep," applying the theme to her dolls and consciously equating being asleep with being dead. While doing so, she sometimes believed she was Christ, grandfather-God's protector of children, and felt her pubis repeatedly to determine whether she had grown a penis. She had to check many times to be sure the window was tightly locked, because if she were to fall asleep with it open, she might throw her babies (dolls) and herself into the snow on the ground below. Her own death would have been acceptable because of its altruistic motives; but to have murdered her babies would have made her a sinner and unsuitable to rejoin her grandfather and have God keep her soul.

Her treatment had begun just before a Christmas separation, and her reactions to my first absence had not been decipherable. As our second Christmas separation approached, she returned to thinking of her mother's departures for the grand tour of Europe. Now those memories became cathected with feeling of rage and then with loneliness. She sought to remove the loneliness by joining a singles group and resuming the drunken activities with men she picked up. For the first time, she could remember what she did with her partners. She was exceedingly aggressive, insisting on assuming the superior position. She demanded that the man be passive while she pumped up and down on his erection, at times believing his penis was hers and she was penetrating him. I interpreted this behavior as representing a continuation of her efforts to save me from her anger at me for deserting her like a parent.

The following summer when I left her for another extended period, she went on a prolonged drunk and behaved so crazily that she was jailed. She requested hospitalization and rejoined her second husband whom she knew to be in the hospital. There she entered a fusion state with him. She had no conscious thought of my existence until the week before our scheduled appointment. Then she arranged her release and met me on time.

She explained that in her rage at my leaving her she had wanted to humiliate me by killing herself or getting murdered; but she protected herself by getting hospitalized and joining her husband. Thus she deemed her behavior to have been adaptive and was pleased with herself. She now valued her contacts with me above all else.

Throughout her treatment until this time, there had been rare contacts with her mother, sisters, daughters and their young children whom she had never been able to touch, fearing she would kill them. When the third Christmas came, she was able to spend more time with her mother and sisters and feel less uneasiness than before. She also had one of her daughters bring her family to visit for the holidays. She found herself infuriated with the excited pleasure and selfishness of the young children. Now she recalled with intensity childhood Christmases which had been immensely frustrating for her, not only because she felt her sisters got more than she, but particularly because she did not turn into a boy or get a penis so she could be Christ, the martyred favorite son of all mankind. She began to realize that her fears of harming her own babies disguised a wish to kill them, as they represented her siblings. Then she became closer to her daughters and enjoyed holding their children. Also her relations with her mother and sisters improved. She invited her son to visit her periodically on leave from a distant psychiatric hospital. Over the next few years during subsequent visits they developed a calmer and mutually affectionate relationship.

She now eschewed alcohol for long periods and only occasionally had sexual relations with men. Her interests were limited to job, school, and analysis. She was gradually promoted at work. There was a growing interest in the lives of her female bosses, and fantasies pertaining to them I interpreted as displaced fantasies about my life. The previous flirtatiousness with me resumed as did the pattern of coming to the office in altered ego states; the fusion of vaginal, urethral and anal sensations reappeared. I suggested that her childhood pattern of checking on her parents' breathing was the result of her having been disturbed by noises in their bedroom which she assumed to have occurred during their sexual activities. She then recalled that during preoedipal years, her bedroom was separated from theirs by a bathroom in which her mother's douche tip and bag, which she believed to have been used to give her enemas, hung on the wall and that sometimes mother's bloody menstrual rags were in a bucket of water. Then I guessed that she had repeatedly observed their activities and had experienced excitement which she discharged with urinary and fecal activities during the night. My ideas were accepted with equanimity. She gradually recalled with much feeling repeated childhood observations of their sexual actions which included sodomy, cunnilingus and fellatio, always accompanied by her mother's groaning protests. She had interpreted their actions in anal-sadistic and oral-fusional terms and had thought that each had a penis like a sword which could kill the other. She had reacted with fused oral, anal and vaginal excitement and had sought to interrupt her parents by noisy bathroom activities.

In the fifth year of treatment she gradually repressed the primal scene memories and the observations of father's masturbating on the boat. She did well at work and school, had occasional dates and developed the capacity to have mild orgasms during nonfrantic intercourse. During my summer absence she briefly re-entered a relationship with her second husband, now devoid of its fusional aspects. He was ill, and she cared for him considerately. She began to have vague and emotionally uninvested fantasies about me. Therapy appeared to have reached a plateau in which she was functioning well but retaining a primitive idealization of me, interpretations of which had no effect. She was quite cognizant that I made mistakes and assumed that I had secret faults which she could not verify, but I remained an idol like her mother. I decided to use the parameter of a trial separation in an effort to dislodge the primitive idealization. Accordingly, I recommended that, beginning with my summer absence six months thence, we remain apart for six months and resume treatment just after the following Christmas. She was gratified but apprehensive because she had not recovered the shipboard memories.

She decided to have an earlier trial separation by making a hiking trip with an organized group in the Himalayas and returning to treatment a month before I was to leave for the summer period. During her preparation for the trip, she began to have occasional dates with a black gardener who, she thought, had previously been a chauffeur, her first contact with blacks since she began treatment. She recalled that she had turned to the swarthy chauffeur at the age of seven after her grandfather's death in an effort to replace him with another sustaining object. Before her trip to India she had passing thoughts about seeking a white elephant and wondered whether she might be seeking a magical reunion with her grandfather. En route to the Himalayas, she went for the first time to the site of her father's suicide and could cry and miss him. She also visited with her mother, sisters, children and grandchildren and had warm interchanges with them. After her return she said she had seen her family to say farewell, since she expected to have some accident and die while in India, hoping thereby to be reunited with her grandfather.

On the journey, she was very happy. However, she took fragments from shrines and worried that she had desecrated the dead. She bartered with Tibetan women for their jewelry and felt she corrupted them by buying their religious objects, one of which included a white elephant. When she came back to treatment, we discussed her wish to return to the loving relationship with her grandfather, but she experienced little affectual release.

In the last interview before our trial separation, she had a fantasy of using the stone fragments as a memorial stone for my grave. Thus she would have me near her and available for her alone; she would commune with me in a time of need.

She did not contact me after six months as we had planned. In January I wrote a note inquiring about her progress. She was intensely gratified and requested further therapy. She had not made the memorial shrine and had again forgotten my existence, being sure that I had died.

Her relationship with the black man had intensified. Over Christmas she had the delusional conviction that her visiting mother and a sister had sought to take him from her. She was furious and tried to hurt them in various ways. When she got my note, she partially decathected her delusion and viewed it as a subject for investigation.

During the next eighteen months, the vicissitudes of her jealousy were worked through fairly well. The death of her grandfather and her subsequent seeking to join him in the Himalayas were cathected, but true mourning did not take place; unconsciously, she still did not accept the fact of his death.

She had earlier been unaware of fantasies during masturbation or sexual relationships and had focused solely on the physical seeking for orgasm. Following a reported episode of masturbation, I asked her to visualize what she might have fantasied were she able to shift her attention from the physical experience and her fear that either she would not have orgasm or that if she did, she would convulse and explode into fragments. She closed her eyes and saw oblong geometric forms. During subsequent interviews the forms became rounded and unified as a hand and an arm, tearing at her vagina. She revealed that for years she had awakened at night, clawing her perineum. She was sure she continued to have invisible pinworms from childhood. When stool examinations were negative, she understood the fantasized oblongs in terms of projected sadistic part objects. She now revealed that she kept her apartment like a pigsty and ate her meals standing up when she was alone. She also found it interesting that she had never learned to wipe herself and always had feces on her perianal hair and underpants. When she deemed this behavior to reflect a continuing wish to be totally taken care of, she felt humiliated and began to straighten up her apartment and keep herself clean.

During an interview in which she recalled the fantasy of the fragmented geometric, dehumanized hand-arm symbols, she returned to the terrifying experience on board ship. She had gone to the head and seen her father having intercourse *a tergo* with a nursemaid. She had been shocked and she felt that her face had become wrinkled and flat and had then slid off her head, to lie on the floor like an emptied breast. She recalled also that her father had seen her watching him and looked aghast. His face seemed similarly to disintegrate. She had thought both of them were dissolving. Now she remembered early childhood episodes of watching her father's masturbation and having experienced a halo effect.

She dreamed that she was being decapitated as she was in danger of being swallowed by huge waves. These she equated with her mother's vaginal labia. Her remembered seekings to get into her mother's vagina face-first were recathected. Dressed like a teenage boy, she lay rigid on the couch. She feared she would vomit, ejaculate with her whole body, and that I would cut off her head in retribution for her ambivalent wish to render me impotent by making her treatment a failure. Soon she saw these ideas in terms of an early wish to demasculinize her father as her mother's behavior had effectively done. She became intensely aware of having identified herself with her father's phallus and was both stunned and relieved. She had the fantasy that if she could supplant her father's sexual role with her mother, then her mother would need no one but her and they could live together in an idyllic symbiotic union. On the other hand, such a situation would be dangerous because a fusion with her mother would mean a destructive loss of personal identity.

When she did not regress during my summer absence, she decided to terminate before the annual Christmas separation. During the final six months, she continued to function well, except that she eschewed relationships with men other than the black lover from whom she was detaching herself. She recathected her jealousy of women at work, mother and sister surrogates, but her behavior remained appropriate and her murderous wishes were confined to fantasies. She became relaxed in her relationship with me, which essentially became that of an old friend. While my behavior remained strictly analytic with her, I shared her feelings and her fantasies that when we were apart, we would miss each other and wish each other well.

Just before termination, she brought me a tiny bonsai tree, representing herself, and in the pot was one of the Himalayan shrine stone fragments. She wanted to remain with me, to have me continue to help her mature. She planned to return in another six months, to sit and talk with me as old friends, and perhaps then we would tenderly hold one another. She understood that this wish included an element of finally telling her father she loved and missed him.

During the last interview, she sat on the couch, looking at me through much of the interview, saying she now securely felt herself to be a separate and real person and could view me as a real person. At its end, she hugged me and kissed my cheek. Then she told me she had to touch me during the drunken interview, to be sure I was not the product of her mind, but had some separateness from her.

By the end of treatment she was a vastly changed woman, capable of warm, responsible, calm relationships with the members of her family. She drank socially, had progressed in her work to a position of authority and was on the verge of obtaining a baccalaureate. She was very proud of herself and happy. However, she had not developed the capacity to have lasting mature relationships with men and had neither completely worked through her idealization of me nor truly mourned the death of her grandfather.

A year after termination, Mrs. X requested follow-up interviews because she was uneasy about the Christmas season. She had renounced her relationship with her lover, had begun to have dates with men who were more eligible for marriage, had lost much of her idealization of me and appeared to have satisfactorily mourned her grandfather. She no longer felt compelled to get her baccalaureate, which she now deemed to have been a goal set with the idea that by achieving it she would be more pleasing to me. Rather, she now took courses solely for her own pleasure. She announced her intention to return for interviews early in the holiday season each year until she felt more secure with her emotional responses to Christmastime.

Editors' Introduction

This is a teaching case in the best sense: An example of Adlerian therapy conducted in the context of a graduate course in psychotherapy. Dr. Harold Mosak, a skilled Adlerian therapist, accepts the risks involved in permitting public scrutiny of his work, and in relatively few sessions he provides for new insights and behavioral change in a troubled young man.

The reader will find it useful to contrast the style of Dr. Mosak with that of Dr. Boyer in the previous selection. Mosak is more directive, therapy is time-limited, and his style is didactic. It is cognitive therapy with the focus on examining the values, beliefs, and attitudes of the client. Mosak and Maniacci do a masterful job in illustrating the core elements of individual psychotherapy.

THE CASE OF ROGER

Harold H. Mosak and Michael Maniacci

Alfred Adler developed a theory and strategy of psychology and psychotherapy which have proven to be quite relevant to contemporary clinical and counseling practice. *Individual Psychology,* the name Adler gave his system, derives from the Latin *individuum,* and means "indivisible," emphasizing the holistic perspective that Adlerian psychology is built upon. Distinctions such as conscious and unconscious, mind and body, or approach and avoidance are subjective experiences; in reality, they are a part of a unified relational system. Individuals are viewed as being in movement towards subjectively determined goals which, though influenced by heredity and environment, are in the final analysis the result of choices made according to biased apperceptions. These biased apperceptions, about self, others, and the world, form a self-consistent cognitive and attitudinal set which organizes and directs movement towards the goal, and is called by Adlerians the *style of life.* The goal, though idiographic and individualized for specific people depending upon the particular circumstances in which they grew up and based upon certain choices they made, in general, is always designed to move individuals from a subjective sense of inferiority towards a sense of superiority, perfection, competence, or completion, from a felt minus situation towards a plus situation. Movement can take place in

---

"The Case of Roger" was written specifically to complement Dr. Mosak's chapter in *Current Psychotherapies.*

either of two directions: useful or useless. Useful, as defined by Adlerians, is that which moves with others in prosocial, egalitarian ways; useless is that which moves against others in self-centered, uncooperative ways. All behavior, both adaptive and maladaptive, is conceptualized as taking place within a social field. Behavior that is useful is that which is in line with social interest, a potentiality which requires development and encouragement.

Individuals who move in useless ways are not considered sick, but rather discouraged; they have underdeveloped social interest. They have selected goals which they attempt to move towards in self-centered rather than cooperative ways. Cognitively, they have a private logic which construes events and situations according to biased apperceptions that generally are distorted, overgeneralized, or exaggerated perceptions and are not in line with the less dogmatic common sense followed by most others. The main tasks of life are conceptualized as social tasks which require cooperation, not competition. Adler delineated three of these life tasks: work, friendship and love. Later Adlerians delineated a fourth and a fifth implied in Adler's writings: a self task and a spiritual task. Maladjustment is characterized by increased inferiority feelings, underdeveloped social interest, and an exaggerated, uncooperative goal of personal superiority.

Adler conceptualized psychotherapy as the awakening of the client's innate social interest. By explaining the client's subjective distress not as sickness but as discouragement due to the erroneous meaning given to life, Adler attempted to encourage the client to move towards a more useful, adaptive style of life. Such a change took place by examining how the client grew up and what choices he or she made. The client's family constellation, family atmosphere, family values and earliest recollections were explored in order to understand what particular goals towards which the individual was striving.

Rudolf Dreikurs described Adlerian psychotherapy as consisting of four processes: (a) forming a relationship; (b) investigating the client's life style; (c) interpreting it to the client; and (d) helping the client to reorient towards a more prosocial stance by modifying certain convictions held by the client and putting into practice more cooperative attitudes and behaviors. Though heuristically valuable, these should not be regarded as "phases" or "stages" in actual clinical practice. Interpretation may occur during every phase of the process, and the establishment and maintenance of a positive relationship will require ongoing effort. New material can be investigated throughout the course of treatment, and reorientation is encouraged beginning with the initial interview.

BACKGROUND AND REFERRAL

The case presented here was selected from the audio recordings of an eleven-week graduate psychotherapy course taught by the senior author at the Alfred Adler Institute of Chicago. "Roger" came to the counseling center at the Institute requesting services. After an intake interview, he agreed to participate in front of a class for a pre-established period of ten weeks at no charge.

Coming in shortly after his thirty-sixth birthday, Roger's major complaint was agoraphobia which had grown progressively worse for the past twelve years. Along with the agoraphobia, his intake sheet noted that he drank heavily, was overweight, was dissatisfied with his job (which he had managed to keep only at the expense of considerable anxiety), had multiple specific phobias, and was actively homosexual. Roger requested no treatment for his sexual orientation which he claimed was not a problem, except for the fact that his agoraphobia interfered with making contact with other gay men.

SESSION I
FORMING A RELATIONSHIP AND
DEFINING THE PROBLEM

The session began with Mosak attempting to clarify the problem.

Therapist: O.K. What brings you to the Institute?
Client: I have a problem. I guess they call it agoraphobia, a fear of going out in the open. It's been getting steadily worse for the past ten or twelve years. Now it's getting to the point where I can hardly exist.
T: Is that why you brought a friend?
C: Yeah, somebody to go with me. . . .

The friend made it possible for Roger to move about outside. Roger went on to explain that his anxiety was not so acute if he knew where he was going; then at least he would know where he could "run and hide" along the way should he start to panic. He dealt with his anxiety by drinking "a fifth of wine" before his trips outside of his house.

C: . . . I think it's basically insecurity. In the past year I've had three different jobs, and I started a new job last week. I was a wreck for about a week before time, worrying about going to this place. I was frightened to death driving there . . . I had my brother take me and pick me up. But now that I've been there about a week I did it myself the past couple of days. But still, I worry all day about leaving work. . . If I hit traffic, I sit there and worry about getting into an accident. I might panic. It scares me.
T: You've said something twice now, and that is your symptom permits you to put other people into your service. You have to get somebody to accompany you down here, and for a week, you had to get your brother to drive you to work. It almost sounds like you feel pretty helpless and have to count on "the big boys" to take care of you.

The therapist is offering a tentative interpretation. Adlerian psychology is a psychology of use, not possession. For example, Adlerians do not say that someone has a bad temper, but rather that someone uses temper to intimidate others. The bad temper serves the individual's purpose. In Roger's case, Mosak reframes the symptom to show how it is used: Roger is putting others into his service and though he may not totally be aware (conscious) of it, he is responsible for it.

T: What have you done about it [*the agoraphobia*] for the past twelve years?
C: Well, try to cope with it the best I can . . . avoid certain things,avoid certain areas, don't go into the woods or take vacations or do things you normally would do.

Adler considered a neurosis an evasion of the tasks of life. Roger has constricted life to the point where it is manageable. He is saying, in effect, that he will only operate where he feels secure.

T: Yeah, but that doesn't overcome it. That's living within the confines of your symptom . . .Have you done anything about trying to overcome the symptom?
C: Yeah, I went to a psychiatrist downtown for a while. He gave me Thorazine and it made me sick. I never went back to him. In fact, he made me nervous . . .He really didn't seem to care about the problem that much. He made a comment, he said: "You seem mainly interested in yourself . . .I think you're an egotist." That kind of bothered me . . .He was flippant with me too—we just didn't hit it off.

The message is clear. Roger is warning his new therapist: Take me and my problems seriously or else I will not return. In effect, he is saying he wants someone to care about him. If he feels others do not care, his mode of action is consistent with his style of life—he becomes "nervous" and avoids them (in this case his former psychiatrist). Roger did not feel understood by his last therapist.

T: If I had a magic wand and could wave it over your head and get rid of this agoraphobia . . .what would be different in your life?

This is known as *The Question*. Adlerians use it to determine the purpose of the symptom and to differentiate somatic from psychogenic disorders. It is also usually indicative of what is being avoided—that is, for what purpose the symptom is generated.

C: It would take away a lot of the fears, frustrations of planning ahead. You see, I have to plan my week . . . I've got to make arrangements with friends to pick me up and drive me back . . . I could just float and enjoy life . . . I had to give up several good [job] positions be cause I'm afraid to fly.
T: Suppose I could get you to take a plane ride with me to Los Angeles? Suppose I would take care of whatever would happen at the other end?
C: You're on.

Without realizing it, Roger has told Mosak the purpose of his agoraphobia: He wants to be in control. Without his symptoms, he would not have to "plan ahead" and get others to look after him. The symptoms provide him with the excuse to dictate to others and have them in his service.

The rest of the session involved an exploration of the tasks of life. The extent to which individuals function adequately in each of these areas is a barometer of their level of social interest. Roger rated himself in this way:

> *Work:* Poor. He has to arrange for others to be with him. His symptoms are beginning to interfere with his role as a manager in the trucking business. He has to drink every morning to get to the office.
>
> *Friendship:* His friendships came mostly through his homosexual contacts, which were being affected by his agoraphobia.
>
> *Love:* He was engaged once, but she broke it off. He never had intercourse with a woman but frequently with men. Roger claimed this area was not a problem.
>
> *Self:* Basically, Roger thought he was a good person, but he was dissatisfied with his weight. He added that he "didn't like him self"—he felt "ugly inside." He was also worried about becoming alcoholic.
>
> *Spiritual:* Roger was raised a devout Catholic. He still prayed and lit candies, but avoided confession due to his sexual orientation. When he claimed, "I don't need confession," Mosak noted that "Even the Pope has a confessor." Roger replied without a hint of humor, "He needs it more than I do."

In conclusion, Roger was offered encouragement. He felt that at thirty-six, it was "too late in life" to continue with much else. He expressed openly his discouragement with himself and his inability to move ahead with his life. Mosak mentioned a former colleague who did not start medical school until he was forty-seven. However, Roger only wanted to work on his agoraphobia, and he seriously doubted his ability to overcome it.

The interview concluded with the therapist structuring the next two sessions, a technique especially effective with controllers. Roger would be meeting with a co-therapist who would be gathering the data for a *Life Style Assessment,* a form of investigation which Adlerians use to understand the goals, intentions, and biased apperceptions of clients. While Mosak implicitly made it clear that he was in control of the process, he respected Roger's desire to be in control.

In summary, Roger is a controller who uses passive means of controlling others. At thirty-six, his passive means of controlling (via his agoraphobia) has begun to exact a toll that even Roger can no longer tolerate, and he has begun therapy. He has strong inferiority feelings and underdeveloped social interest, as indicated by his poor overall functioning in the life tasks. Despite his poor self-concept, he still considers himself somewhat superior (he has higher standards than the Pope). The therapist has shown that he understands Roger's problems, that he takes them seriously, and that he is willing to align his goals with the client's, therefore reducing resistance. Most importantly, he has encouraged Roger, who is seriously discouraged, and he has given him hope.

SESSIONS 2-3
THE LIFE STYLE INTERVIEW

The next two sessions were spent with the co-therapist gathering Life Style Assessment data. Adlerians frequently practice *multiple psychotherapy* and have documented its benefits.

The Life Style Assessment is a diagnostic procedure which investigates the client's past and present situation in order to come to an understanding of the particular person's way of construing the world, other people, and ideas about self. Understanding the premises upon which a client operates helps to tailor treatment to the particular client and brings idiographic relevance to the nomothetic principles of Individual Psychology. The primary areas of investigation are the client's family constellation, which includes sibling descriptions, ratings, and an investigation of parental guiding lines and the family atmosphere, and the client's earliest recollections, the earliest memories the client can visualize and report to the therapist. Through this investigation, the therapist and client can arrive at an understanding of the particular client's personal history and current beliefs.

SESSION 4
THE LIFE STYLE SUMMARY

Mosak and the co-therapist spent the fourth session discussing the Life Style Summary with Roger. First the co-therapist read the recorded data to Mosak. Some highlights follow:

> Roger, age thirty-six, is the oldest in his family. He has a sister, Ginger, minus two (i.e., two years younger), a brother Evan, minus six, a brother, Arthur, minus nine and another brother died in childhood after Arthur. Roger described himself as a dreamer who fantasized a lot, had delusions of grandeur, looked at the world through rose-colored glasses, and who was happy through the age of six/seven. He was sexually promiscuous with boys and girls; they played show and tell. He was overweight as were his siblings. He had the usual arguments/fights with his sister—she is described as dumb and slovenly.
>
> Evan was described as being very precocious, very personable.
>
> He loved everyone, everyone loved him, both adults and kids.... He was more masculine than Roger. Arthur was born handicapped and was always overprotected. He was allowed to have his own way.
>
> Evan was most different—more outgoing and more gregarious. Ginger was most like Roger. She was feminine and he could relate to her more.
>
> As a youngster Roger was afraid of his father, who seemed like a tyrant. Roger was the most intelligent and the most industrious and he had higher standards of achievement. Evan was more athletic, rebellious, better looking, more masculine, and made more mischief. Roger was always overweight and he was the last to be picked for sports.
>
> Roger originally hated school and his mother had to keep taking him out of school. He hated other kids and felt inferior. There were no problems with

behavior and Roger was smart enough to keep his mouth shut. He was a patrol boy in the fourth and fifth grades and he enjoyed the role. He was "the captain" who liked having other people under him.

Roger's father would have been fifty-seven but he died in 1965. He was a truck driver and Roger didn't like him. The father used to beat Roger's mother and he chased them out of the house with a gun when he was drunk. He was seldom sober and he was always in a rotten mood. He was filthy and he took family possessions and sold them for booze.

The mother is fifty-nine years old and a housewife. She held the family together; she did the cooking and baking. She was always complaining about her ill health and how close she was to dying. She tried to play on everyone's sympathy and she was usually successful. Roger was most like her.

The co-therapist went on to describe the stormy and troubled marriage of Roger's parents. The mother saw herself as a "martyred saint." They had violent fights. Two other paternal uncles lived with them. Both were ex-convicts and one had five marriages, all ending in divorce; the other was an alcoholic. Mosak dictated the following summary

SUMMARY OF FAMILY CONSTELLATION

Roger is the oldest of four, in a 2-2 family, which makes him the older of two and the only boy in his group. He grew up in a family characterized by poverty, ethnic and marital discord, and one in which all the men acted as arms of the devil. The father was an alcoholic, a tyrant, abusive, and a squanderer of the family's money. Both uncles were thieves. One was moody in the negative sense, and the other was a playboy with five wives. The only positive model was Roger's mother, but she overdid a good thing. She was not only the standard bearer of good; she was also a martyr and a saint. Nevertheless, Mother was also a fearful person who, in spite of her religious faith, didn't believe that God would preserve her. Roger grew up hating his father, and determined that if all men were like his father and uncles, he wasn't going to be like that. He adopted his mother's standards of rightness and like her, opted for sainthood. Nevertheless, he fell short, but even though he acknowledged at times that he was wrong, he was still "righter" than others. He sat in judgment upon the whole world and himself—they were beneath him and he looked down upon them or expressed temper when he had too much of their wrong. He also looked down upon himself since he too was not all he felt he should be. He was fat in a family where being fat was bad. He was sexually active and this was bad. He was having negative feelings and for an observant Catholic, the thought was as sinful as the deed. He rested his feeling of belonging upon his intelligence, trying to be good, trying to be right, and staying out of trouble because that would make him like the men. He wanted to be a real man, and his sexual promiscuity was evidence of his pursuit. But somewhere along the line, Roger became discouraged, because (a) he misdefined masculinity (e.g., Evan was more masculine because he was more athletic), (b) he could not identify with the male role models in his family, and (c) he couldn't resolve the conflict between "goodness" and masculinity. In Roger's mind, one couldn't be good *and* a man simultaneously. He grew up unhappy partly because of the climate in which he grew up, partly because of his exalted standards for himself and others, partly because of his disdain for other people, and partly because of his disdain for himself.

T: Roger, how does that sound as a summary of the way you grew up?
C: Yeah—very much [*noticeably shaken*]. I think you hit it on the head.

They then went on to review the early recollections. The co-therapist read them aloud.

1. I went to first grade, I didn't go to kindergarten. The teacher asked me to do something—I told her to go to hell . . . [Age 5.]
2. I remember sitting in church. I stared at the statue of Christ on the cross. I was told that if you stared at it long enough, you could see Christ come off the cross. I got very excited and agitated—only saints were supposed to be able to do that. I imagined Christ coming towards me . . . [Age 7; Feeling excited.]
3. I remember an aunt of mine. She had come over with presents. I loved her . . . Everybody loved her. She was a very joyful woman. I was in total awe of her . . . [Age 5–6; Feeling awe.]
4. My Mother got pregnant. My Father was swearing at her and saying something about getting rid of it. He was going to stick his hand up her and pull it out. [Age 7; Feeling scared.]
5. They [the parents] had a couple that used to come over every weekend—a Polish couple. They started fighting. I remember specifically this woman talking about her sex life, that she wanted it, he didn't. The woman was crying in the kitchen . . . The husband telling her that she's a lousy lay anyway . . . [Age 8; Feeling "something I didn't understand—why was it so important."]

Early recollections are those memories which individuals store and use to assist them in moving through life. They reflect how people perceive life currently, and are quite effective as projective techniques. Mosak proceeded to dictate a note about Roger's view of life, self, and others, and noted Roger's "Basic Mistakes," and "Assets."

SUMMARY OF EARLY RECOLLECTIONS

"Nobody should tell me what to do; otherwise I balk. Men and women get along poorly and the conflict generally has to do with sex. I just can't understand what the conflict's all about. Men brutalize women and all women can do is suffer. Women, independent of men, can radiate warmth and joy. I stand in awe of them but I keep my distance and do not get involved with them. If I did want to get involved, it would be too late anyway. I want to be purged of all sin and be in union with God."

BASIC MISTAKES

1. He doesn't see the possibility of good man/woman relationships. Put a man and a woman in a cage and the blood is going to start to flow.

2. Roger idealizes women, feels he can't have them, and distances himself from them.

3. Roger wants to do it his way. "No one has the right to tell me what to do."

4. Roger tries too hard to be perfect because he regards himself as so much less than perfect.

ASSETS

1. He has positive feelings for women.

2. He does try to be better.

3. He uses religion for sanctification rather than downgrading himself.

4. Even though he is confused, he tries to figure things out.

5. He has a vivid fantasy life. He's had excellent training in it.

6. In many ways he comes close (though not in terms of birth order) to Joseph in the Bible: The one who can read omens in dreams, who has great dreams about the sun, moon, and planets.

T: O.K. Roger, that's our summary. [*Roger gets up to leave.*] No—don't get up yet.

C: I thought we were through.

T: No, just with the summary. Now that's how it looks to us. How do you feel about it?

C: I think it's pretty interesting about the women.

T: About the women?

C: Yeah ... about not really relating to them—putting them on a pedestal. In my life I have a lot of women friends and they're all looked at this way—and none of them are really with men.

T: Yeah, that comes out in your recollection. . . .

C: In fact any woman who's close to me doesn't have a relationship with men. . . .

T: Yeah, well men are all bastards anyway.

C: Then why am I sleeping with them?

T: Maybe that's so you can look down on them and look down on yourself?

C: [*Sighing—noticeably shaken*] Maybe it's just too much for me to comprehend right now.

T: O.K. We'll talk about that some more later. You said that the reading of the material was getting to you. What was getting to you?

C: . . . Just thinking about things I've tried to avoid thinking about for a long time.

T: Do you feel understood?

C: Right now—more so than I have in a long time.

T: You see, while what we wrote may not be 100% accurate, it's our first guess about you—

C: I'd say it's a good 95%.

T: And on that basis we have some things that we can already start talking about. If something is wrong, we'll modify it. Now next week we're going to talk a little about this, but we're also going to start talking about your present situation, because basically, that's the thing you've got to change. We may refer to some things in your childhood, but basically we're going to be talking about your fears...your job, and all those kinds of things you told us about in the first interview.

C: Very good—I'm looking forward to it.

T: Good. See you next week.

C: Thank you. Goodnight. [*Addressing the class*] Goodnight.

Roger, from wanting to talk only about his symptoms, is now examining his way of relating to the world and other people. Through the use of the Life Style Assessment, he is examining his view of life. Even the previously taboo subject of his homosexuality is now open for discussion and was raised by Roger himself. What was once unconscious and never clearly formulated has now been brought to light and presented to him in a way he can grasp and in his own language, using his own metaphors and imagery. He is told before he leaves that he is to be prepared at the next session to discuss his present situation since that is what he has to change.

SESSIONS 5–9
MODIFYING CONVICTIONS

The fifth session opened with Mosak asking Roger what he remembered from the previous session, two weeks ago (Roger had been sick and missed a week).

C: Well, let's see. I think I remember the fact that there were more good points than bad points about myself. Also, the tendency to put women on a shrine . . . and feel that they're untouchable. I also made a comment that I never have women who have anything to do with men totally as friends. . . .

Roger was obviously struck by the fact that the therapist included more "good points" (i.e., assets) than "bad points." Roger is discouraged, and hearing assets included in his Life Style Assessment encouraged him and helped strengthen the therapeutic relationship. He reports that he was impressed by his new understanding of his attitude towards women. Mosak re-read the entire Life Style Assessment summaries and discussed some of the points with him.

T: Now, as you hear it a second time today, Roger, what does it sound like?

C: It doesn't sound like anybody I know.

T: It doesn't?

C: No.

T: And yet two weeks ago you gave me a grade of "95." So what's happened in the two weeks?

C: I feet like a different person now.

T: You feel like you've changed.

C: Yeah.

T: Would you identify for me what the change is like or maybe how or what happened?

C: I don't know what happened. First of all I feel a little more sure of myself today. I feel less emotional today, not as embarrassed.

T: What was wrong with the emotional feeling you had?

C: I don't like to show emotion.

T: Why?

C: It's a sign of weakness.

T: Is it?

C: I think so. I try to be rather cold and calculating most of the time.

T: Where did you learn that emotion was a sign of weakness?

C: Well, I don't like to put up with anybody who shows emotion. I don't have the patience for anybody who starts crying in front of me or starts pouring out their heart to me—I don't like it at all.

T: I see. So if you don't show emotion or other people are not permitted to show emotion to you, then you can keep your distance from them?

C: Yeah. It's like somebody saying that they love you—to me it's a negative word. I don't ever use it because it's stupid. Nobody ever really loves anybody.

Mosak raised the issue of Roger's style of relating to people. Hearing one's style of life summarized can have a disorienting effect upon one's self-image and perspective of others and life. Roger grew emotional upon hearing it, and that bothered him. The therapist interpreted Roger's dampening of emotions as a method for keeping distance from others. As Roger went on to point out, getting close to people meant getting hurt, and he wanted no more pain in his life. By "cutting off" his emotions, he attempted to protect himself.

Roger sees life *vertically* rather than *horizontally*—that is, he is concerned with who is better than or on top of whom. People are not equals cooperating for a common cause and working together; they are "out to get you." This is evident in Roger's agoraphobia: If he does not get too far out of his house, people will not get too close to him.

T: So for you the important goal is to be dominant in every relationship. There's a master and a slave and by golly—

C: I like to call the shots.
T: You better be the master.
C: Um hmm, yeah. I'm the leader too. . . .
T: Will you do something for me, Roger? While there's no way for us to pre-
dict what's going to happen, I'd like you to compose, since you have a
great fantasy life, a future autobiography. . . Ten years from now you'll
be forty-five years old. What do you think your life will be like?
C: It could go either way. If this therapy-thing works out, I might be quite
a fantastic individual . . . have a lover, a beautiful home somewhere,
travel a lot . . .
T: Supposing therapy doesn't take, as it were?
C: Well, I think ten years from now I would just be a bum. . . I would just
sell everything, have long hair, and look like Jesus Christ walking down
the street . . . It might be rather interesting.
T: No problems, but what meaning?
C: It's better to be a king of derelicts than not a king at all.
T: As you just put it, in ten years, if therapy takes you'll be doing something
fantastic . . . and if not, you'll be the king of the derelicts.
C: One way or another I'm going to make it.

Roger is exhibiting what Adler called antithetical modes of apperception.
He'll either be the best or the worst. The strong sense of inferiority and superiority are two sides of the same coin and the basic problem is the meaning
Roger has given to life: He must be the best. With that as a prerequisite for relating, he runs into considerable difficulty in life. The goal at this point in treatment is to encourage Roger to begin relating horizontally to others.

T: Roger, you're counting on your mentality [*Roger's term for "intellect"*] to
dominate people . . . What if you met your match?
C: . . . Maybe you're my match.
T: What if somebody gets to you through feelings? What then? . . . You see,
two weeks ago, we got to you through feeling.
C: I know—that bothered me all the way home.
T: You see, I didn't see you as submissive [*Roger earlier had referred to him-
self as "submissive" for showing feelings*]. I saw you as feeling. You're the
one who attached "feeling equals weakness." I attached to it "feeling
equals humanity." By golly, the guy's human.
C: Yeah, but that phase is over.
T: Oh, I don't know—Isn't it possible I might get you again?
C: It's possible.
T: How hard are you going to defend yourself against it?

Roger claimed he did not have to defend himself in therapy, and Mosak
pointed out that no, he did not have to but that in fact he *did*. Roger pointed out that he would be "mortified" if he ran into any of the class on the
street—he is afraid to look any of them in the face. The therapist drew a

parallel between that and his behavior toward others in general: He keeps his distance from others. When asked if anyone in the room really cared about him, Roger flatly, and sincerely, replied, "No."

C: If I threw myself out the window right now, nobody would shed a tear.

T: Do you think any of them would try and stop you?

C: No. Why would they? They might get their names in the paper tomorrow. That's why they would stop me . . . [*They'd be famous.*]

T: Supposing somebody grabbed you [before you jumped out]? What would you feel?

C: Maybe they'd want to go to bed with me, I don't know.

T: But that's the only reason?

C: They'd probably push me out after one night.

T: So it's inconceivable that anybody would really care?

C: People really don't care about people that much. They put on a good front, but basically—

T: Are you speaking about people or are you speaking about Roger?

C: Just in general.

T: Roger—Do I care? [*Mosak is introducing the issue of "love."*]

C: I'd like to think you care. I'm not sure though.

T: What makes me the exception?

C: Financial gain.

T: I don't get one penny for seeing you.

C: I know that—I appreciate that. But, you get [money] from these people in here [the class].

T: I don't get one penny from them.

C: [*Surprised*] I apologize, I didn't know that. [*Apologizes repeatedly.*]

T: So the best you can do is accuse me of being interested in you as a case study . . .

C: [*Still apologizing sheepishly.*]

T: You've got to find some other reason [than financial gain]—that ain't it. What makes me different? Why might I possibly care for you? Because I'll tell you—You try and go out that window and I'm going to grab you.

C: Maybe you don't want the notoriety—bad for business.

T: Yeah, you're right. But on the other hand, maybe I want the fame? . . . My name would get in the paper. [*Long pause*] Why might I possibly care?

C: I was thinking about that—I'm really rather confused. . . I mentioned it to a friend as a matter of fact—I asked "Why is this man even bothering?"

T: That's my question . . .

C: Feelings of being a great humanitarian?

T: Not really. Not by seeing one patient for free . . .

C: Yeah, that's true.

T: What's my game?

C: Maybe you thought it was an interesting case? . . .

T: You know, Roger, after thirty years—

C: Nothing is new—

T: Yeah ... [I've dealt with about everything.] Why am I bothering?

C: [*Subdued*] Give me a week to think about it.

T: I will. I hope you will.

C: I am going to think about it

T: Good, because that's a crucial issue ... it is not only important in terms of your therapy, but it's important for your life. Because if one person can care for you, then you'll have to ask another question, and that is, maybe two can.

C: [*Somewhat choked up*] It's very difficult for me to believe it.

The interview concluded on that note. Roger added that he does listen to what his therapist talks about. He came to the therapy session alone, and has found it easier and easier to move about unescorted outside. He has also been driving to work with greater ease. Roger commented, "I just wanted you to know that." The drinking had decreased noticeably as well. Asked how he accounted for it, Roger replied, "It's an awakening to reality, finding out I am a somebody."

This session, along with the previous one (the Life Style Assessment interview), was a turning point in treatment. Roger, having begun to accept himself as "a somebody," was losing his feelings of inferiority. The less inferior he felt, the easier time he had with healthy, consensual interaction. He no longer had to *safeguard* himself against what he feared would be a horrible fate if he exposed himself and his imperfections to others.

The sixth session began with Roger claiming to have been doing a lot of thinking. "I haven't wasted so much time in my life as I thought," he reported. His gains, from a behavioral standpoint, continued to grow as he attempted more activities independently. Mosak encouraged even more, and used task-setting (i.e., homework) to continue the growth.

T: So my question, Roger, is what can we do—since apparently you do want to live a happier life—to help you live a happier life? ...

Mosak is using the pronoun "we." He is communicating to Roger that therapy is a collaborative enterprise, and that human interaction can be one of mutual respect and cooperation.

C: Well, can the people here [the class] make suggestions?

T: No, they're only permitted to be observers.

C: Well, can you make suggestions?

T: I can, but I don't think I want to, Roger, because I don't think that would do you any good. And being committed to your welfare I don't think I would want to do anything that wasn't for your good. ...

The responsibility for therapy is squarely on Roger's shoulders. The message being communicated is this: *We* may be in this together, but *you* are in charge of your life and are ultimately responsible for it, for better or worse.

Should any action or homework assignment "backfire," Roger will not be able to blame anybody. He will be responsible.

Roger decided to attend the opera—provided that he could sit in the back row. Roger also agreed to go to the Art Institute. Mosak readily agreed and showed "faith" in Roger's ability to do it. Roger wondered why things had become so hard for him to do. "When I was twenty-one, it was easier," he commented.

T: Because at twenty-one, you apparently got discouraged about yourself and at twenty-one you "came out."

C: Yeah, at twenty-one, exactly.

T: Somewhere along that period, you apparently became discouraged.

C: Well, what happened? What caused the total disintegration . . . ?

T: Well, my guess is, that as time went on your confidence in yourself eroded because you weren't going anywhere in life. And then you have a few bad experiences tossed in [*Roger was deeply hurt by his first lover*], and you weave all of those things together, and you say, "Well, what's the use?" And that's the point I would like to turn around. Because I think people function better when they are encouraged than when they're discouraged.

C: I found out an important thing this week . . . I can't stand disappointments or anybody rejecting me. I never realized how deep rooted it was . . . It goes deeper than just lovers, even people, friends—as a consequence I really go overboard with people as far as being overly generous with gifts, entertaining, so forth.

T: You mean you try to buy their approval?

C: Yeah, a little too much so.

T: Why do you think you need their approval so badly?

C: I don't know, I just don't think I could exist without it.

Roger is overcompensating for his perceived inferiority in the eyes of others. His low opinion of himself, combined with his high standards, convinced him that no one would be able to "truly" care for him, therefore, he bought their approval. Mosak placed Roger's goal into perspective.

T: . . . I don't think any of us could exist, Roger, if we didn't have some approval—but do we *have* to have everybody's approval, and do we to *have* everybody's approval constantly?

C: That's my problem. I need it constantly. I've got to be constantly wanted, constantly sought after . . .

T: Roger, your desire to please and to buy people—that kind of thing—and your fearing their rejection or disapproval of you is really a very ambitious kind of goal. You see, as a Catholic you believe in God, and here is God, the most perfect Being, right? Does everybody love God?

C: [*Very softly*] No.

T: Some people even reject Him?

C: [*Again, very softly*] Definitely.

T: And even the people who love God—do they love God constantly? So here is God, the most perfect Being, willing to take his chances with human beings—but you're not willing to take the same chances that even God takes.

C: Good point.

T: Do you think you might want to take the same chances with humanity God does? . . . And if somebody rejects you . . . there are always atheists!

C: Doesn't make them an atheist if they reject me, does it? [*Laughing.*]

T: Well, in a sense, it does.

C: In my mind it would—Saint Roger is not being venerated. True—[*laughing again*] very true.

T: . . . Perhaps, Roger, you have a place, even if somebody does reject you?

Roger, needing caring and approval, is afraid of rejection, and Mosak confronts him with the unrealistic and unattainable nature of his goals. He even gets Roger to joke about it. If he gets too intimate with people, they have some control over him, and if he gives up control, they are liable to hurt him—and the surest way to hurt Roger is to reject him. Therefore Roger will attempt to control ("dominate," to use Roger's language) his relationships. What he cannot control, he does not want. If he does it too actively, he is afraid of being too much like his father; therefore he will do it passively, like his mother, through fears and suffering (i.e., agoraphobia). Roger assumes that in order for him to be "relaxed" he must be in control. Mosak is attempting to convince him that maybe he can be *more* in control by being *less* in control.

Roger raised the issue of his engagement when he was nineteen. The discussion which followed highlighted the above issues.

C: I was engaged to a young woman . . . we got along beautifully. She would get me aroused—to a point—but not to actual intercourse, and I broke it off with her. . . Her closing statement to me was "You're queer." Now evidently she picked something up. In the two years I was with her there was no rejection. This is before I even came out and knew what a homosexual was.

T: Well, first of all, her calling you a queer, when you had not come out, was certainly rejection. She was telling you that she was plenty mad at you . . . But secondly, my feeling is that she called you a queer not because she sensed anything, but having tried to arouse you over and over and over again and your not responding, she just had to rub your nose in it. She was just plain mad at you because here she is having gone to all that trouble and you're not going to respond. I don't think she sensed anything.

C: Yeah, it does seem to fall into place.

They continued to explore Roger's relationship to men and women. Roger moved back to the topic of his homosexuality. Of the many possible reasons they discussed for it, three were meaningful to Roger: (a) He had a very low opinion of men and rejected the masculine role while growing up; (b) It was easier to be homosexual than heterosexual. There were no commitments, fewer responsibilities, and less intimacy; and (c) Roger was very concerned that a woman would control him, whereas he could control a man more easily. The interview concluded with a discussion about a woman who had been trying to seduce Roger for the past few weeks.

T: What would happen if you succumb to this girl who is out to seduce you?
C: I would be afraid that I would get involved emotionally.
T: And?
C: I don't know what would happen. It just goes against my mentality or grain. I just can't accept it, that's all.
T: So, you apparently are not willing to rule out that it could ever happen?
C: [*Laughing*] You really know how to get to me.
T: [*Laughing with him*] I hope so.
C: I don't believe you. You're right, I didn't say "No." So maybe I'm not ruling out the idea of it ever happening.
T: Apparently not.

The session ended with one additional point about Roger's homosexuality: Homosexuality is a choice, not a biological condition. If Roger is to choose it, he needs to choose it for "good" reasons, and not out of fear and insecurity.

The seventh session opened with Roger in very good spirits. He had spent a half hour standing on a busy downtown street watching people go by, and enjoyed it. The discussion led to him asking about the nature of fears.

T: You see, the only people who have difficulties with fears are those that have to be in control. If you feel you have to be in control, there's so much you have to be afraid of because there are so many things that can go wrong.
C: Well why does somebody get that way?...
T: They lose their courage... You see, courage is the willingness to take a risk, even if you don't know what's going to happen... or even if there's a chance it might go against you.
C: I'm not a coward. I mean I'd fight if I had to or defend myself if I had to...
T: You're talking about a total coward, in some areas you think of yourself as a coward. When you're afraid to leave your house, alone, you're a coward. Aren't you?
C: Yeah, but I don't want to think of myself as a coward...
T: Well, what is a coward?
C: Someone who's afraid of something.
T: [*Laughing*] By that definition, I guess, in some areas, you're a coward.
C: [*Somewhat taken aback*] No one's ever called me that before.

T: Well, I haven't called you that—

C: Well, you're intimating it.

T: No, I haven't called you that—I'm saying *you think* of yourself as a coward.

C: [*Very softly*] A tough front.

T: Did you hear what you just said? A "tough front" implies that that's not what you are. Strip the front away and you've got somebody who's afraid.

C: I come on very strong with people though, I suppose.

T: A lot of cowards do. They hope that nobody will pick them out . . .

C: But I deal with dockmen, you know, truck drivers. Now I can really buffalo them . . .

T: But in intimate relationships—and I'm not talking about sexual relationships—

C: No, no—

T: Between people, you're scared.

C: Well, I don't have any intimate relationships with people . . .

T: Sure, you see yourself as a coward. You're unwilling to risk it.

C: Why does it have to be cowardly because you're unwilling to risk an intimate relationship? Why do you have to have an intimate relationship?

T: You don't have to, but there's a difference between "I choose not to have any," and "I'm afraid to have any."

C: I'll buy that.

The therapist is working in two directions here. First, he is working to assure that the gains made with the agoraphobia will last. By reframing the symptoms as indicative of a loss of *courage*, Roger's ability to rationalize was greatly diminished. Adlerians call this technique "spitting in the soup." He may still choose to do it, but it will certainly not "taste" as good. With the therapeutic relationship well established, Mosak became more *confrontive* in his interpretive style.

The other direction the therapist was taking involved motivating Roger to engage others meaningfully. Given the limited number of sessions, Mosak was working on Roger's attitude of being "tough" with others. He may be tough when he is in control (e.g., at work with subordinates), but intimately, one-to-one, he is a "coward." Again, the distinction is made between *having* to choose something out of fear and *choosing* to do something due to preference: Roger is choosing out of fear. The discussion rapidly turned to Roger's overall distaste for people in general.

T: You told me that you did all kinds of things to sort of buy people's favor—Why would you want to do that for people who are basically stinkers? . . .

C: I think it's more interesting inviting [over to his home] people you dislike . . . you can prove your superiority to them, put them down . . .

T: Yeah, but then, at least I've been taught—and I happen to think there's a large element of truth in it—that people that have to buy their superiority by pushing other people down don't think very much of themselves in the first place.

C: That may be true but it still is a nice feeling—

T: And that, as you say—

C: [*Bitterly*] Revenge is sweet . . .

T: Instead of having to talk about *them* [the people Roger looks down upon], let's talk about your inferiority feelings . . . What makes you inferior?

C: A combination of things—the area I was born in, the environment, family, we were a bunch of fat slobs. I didn't want anybody to even see them—I'd be ashamed.

T: What's that got to do with you? . . .

C: I always felt I was cheated because I never really had a good family life . . .

T: Well, I'd say to that perhaps, tough. I feel regret that you didn't have a better family life, but, what's that got to do with today, feeling inferior? A lot of people have transcended their early, unhappy family life. . . .

C: It's my perfection again . . . . I won't even go out of the house if . . .

T: In other words, to be equal to the rest of us you have to be perfect, without blemish.

C: Well, I have to be above—I like admiration. . . [*emotionally*] All my life I've been put down, with people making fun of me—calling me a fat slob, a pig . . . now I want people to look at me and I want to be wanted, I want them to eat their hearts out to get at me—male or female. I want them to really just lust after me. . . .

T: You said something which just threw me there for a moment.

C: What's that?

T: Male or female to lust over me. Why both?

C: Why both? I enjoy a woman who adores me or wants to go to bed with me, especially when I say no. It turns me on . . .

T: It turns you on to turn them on?

C: Yeah, sexually [*sheepishly*].

T: So basically, you want to get revenge on the world for giving you a bad time growing up?

C: It didn't end at growing up. It continued on and on.

T: So you want to hurt the world back?

C: [*Remorsefully*] People know how to hurt. They know how to stick a knife in you. Nobody knows the private misery people go through because somebody will just say, "My God—you've gained weight. You look like hell," or whatever the case may be. . . .

T: So you plan to continue with your fight against the world?

C: No, I'm tired of fighting . . .

T: It sounds like you're preparing to fight for the rest of your life.

C: If need be. . . .

They continued to discuss Roger's stance towards others. Adler described neurotics as going through life as if they were in hostile territory, and that is

Roger's movement through life exactly. Mosak encouraged him to change his attitude—about himself, especially.

T: Maybe you want to stop fighting?
C: I'm willing, but—
T: But they aren't?
C: But they aren't exactly. I'm more than willing [*passionately*], I'm tired of fighting. I've been fighting for a long time.
T: There's only one way to tell you're tired—not if your mouth says so, but if you put your fists down.

Mosak encouraged him to choose different friends, ones that would not find so many faults and who would not be so ready to "fight." "I would much rather have friends who are going to treat me well," his therapist added.

C: You know what—you're right. This week I went through a whole list of people I know—mentally, and I started cutting them out. And I must agree with you, some of them are real assholes. They always have been assholes and why I've been bothering with them ten, fourteen years I don't know.
T: Good . . . Is it possible you might want to choose someone who isn't an asshole?

Roger agreed to make the effort. Mosak invited him to have an "easier life": Life, as Roger had been living it, must have been awfully tough. Roger conceded he has a "chip" on his shoulder when he meets people. He expects them to be hostile. Mosak *created an image* for Roger to keep in mind when he met new people.

C: Now I'm going to have to think they're a nice person.
T: Why do you have to think that? Just look them over . . . Why don't you just experience them, just get to know them without any preconceptions about whether they're nice or lousy? . . . Have you ever seen two dogs engaged in sniffing behavior? [*Both laugh.*] They look each other over, you know? . . .
C: [*Laughing*] So you want me to go "sniffing"?
T: Yeah, sniffing around, exactly . . .
C: Then I'll have my fear of rejection again. . . .
T: So what—you mean everybody has to love you? Remember, even God doesn't have that privilege. If you know you're good enough, you don't have to worry about what they think.
C: It's time to start taking my shrine apart, right? Someone told me that, about my house. He says you're building a shrine to yourself. And at the time I was really upset. Now I realize he was right. [*Long pause*] Completely. That's something I noticed a long time ago, but I was never ready to admit it. . . .
T: So even your house reflects your god-like standards.

Mosak and Roger discussed issues which Roger knew all too well but had never clearly formulated or examined. He was confronted with his "god-like" standards, his strong feelings of inferiority, hypersensitivity, and hostile attitude towards others. While sympathetic to Roger's history, the therapist powerfully confronted Roger with his responsibility for *continuing* to feel and act inferior. Roger cannot keep blaming his past. The other crucial issue worth commenting upon is the Adlerian's emphasis upon behavior—if Roger is truly tired of fighting, then he must "put down his fists." Adlerians emphasize the primacy of behavior; individuals must do more than simply "talk a good game." They must make movement.

Roger raised the issue of his relationship with his mother during the eighth session. He was by then functioning with virtually no agoraphobic symptoms. He had attended a play and enjoyed it; he had ceased having a problem with his drinking.

T: Now, Roger, it would seem to me that nobody could make a person feel guilty unless he chooses to feel guilty himself . . . Why do you choose to feel guilty with respect to your mother?

C: Primarily because she's blind and crippled. She uses this as kind of a crutch against me. it's not like she's alone, she has company all the time—people living with her.

T: How does she make you feel guilty? . . . Give me the words.

C: "You left me—you don't care about me" . . . It just goes on and on.

T: . . . What are your lines?

C: I usually don't say anything because I don't want to hurt her feelings.

After clarifying the problem a bit more, Mosak came to the point.

T: I would like to ask a couple of things, Roger. First of all, when your mother says, "You left me, you don't care for me, etc., etc.," do you think she's trying to get you to feel guilty? . . .

C: She loves it.

T: I got a hunch she wants something else.

C: You do?

T: Yeah—and I got a hunch that that's what you're not delivering. Not because you don't want to deliver it, but because you don't even know that that's what she's asking. My guess is she's inviting you to tell her that you love her . . . Maybe she's just looking for some kind of reassurance that you care? . . .

C: That's true, I never say that to her. I'll have to give that a try. This may be exactly it. I think you hit it pretty well.

They went on to discuss why Roger should choose to feel guilty. The primary purpose seemed to be his desire to be perfect. It was related to his god-like goals. Roger felt that there was so much he should do, he felt guilty for doing anything less than would be ideal. This, combined with the fact that Roger was afraid of getting too close to people and showing/expressing his feelings, created a distance which his mother attempted to close by using her suffering and complaining.

Adlerians believe that you cannot change other people's behavior, but you can change your own, and in that way, possibly the situation. Roger could not change his mother's behavior, but he could change his response to it. When he did, something happened which amazed him. Roger told her he loved her and showed some genuine concern, and his mother became "much more liberal," according to Roger. He reported that after one afternoon conversation, their relationship improved.

The interview then turned to Roger's opinion of the way others perceive him. Roger, while admitting he had come a long way, expressed concern over the fact that he was still afraid of opening himself up too much to others. They just would not like him if they knew the "real Roger." Mosak then "broke" one of his own rules: He allowed the class to participate and say what they thought of Roger. Roger was stunned and waited anxiously. The response was overwhelmingly one of interest and genuine concern. Unlike Roger's (admitted) expectations, no one was bored and no one found him in any way disagreeable. When the class was done, Mosak asked Roger what he thought.

C: [*Very subdued*] I'm very impressed . . . They make me feel very, very good—I feel great . . . They do take me seriously. I never dreamed that I was worth concern. . . .

Roger went on with Mosak to discuss why Roger was so surprised. People had seen all his weaknesses, flaws, and imperfections, and still they cared about him. Roger was sincerely moved. The issue the therapist raised was that now Roger might want to do something about his newly discovered knowledge and take a chance with people. Almost immediately Roger stated, "I've met someone who I think cares and I'm trying."

Roger admitted that he really wanted somebody to love him, and he thought he had found somebody to love, a young man. They had spent an entire week living together (it had been two weeks since the last therapy session) and despite Roger's attempts to "buy" the man's affections, the man had refused to be "bought." He seemed to genuinely care. The session ended with Roger stating, "I do care about people." Mosak gave Roger a homework assignment.

T: What would we see if the real you came out of hiding?
C: [*Laughing*] Probably one hell of a mess . . . an emotional wreck, someone who can't really cope. . . .
T: [*Speaking of Roger's tendency to secretly become emotional and occasionally cry when alone*] Crying . . . has nothing to do with masculinity—or to make a pun, *mess*-culinity, since you said you were a mess.
C: That's a good term—I like that.

T: It only has to do with being human. I would like to set you a task. Do you know any people who aren't messes?

C: Yeah.

T: Good. For the next week, I would like you to act as if you were one of those adequate people. Now it's going to be an act, no doubt about it, but it's not phony any more than a person that plays Hamlet is phony even though he's playing a role. I would just like you to try out that role. I would like you to act, for one week, as if you were not a mess. And if you don't know what that means concretely, then when you get into a certain kind of situation where you feel in doubt, you say "How would so-and-so who is adequate behave in this kind of situation?" And then, act that way.

Roger is moving in a healthy, prosocial direction. Social interest is being fostered. As his attitude changes and his motivation is modified, Mosak is including the behavioral component. Roger is accustomed to thinking of himself as a "mess." His strivings for perfection have usually met with feelings of inferiority; hence, subjectively, he feels like a "wreck"—a mess. Though motivation may change rapidly, the behavioral component requires practice and self-training and quite often lags behind the motivational change. The task to act *as if* he were an adequate person introduces modeling principles, especially when Roger is asked to act as if he were someone adequate that he knows. If Roger follows through with the task, he will incorporate the behavioral component more rapidly into his modified life style. In time, it will be difficult to differentiate acting adequate from being adequate.

Roger came into the ninth session and told of a situation that occurred at work. He had been "ranting and raving" about how life is so "rotten" and how "everybody is out to hurt you and nobody cares," when a woman came up to him and said, "I care." He said all he could think about were the therapy sessions. He said he felt "great." He said he smiled, and it changed the whole course of the evening.

The interview moved to a discussion of Roger's *dreams*. Adlerians view dreams as rehearsal for possible solutions to the problems of living. They are teleologic and serve to generate emotions which carry through to the next day and help motivate individuals to behave in certain ways which are consistent with their styles of life. Roger related this dream:

C: I was laying in bed . . . and I opened my eyes and I looked at the end of my bed. There was kind of a cocktail party going on with everybody dressed in 1800s garb. Out of this crowd came a woman—fantastically beautiful—who sat on the edge of my bed and said, "Well, can I help you with your problem—we're going to talk about it." I said, "Go away—this is the result of too many martinis or something." But we talked and she said, "Tell me what's wrong?" and I went on about things we [Mosak and Roger] had talked about. I really felt much better.

T: Much better about what?

C: About myself and life...

T: O.K. It [the dream] is your creation: Why did you put a woman at the foot of your bed?

C: I thought about that. [*Laughing*] I don't know why...

T: Why a beautiful woman? You could have put an ugly woman there. Roger, are you toying with the notion of becoming heterosexual? Or at least giving it a whirl?

C: Ah—yeah, I have been thinking about it [*sheepishly*].

They went on to discuss Roger's surprising admission. He was afraid that if he got involved with a woman, he would be tied down. It never occurred to Roger that he could get involved with a woman without being committed. It related back to Roger's idealizing women: He believed that women would not just "sleep around."

T: Roger, suppose I went down to see my bookie this afternoon and bet on whether in the next six months you would wind up in bed with a woman, should I give or take odds?

C: You should take them.

T: O.K. What odds should I take?

C: 90 to 1 [that he won't sleep with a woman].

T: 90 to 1 hardly leaves any room, and your [dream] would sort of indicate to me that your odds are better than 90 to 1...

Mosak and Roger played the "Game of Probabilities." It is a way of investigating the potential movement of an individual in the future. Though Roger is preparing himself psychologically and emotionally for a heterosexual encounter, behaviorally he is hesitant. Mosak and Roger explored different situations in which Roger might be more comfortable being with a woman.

The session ended with Roger summarizing what he learned in therapy: He was less fearful and accepted himself more. He learned to say "no" to people, to stop feeling sorry for himself and to "function better." Most importantly, Roger said he learned that he was a human being, and that was the most meaningful thing for him. Before he left, he said that his performance at work had improved so much that he was getting a "major promotion." As he left, he warmly said goodbye to the class and the therapist.

Roger never made it back for the last interview. Unexpectedly, his mother became very ill. Roger decided he wanted to be there for her. She died soon after he arrived. The quarter ended at the Institute and Roger decided to attempt to manage on his own.

SUMMARY AND CONCLUSION

Adlerian psychology is a holistic, teleoanalytic theory which stresses the unity of the person and the examination of the individual's goals and movement through life. Behavior that is useful—that is, conducive to healthy, cooperative functioning—is viewed as the ultimate goal of therapy. Such behavior, with its component emotional and psychological factors, is called *social interest*.

During the course of psychotherapy, Roger moved from a position of viewing others as his enemies, the world as hostile, and himself as inferior, to a position of genuine concern for others and acceptance of himself. His unrealistically high goals of personal superiority, most prominently evident in his choice of agoraphobic symptoms to control and dominate those around him, gave way to a more accepting, caring, and mutually respectful stance as he gained more confidence in himself and as his feelings of inferiority were put to rest. In nine therapy sessions, he reappraised his orientation to life, others, and himself, and emerged a happier, more productive individual. In short, he developed social interest.

Mosak utilized a number of techniques to move Roger towards social interest. He encouraged him and gave him hope. By utilizing a Life Style Assessment, the therapist worked on modifying the client's mistaken attitudes, and not just eliminating symptoms. At various times, the therapist used such tactics as Confrontation, Future Autobiography, Humor, the Game of Probabilities, Acting "As If," Tasksetting, Dreams, Multiple Psychotherapy, Interpretation, "Spitting in the Client's Soup," Placing in Perspective, Creating Images, and The Question.

As Roger's convictions became more adaptive and flexible, his private logic came more in line with common sense. He became more motivated to meet the challenges of life in a useful, cooperative way. Individual psychology provides the psychotherapist and client with a system and philosophy to encourage such change.

Editors' Introduction

This case illustrates the richness and depth of analytical psychotherapy. The therapist uses analysis of dreams and of client drawings, as well as analysis of transference and countertransference, to help her client grow emotionally. Both the client and the therapist have to deal with the intensity of their emotional responses to the client's decision to abandon her children in the interest of her personal growth and development. It is interesting to speculate about whether a male therapist could have fully understood this issue or dealt effectively with it.

At one point in therapy, the client becomes quite critical of her therapist and openly describes her as inadequately trained and unqualified to be practicing analytical psychotherapy. Sullivan handles these issues well; she and her client work through this problem and move on to other therapeutic issues.

This case describes an in-depth relationship between the therapist and client that involved meeting three times each week over the course of five years. This type of analysis is aimed at self-growth as well as the treatment of emotional disorders.

CHRISTINA
Barbara S. Sullivan

The immediate issues leading Christina into therapy were an inability to begin a major creative project in her work and a sense of futility and chaos about the meaning or direction of her life. About nine months before calling me, she had left her husband and two preadolescent children and rented temporary living space. Her despair, which had grown steadily throughout her marriage, had not significantly lifted after leaving it, which led to further despair. Realizing that no new birth would come from simply leaving her family, she called me for therapy.

I saw Christina as an intelligent, talented, professionally well-functioning woman with severe narcissistic difficulties. She presented herself in disorderly bits and pieces, jumping from topic to topic, apparently unable to remember what we had talked about in our last hour or to connect emotionally with what she did remember about yesterday or last week; subjectively, she felt fragmented and lost. Two months into the work she presented a dream that revealed the depth of the wounding to her wholeness:

> I did a long narrow painting that reminds me of the drawings in the children's book, *Four Fur Feet*. At the top was a washy kind of sky and at the bottom was grass, with deer and a woodsy place. An idyllic scene. On the right hand side of the painting

Excerpt from Barbara Stevens Sullivan, "Two Clinical Examples," *Psychotherapy Grounded in the Feminine Principle* (pp. 164–172). © 1989 by Chiron Publications. Reprinted by permission of the publisher.

I put in a figure in plastic. It was a little like a figure eight—like those . . . candles you put on a child's birthday cake—with arms and eyes [see illustration].

This is the one part of the picture that can't be changed, for it's plastic. As I made it, I thought, "I'll put the hand here so it's clear it's not masturbation." I showed the painting to a woman and she showed it to people and they praised it a lot. I gave the woman credit for inspiring me.

The . . . plastic figure reminded Christina of a diagram she had seen in Jung's work:

. . . Jung uses this diagram as a map of the archetype of the self. This interpretation of the plastic figure eight as an image of Christina's self is supported by her association to an eight-year-old's birthday cake. Four is typically a number of wholeness (the four points of the compass, the four seasons of the year, for example). Eight is double four. In associating her one unchangeable element to a *divided* Self, Christina is expressing . . . her unconscious despair of ever unifying herself.

Her essential disunity is further expressed in the elements of the doubly spiralling figure eight. The eye is in the top half and the hand in the bottom. The eye cannot see what the hand does; the hand is cut off from the eye's direction. The hand's position, which we must assume is fixed like all else in this image, makes clear that what is happening is not masturbation. Thus the hand's position also precludes masturbation. Christina is permanently unable to give herself pleasure, to love her body, to make love to herself.

These . . . pessimistic implications are softened by two positive elements in the dream. First there is the idyllic rural scene forming the backdrop to the painting. *Four Fur Feet,* the book Christina remembered, is the story of an unidentified furry animal who "walked around the world/on his four fur feet/ and never made a sound." Just so, Christina as a small child must have experienced herself as "never making a sound" in the sense that no one ever seemed to hear her. But the pictures of the round, round world around which the four fur feet walk are delightfully rich in variety and color. This world includes wild animals and fish, cities and railroad trains, meadows, rivers, and a brilliant warming sun. The four fur feet travel all around a wonderfully intact, vital self.

The second hopeful . . . element in the dream is Christina's relationship with the other woman, a relationship we can hope to bring to life in the course of our work. This other woman, apparently simply through her interest in Christina and her work, inspires her to paint the state of her self. Although . . . Christina could not emotionally appreciate the meaning of her dream, the image was permanent . . . Seen by others, the painting leads to praise and this allows Christina to feel good about herself and generous toward the woman who helped her. She is filled with love as a result of receiving praise, love for herself and love for her companion . . .

The dream's instructions seemed clear: . . . I was to see the painting she made and to communicate to her my appreciation for her effort. In the simplest of terms, Christina needed to be cherished and esteemed—loved—by me. . . .

It is not a simple thing to empathize with another person's experience, however, and for the first two years of our work I had great difficulty aligning myself with Christina as a woman who had left her children. . . . Initially, I did not appreciate the intensity of my response to this woman who had "abandoned" her children. But looking back, I remembered that a friendship of mine had collapsed not long before when my friend left her child. I had not been able to absorb the horror the image of a mother leaving her child contained for me. . . . To look such a woman in the face, any mother must confront her own impulses to leave her children; we must each face the ways in which our mothers abandoned us. Resonating to Christina's plight meant sympathizing with the woman who was playing the role of the Bad Mother in this human drama.

The most immediate information we ever have about what is going on in a case is countertransference data, and the most interesting countertransference experience I had with Christina in the first two years of our work was becoming physically cold in my hours with her. I realized it was invariably when she was talking about her children that I started to shiver, and from there it was a short step to realizing that the incidents she was describing were those in which she was shockingly cold toward her children. . . .

For this beginning phase of the work, the theoretical attitude I was taking toward her, around the issue of her children, could be summed up as follows. Because she had been unable to contain her rejecting, hateful feelings toward her children, her feelings had possessed her and led her to leave the children with no warning. I saw my task as helping her to face and accept those rejecting feelings as legitimate parts of her self. . . .

Had I not been so horrified by the external sight of a woman who leaves her children, I would have been freer to pay attention to its psychological implications. Early in our work, Christina had dreamed of being on a long journey, a metaphor for the journey she was starting with me. In the dream as the bus she was riding turned the corner toward her home, its progress stopped. Chris saw an ambulance and a police car beside an overturned child's doll carriage: a little girl had been hit by a car and severely injured or killed. The wounded little girl had been playing at motherhood, enjoying and delighting in her maternal instincts. . . .

My physical coldness reflected the fact I had caught her emotionally cold and unempathic attitude toward herself. Thoroughly saturated with self-loathing, she was more than willing to collaborate in an image of herself as a hateful mother. But as I became less eager to join her, I began to realize how utterly helpless she had felt in her marriage. She had reached a point where she would drive to the supermarket to do the week's shopping only to find she could not get out of the car because she could not stop crying. She had repeatedly asked her husband for a separation, wanting him to leave the house and children, and he had repeatedly refused. At last, feeling she was drowning in that suburban home, believing the only possible way out was to jump out quickly and feeling subjectively unable to take her children with her, she brought herself to make the ultimate sacrifice and wrenched herself away from her children in a desperate attempt to save her essential self.

This is quite a different perspective toward her behavior from the righteous stance I had started with, demanding that Christina take responsibility for her behavior and own up to her hateful, rejecting impulses. It was not that she did not have hateful, rejecting impulses toward her children. All parents suffer those feelings. But she could integrate them only by centering herself in the fact—which was a fact—that leaving her children had been a terrible loss. Christina had reached a point at which she felt she had to choose between her life and her children, and she and I both needed to appreciate how that impossible choice had led to a dreadful wounding of herself. . . .

For the next three years, we flowed in and out of an emotional merger, suffering despair-unto-death and being occasionally soothed with the healing moisture of hope. These themes repeated themselves in an infinite variety of forms, some of which I will describe.

The issue of coldness reflected Chris's basic injury: there was a cold, dead part of herself. Her feeling function had suffered a terrible wounding in her childhood when she received every privilege that money could buy and no empathy for any of her emotional experiences. She emerged unable to empathize with herself and unable to evaluate the importance of events from a feeling perspective. A little girl had been run over, and Chris could not say with any certainty whether this was an important or a trivial event.

A major root of Chris's frigidity was fear of her destructive potential. Although her hatred and rage were ordinarily turned solidly inward against herself, she needed to maintain an impenetrable coldness toward others in order to protect us from that hatred and rage. This coldly distant stance also protected her from my hurting her, as well as shielding her from feeling the pain of her loneliness.

As the months and years of our work passed, the frozen territory inside Chris began to thaw. I needed to restrain all of my impulses to do things: I needed to *not* interpret her dynamics, to stop myself from trying to help her or to make her feel better. I worked to suffer the pain of empathizing with her *just as she was*, and she responded by introjecting that self-directed empathic capacity. Her self-loathing for a long time led her to try to analyze herself, tearing herself to pieces and harshly critiquing each piece. As she began to develop a different attitude toward herself, she dreamed she came into my office and found Jung sitting on the couch. There were raw gems scattered around on the floor and he was polishing one of them. "That's what we Jungians do," he told her. "We polish."

Holding and accepting herself as a unified person enabled Chris to share herself increasingly intimately with me. One strand of that sharing involved criticizing me, hesitantly turning a faint echo of her frozen hatred and rage in my direction as I encouraged this increasingly authentic expression of her true nature. She expressed a gamut of feelings about my various therapeutic inadequacies: I was inept in my capacity to work with dreams; I was too young to be wise; I was the wrong sex to be powerful; my master's degree was woefully inadequate. Because she came three times a week, and because her income was limited, I did not raise her fee in the five years I saw her. As time passed, her fee became low by contemporary standards. The fee, then, became clear evidence of my second- or third-rate status. She knew when she started with me that I was a candidate at the Jung Institute, and this was also used to discredit me: perhaps she had not fully appreciated the implications of the fact that I had not yet completed my training, that I did not yet know how to do this work. For me, one of her most compelling depreciations was her attitude toward my Jewishness, an attitude faintly colored by her father's anti-Semitism. I was accorded here an intimate view of upper-crust WASP culture I had never had before.

In the last year of our work, Chris realized that these depreciations reflected primarily the ways she depreciated herself. But while this insight was useful, the main value of her criticism lay in the experience itself. She turned her human nastiness in my direction and I survived. Although she hurt my feelings at times, my positive sense of self was strong enough to withstand her destructive impulses. I was able to maintain my affection for her, pretty much unbroken, through her assaults, and that was crucial in helping her develop and maintain some affection for all of herself, including her darker side.

The other side of her sharing herself intimately with me was more directly positive. . . . [S]he became able to express a variety of dependency needs toward me. She talked about the despair that flooded her when I abandoned her by going away on vacations or by ending each hour. She shared with me her wishes to come home with me and to be my child. With considerable distress and anxiety, she told me about sexual feelings toward me. At about the time I worked through my coldness toward her, Chris had an erotic dream in which she did not have an orgasm. The dream continued, and in it she began telling me her dream. The process of telling me about it led her to have an orgasm. . . . The warmth of our relationship brought to life her frozen ability to enjoy her body and her self. The parallel with Chris's early dream of the divided self seemed vivid: I [had] become able, both within her psyche and within my own, authentically to play the part of the early dream's appreciative audience that enabled her to love.

Some of our most moving hours revolved around her sharing herself with me on a bodily level. In a session that occurred in the last six months of our work, she noticed I had a corn pad on my little toe. Mastering her embarrassment, she managed to tell me the insulting thought about my physical grossness that popped into her mind. Then she went on, in an easy, intimate way, talking about the various gross disabilities of her own body, such as what her hemorrhoids looked like recently when she examined them in a mirror. (One can see, in this sequence, the way the expression of negative, critical thoughts can open the door to a positive, interpersonal connection.) This verbal sharing of her body has been important *not* for the psychodynamic "meaning" of the content, but rather because of the interpersonal experience it generated. This kind of utterly intimate view of another person's body is normally available only to the mother of an infant. Telling me about her private physical self was one way a deep merger was created and maintained between us. The fruit of that intimate connection was pictured in a dream in which she was giving birth to a baby girl. I was standing at her feet with my hands deep inside her, helping the baby out. . . .

Chris's communications, both the critical ones and the loving ones, express the fact that we had merged in a union that was both pleasurable and painful. As the dream of giving birth would indicate, Chris had experiences in our work of being reborn. These experiences alternated with long stretches of immersion in her pain, periods in which we lay locked in grim agony in the tomb. Together we cycled between the deathly experiences in the tomb and the soothing experiences of renewal which follow them many times.

I saw Christina for five years. In terms of outer signs, one would consider our work highly successful, though on an intrapsychic level it remained incomplete. Externally, her relationship with her children was transformed. When I first met her, she saw her children rarely—once every three or four weeks—and the visits were a nightmare for all concerned. Every member of the family was in an on-going rage at every other member of the family. By the third year of our work, she was seeing her children several times a week and was almost as involved with them and with their day-to-day concerns as a custodial mother could be. Their contacts became primarily positive and loving and were clearly enjoyed by all participants. Her relationship with her ex-husband shifted from a rageful symbiosis to a disengaged but reasonably cooperative connection that worked well in relation to their two children. By the end of our work, she had completed the creative project she had been unable to begin and was offered a job that represented a substantial promotion professionally. . . .

It is my belief that the dramatic improvements in her life were a direct result of the transference experience she and I navigated together. In our last hours, Chris struggled to express what our work had meant for her. I tried to point out the improvements of her life, but she decisively rejected that measure of our work. In fact, she felt sorely misunderstood by my intervention. She finally formulated it for herself. "These years have been filled with pain for me. There's been pain with the children, pain at work, pain with my ex-husband, and pain with my lover. Our work has offered me a container for all of that pain. Here I have felt soothed and held." In her relationship with me, Chris developed the capacity to know and hold her whole self by introjecting my capacity to see and hold her, to unite with her without being injured by her fearful impulses. In the container of our relationship, she explored more and more of her inner world, expanding her familiarity with herself and her ability to be the whole person she naturally should be.

Editors' Introduction

Carl Rogers was one of the giants in counseling and psychotherapy as well as in personality theory. He was a sensitive therapist, a master teacher, and for those who knew him, a good friend. He was also a superb researcher and a gifted writer, as the following case will illustrate.

"Mrs. Oak" is a classic case study that documents a client's personal growth during a series of therapy sessions with Dr. Rogers. The experience of unconditional positive regard in the therapeutic relationship allowed Mrs. Oak to increasingly come to like herself and to realize that the core of her personality was positive and healthy. Rogers uses the case as a way to illustrate many of his beliefs about psychotherapy and personality.

Unfortunately, this version of "The Case of Mrs. Oak" is the shorter of two, but space limitations precluded the longer and more detailed selection which can be found in Rogers's and Dymond's book Psychotherapy and Personality Change.

THE CASE OF MRS. OAK

Carl R. Rogers

One aspect of the process of therapy which is evident in all cases might be termed the awareness of experience, or even "the experiencing of experience." I have here labeled it as the experiencing of the self, though this also falls short of being an accurate term. In the security of the relationship with a client-centered therapist, in the absence of any actual or implied threat to self, the client can let himself examine various aspects of his experience as they actually feel to him, as they are apprehended through his sensory and visceral equipment, without distorting them to fit the existing concept of self. Many of these prove to be in extreme contradiction to the concept of self, and could not ordinarily be experienced in their fullness, but in this safe relationship they can be permitted to seep through into awareness without distortion. Thus they often follow the schematic pattern, "I am thus and so, but I experience this feeling which is very inconsistent with what I am"; "I love my parents, but I experience some surprising bitterness toward them at times"; "I am really no good, but sometimes I seem to feel that I'm better than everyone else." Thus at first the expression is that "I am a self which is different from a part of my experience." Later this changes to the tentative pattern, "Perhaps I am several quite different selves, or perhaps my self contains more contradictions that I had dreamed." Still later the pattern changes to some such pattern as this: "I was sure that I could not be my experience— it was too contradictory—but now I am beginning to believe that I can be *all* of my experience."

Perhaps something of the nature of this aspect of therapy may be conveyed from two excerpts from the case of Mrs. Oak. Mrs. Oak was a housewife in her late thirties, who was having difficulties in marital and family relationships when she came in for therapy, Unlike many clients, she had a keen and spontaneous interest in the processes which she felt going on within herself, and her recorded interviews contain much material, from her own frame of reference, as to her perception of what is occurring. She thus tends to put into words what seems to be implicit, but unverbalized, in many clients.

From an early portion of the fifth interview comes material which describes the awareness of experience which we have been discussing.

Client: It all comes pretty vague. But you know I keep, keep having the thought occur to me that this whole process for me is kind of like examining pieces of a jigsaw puzzle. It seems to me I, I'm in the process now of examining the individual pieces which really don't have too much meaning. Probably handling them, now even beginning to think of a pattern. That keeps coming to me. And it's interesting to me because I, I really don't like jigsaw puzzles. They've always irritated me. But that's my feeling. And I mean I pick up little pieces (*She gestures throughout this conversation to illustrate her statements.*) with absolutely no meaning except I mean the, the feeling that you get from simply handling them without seeing them as a pattern, but just from the touch, I probably feel, well it is going to fit someplace here.

Therapist: And that at the moment that, that's the process, just getting the feel and the shape and the configuration of the different pieces with a little bit of background feeling of, yeah they'll probably fit somewhere, but most of the attention's focused right on, "What does this feel like? And what's its texture?"

C: That's right. There's almost something physical in it. A, a—

T: You can't quite describe it without using your hands. A real, almost a sensuous sense in—

C: That's right. Again it's, it's a feeling of being very objective, and yet I've never been quite so close to myself.

T: Almost at one and the same time standing off and looking at yourself and yet somehow being closer to yourself that way than—

C: Mm-hmm. And yet for the first time in months I am not thinking about my problems. I'm not, actually. I'm not working on them.

T: I get the impression you don't sit down to work on "my problems." It isn't that feeling at all.

C: That's right. That's right. I suppose what I, I mean actually is that I'm not sitting down to put this puzzle together as, as something, I've got to see the picture. It, it may be that, it may be that I am actually enjoying this feeling process. Or I'm certainly learning something.

T: At least there's a sense of the immediate goal of getting that feel as being the thing, not that you're doing this in order to see a picture, but that it's a, a satisfaction of really getting acquainted with each piece. Is that—

C: That's it. That's it. And it still becomes that sort of sensuousness, that touching. It's quite interesting. Sometimes not entirely pleasant, I'm sure, but—

T: A rather different sort of experience.

C: Yes. Quite.

This excerpt indicates very clearly the letting of material come into awareness, without any attempt to own it as part of the self, or to relate it to other material held in consciousness. It is, to put it as accurately as possible, an awareness of a wide range of experiences, with, at the moment, no thought of their relation to self. Later it may be recognized that what was being experienced may all become a part of self.

The fact that this is a new and unusual form of experience is expressed in a verbally confused but emotionally clear portion of the sixth interview.

C: Uh, I caught myself thinking that during these sessions, uh, I've been sort of singing a song. Now that sounds vague and uh—not actually singing— sort of a song without any music. Probably a kind of poem coming out. And I like the idea, I mean it's just sort of come to me without anything built out of, of anything. And in—following that, it came, it came this other kind of feeling. Well, I found myself sort of asking myself, is that the shape that cases take? Is it possible that I am just verbalizing and, at times kind of become intoxicated with my own verbalizations? And then uh, following this, came, well, am I just taking up your time? And then a doubt, a doubt. Then something else occurred to me. Uh, from whence it came, I don't know, no actual logical kind of sequence to the thinking. The thought struck me: We're doing bits, uh, we're not overwhelmed or doubtful, or show concern or, or any great interest when, when blind people learn to read with their fingers, Braille. I don't know—it may be just sort of, it's all mixed up. It may be that's something that I'm experiencing now.

T: Let's see if I can get some of that, that sequence of feelings. First, sort of as though you're, and I gather that first one is a fairly positive feeling, as though maybe you're kind of creating a poem here—a song without music somehow but something that might be quite creative. and then the, the feeling of a lot of skepticism about that. "Maybe I'm just saying words, just being carried off by words that I, that I speak, and maybe it's all a lot of baloney, really." And then a feeling that perhaps you're almost learning a new type of experiencing which would be just as radically new as for a blind person to try to make sense out of what he feels with his fingertips.

C: Mm-hmm. Mm-hmm. (Pause) . . . And I sometimes think to myself, well, maybe we could go into this particular incident or that particular incident. And then somehow when I come here, there is, that doesn't hold true, it's, it seems false. And then there just seems to be this flow of words which somehow aren't forced and then occasionally this doubt creeps in. Well, it sort of takes the form of a, maybe you're just making music ... Perhaps that's why I'm doubtful today of, of this whole thing, because it's something that's not forced. And really I'm feeling that what I should do is, is sort of systematize the thing. Oughta work harder and—

T: Sort of a deep questioning as to what am I doing with a self that isn't, isn't pushing to get things *done, solved? (Pause)*

C: And yet the fact that 1, I really like this other kind of thing, this, I don't know, call it a poignant feeling, I mean—I felt things that I never felt before. I *like* that, too. Maybe that's the way to do it. I just don't know today.

Here is the shift which seems almost invariably to occur in therapy which has any depth. It may be represented schematically as the client's feeling that "I came here to solve problems, and now I find myself just experiencing myself." And as with this client this shift is usually accompanied by the intellectual formulation that it is wrong, and by an emotional appreciation of the fact that it "feels good."

We may conclude this section saying that one of the fundamental directions taken by the process of therapy is the free experiencing of the actual sensory and visceral reactions of the organism without too much of an attempt to relate these experiences to the self. This is usually accompanied by the conviction that this material does not belong to, and cannot be organized into, the self. The end point of this process is that the client discovers that he can be his experience, with all of its variety and surface contradiction; that he can formulate himself out of his experience, instead of trying to impose a formulation of self upon his experience, denying to awareness those elements which do not fit.

THE FULL EXPERIENCING OF AN AFFECTIONAL RELATIONSHIP

One of the elements in therapy of which we have more recently become aware is the extent to which therapy is a learning, on the part of the client, to accept fully and freely and without fear the positive feelings of another. This is not a phenomenon which clearly occurs in every case. It seems particularly true of our longer cases, but does not occur uniformly in these. Yet it is such a deep experience that we have begun to question whether it is not a highly significant direction in the therapeutic process, perhaps occurring at an unverbalized level to some degree in all successful cases. Before discussing this phenomenon, let us give it some body by citing the experience of Mrs. Oak. The experience struck her rather suddenly, between the twenty-ninth and thirtieth interview, and she spends most of the latter interview discussing it. She opens the thirtieth hour in this way.

C: Well, I made a very remarkable discovery. I know it's—*(laughs)* I found out that you actually *care* how this thing goes. *(Both laugh.)* It gave me the feeling, it's sort of well—"maybe I'll let you get in the act," sort of thing. It's—again you see, on an examination sheet, I would have had the correct answer, I mean—but it suddenly dawned on me that in the client-counselor kind of thing, you *actually care* what happens to this thing. And it was a revelation, a—not that. That doesn't describe it. It was a—well, the closest I can come to it is a kind of relaxation, a—not a letting down, but a—*(pause)* more of a straightening out without tension if that means anything. I don't know.

T: Sounds as though it isn't as though this was a new idea, but it was a new experience of really *feeling* that I did care and if I get the rest of that, sort of a willingness on your part to let me care.

C: Yes.

This letting the counselor and his warm interest into her life was undoubtedly one of the deepest features of therapy in this case. In an interview following the conclusion of therapy she spontaneously mentions this experience as being the outstanding one. What does it mean?

The phenomenon is most certainly not one of transference and countertransference. Some experienced psychologists who had undergone psychoanalysis had the opportunity of observing the development of the relationship in another case than the one cited. They were the first to object to the use of the terms transference and countertransference to describe the phenomenon. The gist of their remarks was that this is something which is mutual and appropriate, whereas transference or countertransference are phenomena which are characteristically one-way and inappropriate to the realities of the situation.

Certainly one reason why this phenomenon is occurring more frequently in our experience is that as therapists we have become less afraid of our positive (or negative) feelings toward the client. As therapy goes on the therapist's feeling of acceptance and respect for the client tends to change to something approaching awe as he sees the valiant and deep struggle of the person to be himself. There is, I think, within the therapist, a profound experience of the underlying commonality—should we say brotherhood—of man. As a result he feels toward the client a warm, positive, affectional reaction. This poses a problem for the client who often, as in this case, finds it difficult to accept the positive feeling of another. Yet, once accepted, the inevitable reaction on the part of the client is to relax, to let the warmth of liking by another person reduce the tension and fear involved in facing life.

But we are getting ahead of our client. Let us examine some of the other aspects of this experience as it occurred to her. In earlier interviews she had talked of the fact that she did *not* love humanity, and that in some vague and stubborn way she felt she was right, even though others would regard her as wrong. She mentions this again as she discusses the way this experience has clarified her attitudes toward others.

C: The next thing that occurred to me that I found myself thinking and still thinking, is somehow—and I'm not clear why—the same kind of a caring that I get when I say "I don't love humanity." Which has always sort of—I mean I was always convinced of it. So I mean, it doesn't—I knew that it was a good thing, see. And I think I clarified it within myself—what it has to do with this situation, I don't know. But I found out, no, I don't love, but I do *care* terribly.

T: Mm-hmm. Mm-hmm. I see . . .

C: It might be expressed better in saying I care terribly what happens. But the caring is a—takes form—its structure is in understanding and not wanting to be taken in, or to contribute to those things which I feel are false and—It seems to me that in—in loving, there's a kind of *final* factor. If you do that, you've sort of done enough. It's a—

T: That's *it*, sort of.

C: Yeah. It seems to me this other thing, this caring, which isn't a good term—I mean, probably we need something else to describe this kind of thing. To say it's an impersonal thing doesn't mean anything because it isn't impersonal. I mean I feel it's very much a part of a whole. But it's something that somehow doesn't stop . . . It seems to me you could have this feeling of loving humanity, loving people, and at the same time—go on contributing to the factors that make people neurotic, make them ill—where, what I feel is a resistance to those things.

T: You care enough to want to understand and to want to avoid contributing to anything that would make for more neuroticism, or more of that aspect in human life.

C: Yes. And it's—*(pause)*. Yes, it's something along those lines. . . . Well, again, I have to go back to how I feel about this other thing. It's—I'm not really called upon to give of myself in a—sort of on the auction block. There's nothing final . . . It sometimes bothered me when I—I would have to say to myself, "I don't love humanity," and yet, I always knew that there was something positive. That I was probably right. And—I may be all off the beam now, but it seems to me that, that is somehow tied up in the—this feeling that I—I have now, into how the therapeutic value can carry through. Now, I couldn't tie it up, I couldn't tie it in, but it's as close as I can come to explaining to myself, my—well, shall I say the learning process, the follow through on my realization that—yes, you *do care* in a given situation. It's just that simple. And I hadn't been aware of it before. I might have closed this door and walked out, and in discussing therapy, said, yes, the counselor must feel thus and so, but, I mean, I hadn't had the dynamic experience.

In this portion, though she is struggling to describe her own feeling, it would seem that what she is saying would be characteristic of the therapist's attitude toward the client as well. His attitude, at its best, is devoid of the *quid pro quo* aspect of most of the experiences we call love. It is the simple outgoing human feeling of one individual for another, a feeling, it seems to me, which is even more basic than sexual or parental feeling. It is a caring enough about the person that you do not wish to interfere with his development, nor to use him for any self-aggrandizing goals of your own. Your satisfaction comes in having set him free to grow in his own fashion.

Our client goes on to discuss how hard it has been for her in the past to accept any help or positive feeling from others, and how this attitude is changing.

C: I have a feeling . . . that you have to do it pretty much yourself, but that somehow you ought to be able to do that with other people. *(She mentions that there have been "countless" times when she might have accepted personal warmth and kindliness from others.)* I get the feeling that I just was afraid I would be devastated. *(She returns to talking about the counseling itself and her feeling toward it.)* I mean there's been this tearing through the thing myself. Almost to—I mean, I felt it—I mean I tried to verbalize it on occasion—a kind of—at times almost not wanting you to restate, not wanting you to reflect, the thing is *mine.* Course all right, I can say it's resistance. But that doesn't mean a damn thing to me now . . . The—I think in—in relationship to this particular thing, I mean, the—probably at times, the strongest feeling was, it's mine, it's *mine.* I've got to cut it down myself. See?

T: It's an experience that's awfully hard to put down accurately into words, and yet I get a sense of difference here in this relationship, that form the feeling that "this is mine," "I've got to do it," "I am doing it," and so on, to a somewhat different feeling that—"I could let you in."

C: Yeah. Now. I mean, that's—that it's—well, it's sort of, shall we say, volume two. It's—it's a—well, sort of, well, I'm still in the thing alone, but I'm *not*—see—I'm—

T: Mm-hmm.Yes, that paradox sort of sums it up, doesn't it?

C: Yeah.

T: In all of this, there is a feeling, it's still—every aspect of my experience is mine and that's kind of inevitable and necessary and so on. And yet that isn't the whole picture either. Somehow it can be shared or another's interest can come in and in some ways it is new.

C: Yeah. And it's—it's as though, that's how it should be. I mean, that's how it—has to be. There's a—there's a feeling, "and this is good." I mean, it expresses, it clarifies it for me. There's a feeling—in this caring, as though—you were sort of standing back—standing off, and if I want to sort of cut through to the thing, it's a—a slashing of—oh, tall weeds, that I can do it, and you can—I mean you're not going to be disturbed by having to walk through it, too. I don't know. And it doesn't make sense. I mean—

T: Except there's a very real sense of rightness about this feeling that you have, hm?

C: Mm-hmm.

May it not be that this excerpt portrays the heart of the process of socialization? To discover that it is not devastating to accept the positive feeling from another, that it does not necessarily end in hurt, that it actually "feels good" to have another person with you in your struggles to meet life—this may be one of the most profound learnings encountered by the individual, whether in therapy or not.

Something of the newness, the nonverbal level of this experience is described by Mrs. Oak in the closing moments of this thirtieth interview.

C: I'm experiencing a new type, a—probably the only worthwhile kind of learning, a—I know I've—I've often said what I know doesn't help me here. What I meant is, my acquired knowledge doesn't help me. But it seems to me that the learning process here has been—so dynamic, I mean, so much a part of the—of everything, I mean, of me, that if I just get that out of it, it's something, which, I mean—I'm wondering if I'll ever be able to straighten out into a sort of acquired knowledge what I have experienced here.

T: In other words, the kind of learning that has gone on here has been something of quite a different sort and quite a different depth; very vital, very real. And quite worthwhile to you in and of itself, but the question you're asking is: Will I ever have a clear intellectual picture of what has gone on at this somehow deeper kind of learning level?

C: Mm-hmm. Something like that.

Those who would apply to therapy the so-called laws of learning derived from the memorization of nonsense syllables would do well to study this excerpt with care. Learning as it takes place in therapy is a total, organismic, frequently nonverbal type of thing which may or may not follow the same principles as the intellectual learning of trivial material which has little relevance to the self. This, however, is a digression.

Let us conclude this section by rephrasing its essence. It appears possible that one of the characteristics of deep or significant therapy is that the client discovers that it is not devastating to admit fully into his own experience the positive feeling which another, the therapist, holds toward him. Perhaps one of the reasons why this is so difficult is that essentially it involves the feeling that "I am worthy of being liked." This we shall consider in the following section. For the present it may be pointed out that this aspect of therapy is a free and full experiencing of an affectional relationship which may be put in generalized terms as follows: "I can permit someone to care about me, and can fully accept that caring within myself. This permits me to recognize that I care, and care deeply, for and about others."

THE LIKING OF ONE'S SELF

In various writings and researches that have been published regarding client-centered therapy, there has been a stress upon the acceptance of self as one of the directions and outcomes of therapy. We have established the fact that in successful psychotherapy negative attitudes toward the self decrease and positive attitudes increase. We have measured the gradual increase in self-acceptance and have studied the correlated increase in acceptance of others. But as I examine these statements and compare them with our more recent cases, I feel they fall short of the truth. The client not only accepts himself—a phrase which may carry the connotation of a grudging and reluctant acceptance of the inevitable—he actually comes to *like* himself. This is not a bragging or self-assertive liking; it is rather a quiet pleasure in being one's self.

Mrs. Oak illustrates this trend rather nicely in her thirty-third interview. Is it significant that this follows by ten days the interview where she could for the first time admit to herself that the therapist cared? Whatever our speculations on this point, this fragment indicates very well the quiet joy in being one's self, together with the apologetic attitude which, in our culture, one feels is necessary to take toward such an experience. In the last few minutes of the interview, knowing her time is nearly up she says:

C: One thing worries me—and I'll hurry because I can always go back to it—a feeling that occasionally I can't turn out. Feeling of being quite pleased with myself. Again the Q technique.[1] I walked out of here one time, and impulsively I threw my first card, "I am an attractive personality"; looked at it sort of aghast but left it there, I mean, because honestly, I mean, that is exactly how it felt—a—well, that bothered me and I catch that now. Every once in a while a sort of pleased feeling, nothing superior, but just—I don't know, sort of pleased. A neatly turned way. And it bothered me. And yet—I wonder—I rarely remember things I say here, I mean I wondered why it was that I was convinced, and something about what I've felt about being hurt that I suspected in—my feelings when I would hear someone say to a child, "Don't cry." I mean, I always felt, but it isn't right; I mean, if he's hurt, let him cry. Well, then, now this pleased feeling that I have. I've recently come to feel, it's—there's something almost the same there. It's—We don't object when *children* feel pleased with themselves. It's—I mean, there really isn't anything vain. It's—maybe that's how people *should* feel.

T: You've been inclined almost to look askance at yourself for this feeling, and yet as you think about it more, maybe it comes close to the two sides of the picture, that if a child wants to cry, why shouldn't he cry? And if he wants to feel pleased with himself, doesn't he have a perfect right to feel pleased with himself? And that sort of ties in with this, what I would see as an appreciation of yourself that you've experienced every now and again.

---

[1]This portion needs explanation. As part of a research study by another staff member this client had been asked several times during therapy to sort a large group of cards, each containing a self-descriptive phrase, in such a way as to portray her own self. At one end of the sorting she was to place the card or cards most like herself, and at the other end, those most unlike herself. Thus when she says that she put as the first card, "I am an attractive personality," it means that she regarded this as the item most characteristic of herself.

C: Yes. Yes.

T: "I'm really a pretty rich and interesting person."

C: Something like that. And then I say to myself, "Our society pushes us around and we've lost it." And I keep going back to my feelings about children. Well, maybe they're richer than we are. Maybe we—it's something we've lost in the process of growing up.

T: Could be that they have a wisdom about that that we've lost.

C: That's right. My time's up.

Here she arrives, as do so many other clients, at the tentative, slightly apologetic realization that she has come to like, enjoy, appreciate herself. One gets the feeling of a spontaneous relaxed enjoyment, a primitive *joie de vivre*, perhaps analogous to the lamb frisking about the meadow or the porpoise gracefully leaping in and out of the waves. Mrs. Oak feels that it is something native to the organism, to the infant, something we have lost in the warping process of development.

Earlier in this case one sees something of a forerunner of this feeling, an incident which perhaps makes more clear its fundamental nature. In the ninth interview Mrs. Oak in a somewhat embarrassed fashion reveals something she has always kept to herself. That she brought it forth at some cost is indicated by the fact that it was preceded by a very long pause, of several minutes duration. Then she spoke.

C: You know this is kind of goofy, but I've never told anyone this *(nervous laugh)* and it'll probably do me good. For years, oh, probably from early youth, from seventeen probably on, I, I have had what I have come to call to myself, told myself were "flashes of sanity." I've never told anyone this *(another embarrassed laugh)*, wherein, in, really I feel sane. And, and pretty much aware of life. And always with a terrific kind of concern and sadness of how far away, how far astray that we have actually gone. It's just a feeling once in a while of finding myself a whole kind of person in a terribly chaotic kind of world.

T: It's been fleeting and it's been infrequent, but there have been times when it seems the whole you is functioning and feeling in the world, a very chaotic world to be sure—

C: That's right. And I mean, and knowing actually how far astray we, we've gone from, from being whole healthy people. And of course, one doesn't talk in those terms.

T: A feeling that it wouldn't be *safe* to talk about the singing you[2]—

C: Where does that person live?

T: Almost as if there was no place for such a person to, to exist.

C: Of course, you know, that, that makes me—now wait a minute—that probably explains why I'm primarily concerned with feelings here. That's probably it.

---

[2]The therapist's reference is to her statement in a previous interview that in therapy she was singing a song.

T: Because that whole you does exist with all your feelings. Is that it, you're more aware of feelings?

C: That's right. It's not, it doesn't reject feelings and—that's *it*.

T: That whole you somehow lives feelings instead of somehow pushing them to one side.

C: That's right. (*Pause*) I suppose from the practical point of view it could be said that what I ought to be doing is solving some problems, day-to-day problems. And yet, I, I—what I'm trying to do is solve, solve something else that's a great, that is a great deal more important than little day-to-day problems. Maybe that sums up the whole thing.

T: I wonder if this will distort your meaning, that from a hard-headed point of view you ought to be spending time thinking through specific problems. But you wonder if perhaps maybe you aren't on a quest for this whole you and perhaps that's more important than a solution to the day-to-day-problems.

C: I think that's it. That's probably what I mean.

If we may legitimately put together these two experiences, and if we are justified in regarding them as typical, then we may say that both in therapy and in some fleeting experiences throughout her previous life, she has experienced a healthy, satisfying, enjoyable appreciation of herself as a whole and functioning creature; and that this experience occurs when she does not reject her feelings but lives them.

Here, it seems to me, is an important and often overlooked truth about the therapeutic process. It works in the direction of permitting the person to experience fully, and in awareness, all of his reactions including his feelings and emotions. As this occurs, the individual feels a positive liking for himself, a genuine appreciation of himself as a total functioning unit, which is one of the important end points of therapy.

THE DISCOVERY THAT THE CORE OF PERSONALITY IS POSITIVE

One of the most revolutionary concepts to grow out of our clinical experience is the growing recognition that the innermost core of man's nature, the deepest layers of his personality, the base of his "animal nature," is positive in nature—is basically socialized, forward moving, rational, and realistic.

This point of view is so foreign to our present culture that I do not expect it to be accepted, and it is indeed so revolutionary in its implications that it should not be accepted without thoroughgoing inquiry. But even if it should stand these tests, it will be difficult to accept. Religion, especially the Protestant Christian tradition, has permeated our culture with the concept that man is basically sinful, and only by something approaching a miracle can his sinful nature be negated. In psychology, Freud and his followers have presented convincing arguments that the id, man's basic and unconscious nature, is primarily made up of instincts which would, if permitted expression, result in incest, murder, and other crimes. The whole problem of therapy, as seen by this group, is how to hold these untamed forces in check in a wholesome and constructive manner, rather than in the costly fashion of the neurotic. But the fact that at heart man is irrational, unsocialized, destructive of others and self—this is a concept accepted almost without question. To be sure there are occasional voices of protest. But these solitary voices are little heard. On the whole the viewpoint of the professional worker as well as the layman is that man as he is, in his basic nature, had best be kept under control or under cover or both.

As I look back over my years of clinical experience and research, it seems to me that I have been very slow to recognize the falseness of this popular and professional concept. The reason, I believe, lies in the fact that in therapy there are continually being uncovered hostile and antisocial feelings, so that it is easy to assume that this indicates the deeper and therefore the basic nature of man. Only slowly has it become evident that these untamed and unsocial feelings are neither the deepest nor the strongest, and that the inner core of man's personality is the organism itself, which is essentially both self-preserving and social.

To give more specific meaning to this argument, let me turn again to the case of Mrs. Oak. Since the point is an important one, I shall quote at some length from the recorded case to illustrate the type of experience on which I have based the foregoing statements. Perhaps the excerpts can illustrate the opening up of layer after layer of personality until we come to the deepest elements.

It is in the eighth interview that Mrs. Oak rolls back the first layer of defense, and discovers a bitterness and desire for revenge underneath.

C: You know over in this area of, of sexual disturbance, I have a feeling that I'm beginning to discover that it's pretty bad, pretty bad. I'm finding out that, that I'm bitter, really. Damn bitter. I—and I'm not turning it back in, into myself . . . I think what I probably feel is a certain element of "I've been cheated." (*Her voice is very tight and her throat chokes up.*) And I've covered up very nicely, to the point of consciously not caring. But I'm, I'm sort of amazed to find that in this practice of, what shall I call it, a kind of sublimation that right under it—again words—there's a, a kind of passive force that's, it's pas—it's very passive, but at the same time it's just kind of *murderous*.

T: So there's the feeling, "I've really been cheated. I've covered that up and seem not to care and yet underneath that there's a kind of a, a latent but very much present *bitterness* that is very, very strong."

C: It's very strong. I—that I know. It's terribly powerful.

T: Almost a dominating kind of force.

C: Of which I am rarely conscious. Almost never . . . Well, the only way I can describe it, it's a kind of murderous thing, but without violence . . . It's more like a feeling of wanting to get even . . . And of course, I won't pay back, but I'd like to. I really would like to.

Up to this point the usual explanation seems to fit perfectly. Mrs. Oak has been able to look beneath the socially controlled surface of her behavior, and find underneath a murderous feeling of hatred and a desire to get even. This is as far as she goes in exploring this particular feeling until considerably later in therapy. She picks up the theme in the thirty-first interview. She has had a hard time getting under way, feels emotionally blocked, and cannot get at the feeling which is welling up in her.

C: I have the feeling it isn't guilt. *(Pause. She weeps.)* Of course I mean, I can't verbalize it yet. *(Then with a rush of emotion)* It's just being terribly hurt!

T: Mm-hmm. It isn't guilt except in the sense of being very much wounded somehow.

C: *(Weeping)*: It's—you know, often I've been guilty of it myself but in later years when I've heard parents say to their children, "stop crying," I've had a feeling, a hurt as though, well, why should they tell them to stop crying? They feel sorry for themselves, and who can feel more adequately sorry for himself than the child? Well, that is sort of what—I mean, as though I mean, I thought that they should let him cry. And—feel sorry for him too, maybe. In a rather objective kind of way. Well, that's—that something of the kind of thing I've been experiencing. I mean, now—just right now. And in—in—

T: That catches a little more the flavor of the feeling that it's almost as if you're really weeping for yourself.

C: Yeah. And again you see there's conflict. Our culture is such that—I mean, one doesn't indulge in self-pity. But this isn't—I mean, I feel it doesn't quite have that connotation. It may have.

T: Sort of think that there is a cultural objection to feeling sorry about yourself. And yet you feel the feeling you're experiencing isn't quite what the culture objected to either.

C: And then of course, I've come to—to see and to feel that over this—see, I've covered it up. *(Weeps.)* But I've covered it up with so much bitterness, which in turn I had to cover up. *(Weeping)* That's what I want to get rid of! I almost don't *care* if I hurt.

T: *(Softly, and with an empathic tenderness toward the hurt she is experiencing)*: You feel that here at the basis of it as you experience it is a feeling of real tears for yourself. But that you can't show, mustn't show, so that's been covered by bitterness that you don't like, that you'd like to be rid of. You almost feel you'd rather absorb the hurt than to—than to feel the bitterness. *(Pause)* And what you seem to be saying quite strongly is, I do *hurt*, and I've tried to cover it up.

C: I didn't know it.

T: Mm-hmm. Like a new discovery really.

C: (*Speaking at the same time*): I never really did know. But it's—you know, it's almost a physical thing. It's—it's sort of as though I were looking within myself at all kinds of—nerve endings and bits of things that have been sort of mashed. (*Weeping*)

T: As though some of the most delicate aspects of you physically almost have been crushed or hurt.

C: Yes. And you know, I do get the feeling, "Oh, you poor thing." (*Pause*)

T: Just can't help but feel very deeply sorry for the person that is you.

C: I don't think I feel sorry for the whole person; it's a certain aspect of the thing.

T: Sorry to see that hurt.

C: Yeah.

T: Mm-hmm. Mm-hmm.

C: And then of course there's this damn bitterness that I want to get rid of. It's—it gets me into trouble. It's because it's a tricky thing. It tricks me. (*Pause*)

T: Feel as though that bitterness is something you'd like to be rid of because it doesn't do right by you.

C: (*Weeps. Long pause*): I don't know. It seems to me that I'm right in feeling, what in the world good would it do to term this thing guilt. To chase down things that would give me an interesting case history, shall we say. What *good* would it do? It seems to me that the—that the key, the real thing is in this feeling that I have.

T: You could track down some tag or other and could make quite a pursuit of that, but you feel as though the core of the whole thing is the kind of experience that you're just having right here.

C: That's right. I mean if—I don't know what'll happen to the feeling. Maybe nothing. I don't know, but it seems to me that whatever understanding I'm to have is a part of this feeling of hurt, of—it doesn't matter much what it's called. (*Pause*) Then I—one can't go around with a hurt so openly exposed. I mean this seems to me that somehow the next process has to be a kind of healing.

T: Seems as though you couldn't possibly expose yourself if part of yourself is so hurt, so you wonder if somehow the hurt mustn't be healed first. (*Pause*)

C: And yet, you know, it's—it a funny thing (*pause*). It sounds like a statement of complete confusion or the old saw that the neurotic doesn't want to give up his symptoms. But that isn't true. I mean, that isn't true here, but it's—I can just hope that this will impart what I feel. I somehow don't mind being hurt. I mean, it's just occurred to me that I don't mind terribly. It's a—I mind more the—the feeling of bitterness which is, I know, the cause of this frustration, I mean the—I somehow mind that more.

T: Would this get it? That, though you don't like the hurt, yet you feel you can accept that. That's bearable. Somehow it's the things that have covered up that hurt, like the bitterness, that you just—at this moment, can't stand.

C: Yeah. That's just about it. It's sort of as though, well, the first, I mean, as though, it's—well, it's something I can cope with. Now, the feeling of, well, I can still have a hell of a lot of fun, see. But that this other, I mean, this frustration—I mean, it comes out in so many ways, I'm beginning to realize, you see. I mean, just this sort of, this kind of thing.

T: And a hurt you can accept. It's a part of life within a lot of other parts of life, too. You can have lots of fun. But to have all of your life diffused by frustration and bitterness, that you don't like, you don't want, and are now more aware of

C: Yeah. And there's somehow no dodging it now. You see, I'm much more aware of it. *(Pause)* I don't know. Right now, I don't know just what the next step is. I really don't know. *(Pause)* Fortunately, this is a kind of development, so that it—doesn't carry over too acutely into—I mean, I— what I'm trying to say, I think, is that I'm still functioning. I'm still enjoying myself and—

T: Just sort of want me to know that in lots of ways you carry on just as you always have.

C: That's it. *(Pause)* Oh, I think I've got to stop and go.

In this lengthy excerpt we get a clear picture of the fact that underlying the bitterness and hatred and the desire to get back at the world which has cheated her, is a much less antisocial feeling, a deep experience of having been hurt. And it is equally clear that at this deeper level she has no desire to put her murderous feelings into action. She dislikes them and would like to be rid of them.

The next excerpt comes from the thirty-fourth interview. It is very incoherent material, as verbalizations often are when the individual is trying to express something deeply emotional. Here she is endeavoring to reach far down into herself. She states that it will be difficult to formulate.

C: I don't know whether I'll be able to talk about it yet or not. Might give it a try. Something—I mean, it's a feeling—that—sort of an urge to really get out. I know it isn't going to make sense. I think that maybe if I can get it out and get it a little, well, in a little more matter of fact way, that it'll be something that's more useful to me. And I don't know how to—I mean, it seems as though I want to say, I want to talk about my *self*. And that is of course as I see, what I've been doing for all these hours. But, no, this—it's my *self*. I've quite recently become aware of rejecting certain statements, because to me they sounded—not quite what I meant, I mean, a little bit too idealized. And I mean, I can remember always saying it's more selfish than that, more selfish than that. Until I—it sort of occurs to me, it dawns, yeah, that's exactly what I mean, but the selfishness I mean, has an entirely different connotation. I've been using a word "selfish." Then I have this feeling of—I—that I've never expressed it before of selfish—which means nothing. A—I'm still going to talk about it. A kind of pulsation. And it's something aware all the time. And still it's there. And I'd like to be able to utilize it, too—as a kind of descending into this thing. You know, it's as though—I don't know, damn! I'd sort of acquired someplace, and picked up a kind of acquaintance with the structure. Almost as though I knew it brick for brick kind of thing. It's something that's an awareness. I mean, that—of a feeling of not being fooled, of not being drawn into the thing, and a critical sense of knowingness. But in a way— the reason, it's hidden and—can't be a part of everyday life. And there's something of—at times I feel almost a little bit terrible in the thing, but again terrible not as terrible. And why? I think I know. And it's—it also explains a lot to me. It's—it's something that is *totally* without hate. I mean, just *totally*. Not with love, but *totally without hate*. But it's—it's an exciting thing, too . . . I guess maybe I am the kind of person that likes to, I mean, probably even torment myself, or to chase things down, to try to find the whole. And I've told myself, now look, this is a pretty strong kind of feeling which you have. lt isn't constant. But you feel it sometimes, and as you let yourself feel it, you feel it yourself. You know, there are words for that kind of thing that one could find in abnormal psychology. Might almost be like the feeling that is occasionally, is attributed to things that you read about. I mean, there are some elements there—I mean, this pulsation, this excitement, this knowing. And I've said—I tracked down one thing, I mean, I was very, very brave, what shall we say—a sublimated sex drive. And I thought, well, *there* I've got it. I've really solved the thing. And that there is nothing more to it than that. And for awhile, I mean, I was quite pleased with myself. That was it. And then I had to admit, no, that wasn't it. 'Cause that's something that had been with me long before I became so terribly frustrated sexually. I mean, that wasn't—and, but in the thing, then I began to see a little, within this very core is an acceptance of sexual relationship, I mean, the only kind that *I* would think would be possible. It was in this thing. It's not something that's been—I mean, sex hasn't been sublimated or substituted there. No. Within this, within what I know there—I mean, it's a different kind of sexual feeling to be sure. I mean, it's one that is stripped of all the things that have happened to sex, if you know what I mean. There's no chase, no pursuit, no battle, no— well, no kind of hate, which I think, seems to me, has crept into such things. And yet, I mean, this feeling has been, oh, a little bit disturbing.

T: I'd like to see if I can capture a little of what that means to you. It is as you've gotten very deeply acquainted with yourself on kind of a brick-by-brick experiencing basis, and in that sense have become more *self*-ish, and the notion of really,—in the discovering of what is the core of you as separate from all the other aspects, you come across the re- alization, which is a very deep and pretty thrilling realization, that the core of that self is not only without hate, but is really something more resembling a saint, something really very pure, is the word I would use. And that you can try to depreciate that. You can say, maybe it's a sub- limation, maybe it's an abnormal manifestation, screwball and so on. But inside of yourself, you knew that it isn't. This contains the feelings which could contain rich sexual expression, but it sounds bigger than, and really deeper than that. And yet fully able to include all that could be a part of sex expression.

C: It's probably something like that . . . It's kind of—I mean, it's a kind of descent. It's a going down where you might almost think it should be going up, but no, it's—I'm sure of it; it's kind of going down.

T: This is a going down and immersing yourself in your self almost.

C: Yeah. And I—I can't just throw it aside. I mean, it just seems, oh, it just *is*. I mean, it seems an awfully important thing that I just had to say.

T: I'd like to pick up one of those things too, to see if I understand it. That it sounds as though this sort of idea you're expressing is something you must be going up to capture, something that *isn't* quite. Actually though, the feeling is, this is a going down to capture something that's more deeply there.

C: It is. It really—there's something to that which is—I mean, this—I have a way, and of course sometime we're going to have to go into that, of rejecting almost violently, that which is righteous, rejection of the ideal, the—as—and that expressed it; I mean, that's sort of what I mean. One is a going up into I don't know. I mean, I just have a feeling, I can't follow. I mean, it's pretty thin stuff if you ever start knocking it down. This one went—I wondered why—I mean, has this awfully definite feeling of descending.

T: That this isn't a going up into the thin ideal. This is a going down into the astonishingly solid reality, that—

C: Yeah.

T: —is really more surprising than—

C: Yeah. I mean, a something that you don't knock down. That's there—I don't know—seems to me after you've abstracted the whole thing. That lasts . . .

Since this is presented in such confused fashion, it might be worth while to draw from it the consecutive themes which she has expressed.

I'm going to talk about myself as *self*-ish, but with a new connotation to the word. I've acquired an acquaintance with the structure of myself, know myself deeply. As I descend into myself, I discover something exciting, a core that is totally without hate.
It can't be a part of everyday life—it may even be abnormal.
I thought first it was just a sublimated sex drive.
But no, this is more inclusive, deeper than sex.
One would expect this to be the kind of thing one would discover by going up into the thin realm of ideals.
But actually, I found it by going deep within myself.
It seems to be something that is the essence, that lasts.

Is this a mystic experience she is describing? It would seem that the counselor felt so, from the flavor of his responses. Can we attach any significance to such a Gertrude Stein kind of expression? The writer would simply point out that many clients have come to a somewhat similar conclusion about themselves, though not always expressed in such an emotional way. Even Mrs.

Oak, in the following interview, the thirty-fifth, gives a clearer and more concise statement of her feeling, in a more down-to-earth way. She also explains why it was a difficult experience to face.

C: I think I'm awfully glad I found myself or brought myself or wanted to talk about self. I mean, it's a very personal, private kind of thing that you just don't talk about. I mean, I can understand my feeling of, oh, probably slight apprehension now. It's—well, sort of as though I was just rejecting, I mean, all of the things that western civilization stands for, you see. And wondering whether I was right, I mean, whether it was quite the right path, and still of course, feeling how right the thing was, you see. And so there's bound to be a conflict. And then this, and I mean, now I'm feeling, well, of course that's how I feel. I mean there's a—this thing that I term a kind of a lack of hate, I mean, is very real. It carried over into the things I do, I believe in . . . I think it's all right. It's sort of maybe my saying to myself, well, you've been bashing me all over the head, I mean, sort of from the beginning, with superstitions and taboos and misinterpreted doctrines and laws and your science, your refrigerators, your atomic bombs. But I'm just not buying; you see, I'm just, you just haven't quite succeeded. I think what I'm saying is that, well, I mean, just not conforming, and it's—well, it's just that way.

T: Your feeling at the present time is that you have been very much aware of all the cultural pressures—not always very much aware, but "there have been so many of those in my life—and now I'm going down more deeply into myself to find out what I really feel" and it seems very much at the present time as though that somehow separates you a long ways from your culture, and that's a little frightening, but feels basically good. Is that—

C: Yeah. Well, I have the feeling now that it's okay, really. . . Then there's something else—a feeling that's starting to grow; well, to be almost formed, as I say. This kind of conclusion, that I'm going to stop looking for something terribly wrong. Now I don't know why. But I mean, just— it's this kind of thing. I'm sort of saying to myself now, well, in view of what I know, what I've found—I'm pretty sure I've ruled out fear, and I'm positive I'm not afraid of shock—I mean, I sort of would have welcomed it. But—in view of the places I've been, what I learned there, then also kind of, well, taking into consideration what I don't know, sort of, maybe this is one of the things that I'll have to date, and say, well, now, I've just—I just can't find it. See? And now without any—without, I should say, any sense of apology or covering up, just sort of simple statement that I can't find what at this time, appears to be bad.

T: Does this catch it? That as you've gone more and more deeply into yourself, and as you think about the kind of things that you've discovered and learned and so on, the conviction grows very, very strong that no matter how far you go, the things that you're going to find are not dire and awful. They have a very different character.

C: Yes, something like that.

Here, even as she recognized that her feeling goes against the grain of her culture, she feels bound to say that the core of herself is not bad, nor terribly wrong, but something positive. Underneath the layer of controlled surface behavior, underneath the bitterness, underneath the hurt, is a self that is positive, and that is without hate. This I believe is the lesson which our clients have been facing us with for a long time, and which we have been slow to learn.

If hatelessness seems like a rather neutral or negative concept, perhaps we should let Mrs. Oak explain its meaning. In her thirty-ninth interview, as she feels her therapy drawing to a close, she returns to this topic.

C: I wonder if I ought to clarify—it's clear to me, and perhaps that's all that matters really, here—my strong feeling about a hate-free kind of approach. Now that we have brought it up on a rational kind of plane, I know—it sounds negative. And yet in my thinking, my—not really my thinking but my feeling, it—and my thinking, yes, my thinking, too—it's a far more positive thing than this—than a love—and it seems to me a far easier kind of a—it's less confining. But it—I realize that it must sort of sound and almost seem like a complete rejection of so many things, of so many creeds and maybe it is. I don't know. But it just to me seems more positive.

T: You can see how it might sound more negative to someone but as far as the meaning that it has for you is concerned, it doesn't seem as binding, as possessive I take it, as love. It seems as though it actually is more— more expandable, more usable, than—

C: Yeah.

T: —any of these narrower terms.

C: Really does to me. It's easier. Well, anyway, it's easier for me to feel that way. And I don't know. It seems to me to really be a way of—of not—of finding yourself in a place where you aren't forced to make rewards and you aren't forced to punish. It is—it means so much. It just seems to me to make for a kind of freedom.

T   Mm-hmm. Mm-hmm. Where one is rid of the need of either rewarding or punishing, then it just seems to you there is so much more freedom for all concerned.

C: That's right. (Pause) I'm prepared for some breakdowns along the way.

T: You don't expect it will be smooth sailing.

C: No.

This section is the story—greatly abbreviated—of one client's discovery that the deeper she dug within herself, the less she had to fear; that instead of finding something terribly wrong within herself, she gradually uncovered a core of self which wanted neither to reward nor punish others, a self without hate, a self which was deeply socialized. Do we dare to generalize from this type of experience that if we cut through deeply enough to our organismic nature, that we find that man is a positive and social animal? This is the suggestion from our clinical experience.

BEING ONE'S ORGANISM, ONE'S EXPERIENCE

The thread which runs through much of the foregoing material of this chapter is that psychotherapy (at least client-centered therapy) is a process whereby man becomes his organism—without self-deception, without distortion. What does this mean?

We are talking here about something at an experiential level—a phenomenon which is not easily put into words, and which, if apprehended only at the verbal level, is by that very fact, already distorted. Perhaps if we use several sorts of descriptive formulation, it may ring some bell, however faint, in the reader's experience, and cause him to feel "Oh, now I know, from my own experience, something of what you are talking about."

Therapy seems to mean a getting back to basic sensory and visceral experience. Prior to therapy the person is prone to ask himself, often unwittingly, "What do others think I should do in this situation?" "What would my parents or my culture want me to do?" "What do I think *ought* to be done?" He is thus continually acting in terms of the form which should be imposed upon his behavior. This does not necessarily mean that he always acts in *accord* with the opinions of others. He may indeed endeavor to act so as to contradict the expectations of others. He is nevertheless acting *in terms of* the expectations (often introjected expectations) of others. During the process of therapy the individual comes to ask himself, in regard to ever-widening areas of his life-space, "How do I experience this?" "What does it mean to me?" "If I behave in a certain way how do I symbolize the meaning which it *will* have for me?" He comes to act on a basis of what may be termed realism—a realistic balancing of the satisfactions and dissatisfactions which any action will bring to himself.

Perhaps it will assist those who, like myself, tend to think in concrete and clinical terms, if I put some of these ideas into schematized formulations of the process through which various clients go. For one client this may mean: "I have thought I must feel only love for my parents, but I find that I experience both love and bitter resentment. Perhaps I can be that person who freely experiences both love and resentment." For another client the learning may be: "I have thought I was only bad and worthless. Now I experience myself at times as one of much worth; at other times as one of little worth or usefulness. Perhaps I can be a person who experiences varying degrees of worth." For another: "I have held the conception that no one could really love me for myself. Now I experience the affectional warmth of another for me. Perhaps I can be a person who is lovable by others—perhaps I am such a person." For still another: "I have been brought up to feel that I must not appreciate myself—but I do. I can cry for myself, but I can enjoy myself, too. Perhaps I am a richly varied person whom I can enjoy and for whom I can feel sorry." Or, to take the last example from Mrs. Oak, "I have thought that in some deep way I was bad, that the most basic elements in me must be dire and awful. I don't experience that badness, but rather a positive desire to live and let live. Perhaps I can be that person who is, at heart, positive."

What is it that makes possible anything but the first sentence of each of these formulations? It is the addition of awareness. In therapy the person adds to ordinary experience the full and undistorted awareness of his experiencing—of his sensory and visceral reactions. He ceases, or at least decreases, the distortions of experience in awareness. He can be aware of what he is actually experiencing, not simply what he can permit himself to experience after a thorough screening through a conceptual filter. In this sense the person becomes for the first time the full potential of the human organism, with the enriching element of awareness freely added to the basic aspect of sensory and visceral reaction. The person comes to *be* what he *is*, as clients so frequently say in therapy. What this seems to mean is that the individual comes to *be*— in awareness—what he *is*—in experience. He is, in other words, a complete and fully functioning human organism.

Already I can sense the reactions of some of my readers. "Do you mean that as a result of therapy, man becomes nothing but a human *organism*, a human *animal*? Who will control him? Who will socialize him? Will he then throw over all inhibitions? Have you merely released the beast, the id, in man?" To which the most adequate reply seems to be, "In therapy the individual has actually *become* a human organism, with all the richness which that implies. He is realistically able to control himself, and he is incorrigibly socialized in his desires. There is no beast in man. There is only man in man, and this we have been able to release."

So the basic discovery of psychotherapy seems to me, if our observations have any validity, that we do not need to be afraid of being "merely" homo sapiens. It is the discovery that if we can add to the sensory and visceral experiencing which is characteristic of the whole animal kingdom, the gift of a free and undistorted awareness of which only the human animal seems fully capable, we have an organism which is beautifully and constructively realistic. We have then an organism which is as aware of the demands of the culture as it is of its own physiological demands for food or sex—which is just as aware of its desire for friendly relationships as it is of its desire to aggrandize itself—which is just as aware of its delicate and sensitive tenderness toward others, as it is of its hostilities toward others. When man's unique capacity of awareness is thus functioning freely and fully, we find that we have, not an animal whom we must fear, not a beast who must be controlled, but an organism able to achieve, through the remarkable integrative capacity of its central nervous system, a balanced, realistic, self-enhancing, other-enhancing behavior as a resultant of all these elements of awareness. To put it another way, when man is less than fully man— when he denies to awareness various aspects of his experience—then indeed we have all too often reason to fear him and his behavior, as the present world situation testifies. But when he is most fully man, when he is his complete organism, when awareness of experience, that peculiarly human attribute, is most fully operating, then he is to be trusted, then his behavior is constructive. It is

not always conventional. It will not always be conforming. It will be individualized. But it will also be socialized.

A CONCLUDING COMMENT

I have stated the preceding section as strongly as I am able because it represents a deep conviction growing out of many years of experience. I am quite
aware, however, of the difference between conviction and truth. I do not ask
anyone to agree with my experience, but only to consider whether the formulation given here agrees with his own experience.

Nor do I apologize for the speculative character of this paper. There is a
time for speculation, and a time for the sifting of evidence. It is to be hoped
that gradually some of the speculations and opinions and clinical hunches of
this paper may be put to operational and definitive test.

Editors' Introduction

Albert Ellis was trained as a psychoanalyst but found he was not getting the results he wanted so, in characteristic style, he created his own system known as Rational Emotive Behavior Therapy. REBT is the precursor of many of today's cognitive and cognitive-behavioral therapies.

Ellis's style is inimitable, as anyone knows who has heard him speak or who has had the good fortune to observe him in a therapy session. He is direct, forceful, confident, and convinced of the correctness of his views.

In the case that follows we have an opportunity to observe Ellis working with a young woman whose thinking is clearly irrational and who presents the type of problem with which REBT therapists seem to excel. The reader will find it interesting to contrast Ellis's style with Rogers's treatment of Mrs. Oak in the preceding case study. Ellis is known as a master clinician, and Rogers had the same reputation. However, as this case clearly demonstrates, their therapy styles are dramatically different.

A TWENTY-THREE-YEAR-OLD WOMAN GUILTY ABOUT NOT FOLLOWING HER PARENTS' RULES[1]

Albert Ellis

Martha, a twenty-three-year-old woman, came for help because she claimed she was self-punishing, compulsive, afraid of males, had no goals in life, and was guilty about her relationship with her parents.

From Ellis, A. (1974). *Growth through Reason* (pp. 223–286). Hollywood: Wilshire Books. Reprinted by permission of the author.

[1]I stress, in this early case of REBT, the cognitive and philosophic techniques it commonly uses. From its start, however, it has been highly behavioral, especially in its use of in vivo desensitization or exposure with clients like Martha, who are afraid to risk failure and rejection; and it uses operant conditioning, stimulus control, relapse prevention, and many other behavioral methods. It is also very forceful, emotive, and experiential, and uses many affective methods—such as shame-attacking exercises, rational emotive imagery, forceful coping statements, and vigorous disputing of clients' irrational beliefs.

    Details on these methods are given in my books *The Practice of Rational Emotive Behavior Therapy* (New York: Springer); *A Guide to Rational Living* (Hollywood, CA: Wilshire Books); *Rational Emotive Behavior Therapy: A Therapist's Guide* (San Luis Obispo, CA: Impact Publishers); *How to Control Your Anxiety Before It Controls You* (Secaucus, NJ: Carol Publishing Group); and in other REBT publications.

SEGMENTS FROM
THE FIRST SESSION

C-1:   Well, for about a year and a half since I graduated from college, I've had the feeling that something was the matter with me. I seem to have a tendency toward punishing myself. I'm accident-prone. I'm forever banging myself or falling down stairs, or something like that. And my relationship with my father is causing me a great deal of trouble. I've never been able to figure out where is the responsibility and what my relationship with my parents should be.

T-2:   Do you live with them?

C-3:   No, I don't. I moved out in March.

T-4:   What does your father do?

C-5:   He is a newspaper editor.

T-6:   And your mother is a housewife?

C-7:   Yes.

T-8:   Any other children?

C-9:   Yes, I have two younger brothers. One is twenty; the other is sixteen. I'm twenty-three. The sixteen-year-old has polio, and the other one has an enlarged heart. We never had much money, but we always had the feeling that love and security in life are what count. And the first thing that disturbed me was, when I was about sixteen years old, my father began to drink seriously. To me he had been the infallible person. Anything he said was right. And since I moved out and before I moved out, I've wondered where my responsibility to my family lies. Because if they would ask me to do something, if I didn't do it, I would feel guilty about it.

T-10:   What sort of things did they ask you to do?

C-11:   Well, they felt that it just wasn't right for an unmarried girl to move out. Also, I find it easier to lie than to tell the truth, if the truth is unpleasant. I'm basically afraid of men and afraid to find a good relationship with a man that would lead to marriage. My parents have never approved of anyone I have gone out with. In thinking about it, I wonder whether I, subconsciously maybe, went out of my way to find somebody they wouldn't approve of.

T-12:   Do you go with anyone now?

C-13:   Yes, two people.

T-14:   And are you serious about either one?

C-15:   I really don't know. One is sort of serious about me, but he thinks there's something the matter with me that I have to straighten out. I have also at various times been rather promiscuous, and I don't want to be that way.

T-16:   Have you enjoyed sex?

C-17:   Not particularly. I think—in trying to analyze myself and find out why I was promiscuous, I think I was afraid not to be.

T-18:   Afraid they wouldn't like you?

C-19: Yes. This one fellow that I've been going with—in fact, both of them—
said I don't have a good opinion of myself.

T-20: What do you work at?

C-21: I'm a copywriter for an advertising agency. I don't know if this means
anything, but when I was in college, I never could make up my mind
what to major in. I had four or five majors. I was very impulsive about
the choice of college.

T-22: What did you finally pick?

C-23: I went to the University of Illinois.

T-24: What did you finally major in?

C-25: I majored in—it was a double major: advertising and English.

T-26: Did you do all right in college?

C-27: Yes, I was a Phi Beta Kappa. I graduated with honors.

T-28: You had no difficulty—even though you had trouble in making up
your mind—you had no difficulty with the work itself?

C-29: No, I worked very hard. My family always emphasized that I couldn't
do well in school, so I had to work hard. I always studied hard. Whenever I set my mind to do anything, I really worked at it. And I was always unsure of myself with people. Consequently, I've almost always
gone out with more than one person at the same time, maybe because
of a fear of rejection by one. Also, something that bothers me more
than anything is that I think that I have the ability to write fiction. But
I don't seem to be able to discipline myself. Instead of spending my
time wisely, as far as writing is concerned, I'll let it go, let it go, and
then go out several nights a week—which I know doesn't help me.
When I ask myself why I do it, I don't know.

T-30: Are you afraid the writing wouldn't be good enough?

C-31: I have that basic fear.

T-32: That's right: it is a *basic* fear.

C-33: Although I have pretty well convinced myself that I have talent, I'm
just afraid to apply myself. My mother always encouraged me to write,
and she always encouraged me to keep on looking for something better in everything I do. From the time I started to go out with boys,
when I was about thirteen or fourteen, she never wanted me to get interested in one boy. There was always something better somewhere
else. "Go out and look for it." And if somebody didn't please me in
all respects, "Go out and look for somebody else." I think that this
has influenced the feeling that I've always had that when I might be
interested in one person, I'm always looking for someone else.

T-34: Yes, I'm sure it probably has.

C-35: But I don't know what I'm looking for.

T-36: You seem to be looking for perfection. You're looking for security,
certainty.

Generally, in doing psychotherapy, I first obtain a moderate degree of
background information to identify a symptom that I can concretely use to

show her what her basic philosophy or value system is and how she can change it. I thus asked her, in T-30, "Are you afraid the writing wouldn't be good enough?" because I assume, on the basis of rational emotive behavior theory, that there are only a few reasons why she is not writing, and that this is probably one of them. Once she admits she has a fear of failure in writing, I emphasize that this is probably her general or basic fear—so that she will begin to see that her fear of failure is all-pervasive and may explain some other dysfunctional behavior she has mentioned. In T-36, I flatly tell her that I think she's looking for perfection and certainty. I hope she will be somewhat startled by this statement. I intend eventually to show her that her writing fears (and other symptoms) largely stem from her perfectionism. As it happens, she does not appear ready yet to take up my hypothesis; so I bide my time, knowing that I will sooner or later get back to forcing her to look at some of the concepts behind her disturbed behavior.

C-37: The basic problem is that I'm worried about my family. I'm worried about money. And I never seem to be able to relax.

T-38: Why are you worried about your family? Let's go into that, first of all. What's to be concerned about? They have certain demands which you don't want to adhere to.

C-39: I was brought up to think that I mustn't be selfish.

T-40: Oh, we'll have to knock that out of your head!

C-41: I think that that is one of my basic problems.

T-42: That's right. You were brought up to be Florence Nightingale.

C-43: Yes, I was brought up in a family of sort of would-be Florence Nightingales, now that I analyze the whole pattern of my family history. . . . My father became really alcoholic sometime when I was away in college. My mother developed a breast cancer last year, and she had one breast removed. Nobody is healthy.

T-44: How is your father doing now?

C-45: Well, he's doing much better. He's been going to AA meetings, and the doctor he has been seeing has been giving him pills to keep him going. He spends quite a bit of money every week on pills. And if he misses a day of pills, he's absolutely unbearable. My mother feels that I shouldn't have left home—that my place is with them. There are nagging doubts about what I should—

T-46: Why are there doubts? Why *should* you?

C-47: I think it's a feeling I was brought up with that you always have to give of yourself. If you think of yourself, you're wrong.

T-48: That's a *belief*. Why do you have to keep believing that—at your age? You believed a lot of superstitions when you were younger. Why do you have to retain them? Your parents indoctrinated you with this nonsense, because that's *their* belief. But why do you still have to believe that one should not be self-interested; that one should be self-sacrificial? Who needs that philosophy? All it's gotten you, so far, is guilt. And that's all it ever *will* get you!

C-49:   And now I try to break away. For instance, they'll call up and say, "Why don't you come Sunday?" And if I say, "No, I'm busy," rather than saying, "No, I'll come when it's convenient," they get terribly hurt, and my stomach gets all upset.

T-50:   Because you tell yourself, "There I go again. I'm a louse for not devoting myself to them!" As long as you tell yourself that crap, then your stomach or some other part of you will start jumping! But it's your *philosophy*, your *belief*, your sentence to *yourself*—"I'm no goddamned good! How could I do that lousy, stinking thing?" *That's* what's causing your stomach to jump. Now, that is a false sentence. Why are you no goddamned good because you prefer you to them? For that's what it amounts to. *Who* said you're no good—Jesus Christ? Moses? Who said so? The answer is: your parents said so. And you believe it because they said so. But who the hell are they?

C-51:   That's right. I was brought up to believe that everything your parents say is right. And I haven't been able to stop believing this.

T-52:   You haven't *done* it. You're *able* to, but you haven't. And *you're* now saying, every time you talk to them, the same crap to yourself. And you've got to see you're saying this drivel! Every time a human being gets upset—except when she's in physical pain—she has always told herself some bullshit the second before she gets upset. Normally, the bullshit takes the form, "This is terrible!"—in your case, "It's terrible that I don't want to go out there to see them!" Or people tell themselves, "I *shouldn't* be doing this!"—in your case, "I *shouldn't* be selfish!" Now, those terms—"This is *terrible!*" and "I *shouldn't* be doing this!"—are assumptions, premises. You cannot sustain them scientifically. You *believe* they're true, without any evidence, mainly because your parents indoctrinated you to believe that they're true. . . . Not only believe it, but *keep* indoctrinating yourself with it. That's the real perniciousness of it. That's the reason it persists—not because they taught it to you. It would just naturally die after a while. But you keep saying it to yourself. It's these simple declarative sentences that you tell yourself every time you make a telephone call to your parents. And unless we can get you to see that you are saying them, and contradict and challenge them, you'll go on saying them forever. Then you will keep getting pernicious results: headaches, self-punishment, lying, and whatever else you get. These results are the logical consequences of an irrational cause, a false premise. And it's this premise that has to be questioned.

As soon as Martha, in C-45, says that she has nagging doubts whenever she thinks of herself first, I try to show her that this idea is only an opinion, that it cannot be empirically justified, and that it will lead to poor results. I am herewith being classically rational emotive: not only explicating but attacking Martha's self-defeating premises and values, and trying to actively teach her how to attack her basic mistaken views.

C-59:   I get so mad at myself for being so illogical.

T-60:   There you go again! You are not only saying that you *are* illogical, but that you *shouldn't* be. Why *shouldn't* you be? It's a pain in the ass to be illogical; it's a nuisance. But who says it's *wicked* for you to be wrong? That's *your parents'* philosophy.

C-61:   Yes, and also there's the matter of religion. I was brought up to be a strict, hard-shelled Baptist. And I can't quite take it any more. This has been going on for—*(Pause)* Well, the first seeds of doubt were sown when I was in high school. Nobody answered my questions. And I kept asking the minister, and he didn't answer my questions. And when I went to college, I started reading. I tried very hard, the first two years in college. I went to church all the time. If I had a question, I'd ask the minister. But pretty soon I couldn't get any answers. And now I really don't believe in the Baptist Church.

T-62:   All right, But are you *guilty* about not believing?

C-63:   Not only am I guilty, but the worst part about it is that I can't tell my parents that I don't believe.

T-64:   But why do you have to? What's the necessity? Because they're probably not going to accept it.

C-65:   Well, they didn't accept it. I was going to get married to a Jewish fellow as soon as I graduated from college. And, of course, the problem of religion came up then. And I didn't stand up for what I believed. I don't know; rather than have scenes, I took the coward's way out. And when I spend Saturdays and Sundays with them now—which is rare— I go to church with them. And this is what I mean by lying, rather than telling the truth.

T-66:   I see. You're probably going to extremes there—going to church. Why do you have to go to church?

C-67:   I always hate to create a scene.

T-68:   You mean you always sell your soul for a mess of porridge?

C-69:   Yes, I do.

T-70:   I don't see why you should. That leaves you with no integrity. Now it's all right to do whatever you want about being quiet, and not telling your parents about your loss of faith—because they're not going to approve and could well upset themselves. There's no use in throwing your irreligiosity in their faces. But to let yourself be forced to go to church and thereby to give up your integrity—that's bullshit. You can even tell them, if necessary, "I don't believe in that any more." And if there's a scene, there's a scene. If they commit suicide, they commit suicide! You can't really hurt them, except physically. You can't hurt anybody else except with a baseball bat! You can do things that they don't like, that they take too seriously, and that they hurt themselves with. But you can't really hurt them with words and ideas. That's non-sense. They taught you to believe that nonsense: "You're hurting us, dear, if you don't go along with what we think you ought to do!" That's drivel of the worst sort! They're hurting themselves by fascistically demanding that you do a certain thing, and then making themselves upset when you don't do it. You're not doing the hurting—they are. If they get hurt because you tell them you're no longer a Baptist, that's their doing. They're hurting themselves; you're not hurting them. They'll say, "How can you do this to us?" But is that *true*? *Are* you doing anything to them or are *they* doing it to themselves?

C-71:   No, I'm not.

T-72:   But you *believe* that you're hurting them. It's crap!

T-104: . . . What you had better do is relatively simple—but it's not easy to do. And that is—you've already done parts of what needs to be done. You have changed some of your fundamental philosophies—particularly regarding religion—which is a big change for a human being to make. But you haven't changed enough of your philosophy; you still believe some basic dogmas. Most people—whether Jew, Catholic, or Protestant—believe certain dogmas. The main dogmas are that we should devote ourselves to others before ourselves; that we must be loved, accepted, and adored by others, especially by members of our own family; and that we must do well, we must achieve greatly, succeed, do right. And you firmly believe these major ideas. You'd better get rid of them!

C-105: How do I do that?

T-106: By seeing, first of all, that every single time you get upset . . . you told yourself some superstitious creed—some bullshit. That, for example, you're no good because you aren't successful at something; or that you're a louse because you are unpopular, or are selfish, or are not as great as you should be. Then, when you see that you have told yourself this kind of nonsense, you have to ask yourself the question, "*Why* should I have to be successful? *Why* should I always have to be accepted and approved? *Why* should I be utterly loved and adored? Who said so? Jesus Christ? Who the hell was he?" There is no evidence that these things *should* be so; and you are just parroting, on faith, this nonsense, this crap that most people in your society believe. And it's not only your parents who taught it to you. It's also all those stories you read, the fairy tales you heard, the TV shows you saw. They all include this hogwash!

C-107: I know. But every time you try to overcome this, you're faced with it somewhere else again. And I realize—I've come to realize—you know, the thing that made me try to straighten myself out was that I know I've got to learn to have confidence in my own judgment.

T-108: While you've really got confidence in this other crap!

C-109: Yes, I'm very unconfident.

T-110: You have to be—because you believe this stuff.

I continue actively teaching and depropagandizing Martha. Not only do I deal with the irrational philosophies that she brings up, but I prophylactically mention and attack others as well. I keep trying to expose to her a few basic groundless ideas—such as the ideas that she must be loved and must perform well—and to show her that her symptoms, such as her self-sacrificing and her lack of self-confidence, are the natural results of these silly ideas. . . .

C-127: . . . I also want to find out—I suppose it's all basically the same thing— why I have been promiscuous, why I lie—

T-128: For love. I get the impression you think you're such a worm that the only way to get worth, value, is to be loved, approved, accepted. And perhaps you're promiscuous to gain love, because it's an easy way: you can gain acceptance easily that way. You may lie because you're ashamed. You possibly feel that they wouldn't accept you if you told the truth. These are very common results; anybody who desperately needs to be loved—as you think you do with your crummy philosophy—will be promiscuous, will lie, will do other things which are silly, rather than do the things she really wants to do and rather than gain her own self-approval.

C-129: That's what I don't have; I don't have any.

T-130: You never tried to get it! You've been working your butt off to get other people's approval. Your parents' first, but other people's second. That's why the promiscuity; that's why the lying. And you're doing no work whatever at getting your own self-acceptance, because the only way you get self-respect is by not giving that much of a damn what other people think. There is no other way to get it; that's what self-acceptance really means: to thine *own* self be true!

In my response, T-130, I epitomize one of the main differences between REBT and most other "dynamic" systems of psychological treatment. Whereas a psychoanalytically-oriented therapist would probably have tried to show Martha that her promiscuity and lying stemmed from her early childhood experiences, I believe nothing of the sort. I assume that her childhood lying, for example, was mainly caused by her own innate tendencies toward crooked thinking—which in turn led her to react inefficiently to the propaganda her parents may have imposed on her. What is important, therefore, is her own reactivity and not her parents' actions. I also believe, on theoretical grounds, that the reason for Martha's present promiscuity and lying is probably her current need to be inordinately loved; and she freely seems to admit (as she also previously did in C-19) that my educated guess about this is true.

If I were proved to be wrong in this guess, I would not be perturbed but would look for another hypothesis—for example, her promiscuity might be a form of self-punishment, because she thought she was unworthy on some other count. As a rational emotive behavior therapist, I am willing to take a chance on being wrong with my first hypothesis because, if I am right, I usually save my client a good deal of time. Moreover, by taking a wrong tack, I may well help myself and the client get to the right tack. If, however, I try the psychoanalytic, history-taking path, to arrive at the "real" reasons for my client's behavior, (a) I may never find what these "real" reasons are (for they may not exist, or years of probing may never turn them up); (b) I may still come up with the wrong reasons; and (c) I may sidetrack the client so seriously that she may never discover what her basic disturbance-creating philosophy is and therefore never do anything about changing it. For a variety of reasons, then, I took a very direct approach with Martha.

C-131: You have to develop a sort of hard shell towards other people?

T-132: Well, it isn't really a callous shell. It's really that you have to develop your own goals and your own confidence so much that you do not allow the views and desires of others to impinge that much on you. Actually, you'll learn to be kinder and nicer to other people if you do this. We're not trying to get you to be against others, to be hostile or resentful. The less vulnerable you get to what others think of you, actually the more sensitive, kindly, and loving you can often be. Because you haven't been really loving, but largely maintaining a façade with your parents. Underneath, you've been resentful, unloving.

C-133: I can be loving, though.

T-134: That's right. But you'd better be true to yourself first; and through being true to yourself then you'll be able to care more for other people. Not all people, and maybe not your parents. There's no law that says you have to love your parents. They may just not be your cup of tea. In fact, it looks like in some ways they aren't. Tough! It would be nice if they were: it would be lovely if you could love them and have good relationships. But that may never really be. You may well have to withdraw emotionally from them, to some extent—not from everybody, but probably from them somewhat—in order to be true to yourself. Because it seems to me they act like leeches, fascists, emotional blackmailers.

C-135: Yes, that's the term: emotional blackmailers. This I know; this has been evidenced all through my life. Emotional blackmail!

At every point, I try to show Martha that she does not have to feel guilty with withdrawing emotionally from her parents, nor for doing what she wants to do or thinking what she wants to think. I do not try to get her to condemn her parents or to be hostile to them. Quite the contrary! But I do consistently show her that they have their own problems in logical thinking and that she'd better resist their emotional blackmailing. As it turns out, she seems to have always known this; but my actively bringing it to her attention will presumably help her to act, now, on what she knows and feels. I am thereby helping her, through frank and therapist-directed discussion, to get in touch with her real feelings and to follow them in practice.

T-136: Right. And you've been accepting this blackmail. You had to accept it as a child—you couldn't help it, you were dependent. But you don't *still* have to accept it. You now can see that they're blackmailing; and now you can calmly resist it, without being resentful of them. Then their blackmail won't take effect. They'll probably foam at the mouth, have fits, and everything. Tough!—so they'll foam. Well, there's no question that you can change. We haven't got any more time now. But the main problem—as I said awhile ago—is your philosophy, which is an internalizing, really, of their philosophy. And if there ever was evidence of how an abject philosophy affects you, there it is: they're thoroughly miserable. And you'll be just as miserable if you continue this way. If you want to learn to *change* your philosophy, this is what I do in therapy: beat people's crazy ideas over the head until they stop defeating themselves. That's all you're doing: defeating yourself!

I keep utilizing material from Martha's own life to consistently show her what is going on in her head, philosophically, and what she'd better do about changing her thinking. This first interview with Martha indicates how REBT, right from the start, encourages the therapist to talk much more about the client's value system than about her symptoms and how it uses the information she gives to highlight her own disturbance-creating ideas and to attack them. I think that this session also shows that although I do not hesitate to contradict Martha's assumptions at several points, I am essentially supportive in that I keep showing her (a) that I am on her side, (b) that I think I can help her, (c) that I am fairly sure what the real sources of her disturbances are, and (d) that if she works at seeing these sources and at doing something to undermine them, the chances are excellent that she will become much less upsettable. My "attack," therefore, is one that would ordinarily be called "ego-bolstering." Or, in REBT terminology, it is one that is designed to help Martha fully accept rather than severely condemn herself.

To this end, I consistently have what Carl Rogers (1961) calls "unconditional positive regard" for Martha, for I accept her in spite of her difficulties and inanities, and believe that she is capable of overcoming her crooked thinking by living and working primarily for herself. I also show that I am on Martha's side, not because I personally find her attractive, bright, or competent, but because I feel that every human has the right to choose to live primarily for himself or herself.

SEGMENTS FROM THE SECOND SESSION

This session takes place five days after the first session. Martha has already made some progress, has calmed down considerably, and is now in a better condition to work on some of her basic problems.

T-1: How are things?

C-2:   Things are okay. I went to visit my parents on Monday night. And every time I was tempted to fall prey to their emotional blackmail, I remembered what you said, and I was able to fight it.

T-3:   Fine!

C-4:   My mother is having a rough time yet, because of having her breast removed. She hardly says anything. She's really in a fog. She gets confused, and she uses the confusion to give her a hold on the family. She was putting on a martyr act the other night; and usually I would have given in to her, but I said, "Quit being a martyr! Go to bed." She just looked at me as though I was a strange creature!

T-5:   And you didn't get upset by it?

C-6:   No, I didn't get upset by it. I had the feeling that I was doing the right thing. And that was, I think, the major accomplishment in the past few days.

T-7:   Yes; well that was quite a good accomplishment.

C-8:   Now if there are any bigger crises that will come, I don't know how I'll face them; but it looks like I can.

T-9:   Yes; and if you keep facing these smaller crises as they arise—and they tend to be continual—there's no reason why you shouldn't be able to face the bigger ones as well. Why not?

C-10:   I guess it's a case of getting into a good habit.

T-11:   Yes, that's right: getting ready to believe that no matter what your parents do, no matter how hurt they get, that's not your basic problem. You're not deliberately doing them in; you're just standing up for yourself.

As often occurs in REBT, although this is only the second session, Martha is already beginning to implement some of the major ideas that were discussed during the first session and is beginning to change herself. I deliberately support her new notion that she can handle herself with her parents, and I keep reiterating that she does not have to react to their views and behavior by getting upset. I thereby am approving her new patterns and rewarding or reinforcing her. But I am also repetitively teaching—taking every opportunity to reassert that she can think for herself and does not have to react negatively because her parents or others view her unfavorably....

C-40:   In school, if I didn't do well in one particular thing, or even on a particular test—and little crises that came up—if I didn't do as well as I had wanted to do.

T-41:   You beat yourself over the head?

C-42:   Yes.

T-43:   But why? What's the point? Are you supposed to be perfect? Why shouldn't human beings make mistakes, be imperfect?

C-44:   Maybe you always expect yourself to be perfect.

T-45:   Yes. But is that *sane*?

C-46:   No.

T-47:   Why do it? Why not give up that unrealistic expectation?

C-48:   But then I can't accept myself.

T-49:   But you're saying, "It's shameful to make mistakes." *Why* is it shameful? Why can't you go to somebody else when you make a mistake and say, "Yes, I made a mistake"? Why is that so awful?

C-50:   I don't know.

T-51:   There *is* no good reason. You're just *saying* it's so. Recently I wrote an article for a professional publication, and they accepted it, and they got another psychologist to write a critique of it. He wrote his critique—a fairly savage one—and he pointed out some things with which I disagree, so I said so in my reply. But he pointed out some things which he was right about; where I had overstated my case and made a mistake. So, I merely said about this in my rejoinder, "He's right; I made a mistake here." Now, what's the horror? Why shouldn't I make a mistake? Who am I—Jesus Christ? Who are you—the Virgin Mary? Then, why shouldn't you be a fallible human being like the rest of us and make mistakes?

C-52:   It might all go back to, as you said, the need for approval. If I don't make mistakes, then people will look up to me. If I do it all perfectly—

T-53:   That is an erroneous belief; that if you never make mistakes everybody will love you and that it is necessary that they do. That's a big part of it. But is it true? Suppose you never did make mistakes—*would* people love you? Maybe they would hate your guts because you were so perfect, wouldn't they?

C-54:   And yet, not all the time. There are times—this is rare, I grant you— but sometimes I'll take a stand on something that other people don't like. But this is rare!

T-55:   Yes, but what about the times when you know you're wrong? Let's take those times—that's what we're talking about. You know you're wrong, you made a mistake, there's no question about it. Why are you a louse at *those* times? Why is it shameful to admit your mistake? Why can't you accept yourself as a fallible human being—which we all are?

C-56:   *(Pause)* Maybe I have the idea that if I keep telling myself how perfect I am, I won't realize how imperfect I am.

T-57:   Yes, but why shouldn't one accept the fact that one is imperfect? That's the real question. What's shameful about being imperfect? Why must one be an angel—which you're trying to be?

C-58:   Probably there's no good reason.

T-59:   No. Then why don't you look at *that*? There's no good reason. It's a definitional thing, saying "To be good, to be perfect, to be a worthwhile human being, I must be perfect. If I have flaws, I'm no damned good." And you can't substantiate that proposition. It's a senseless proposition; but you believe it. The reason you believe it is your society believes it. This is the basic creed of your silly society. Certainly, your parents believe lt. If they knew one-sixtieth of your errors and mis-takes—especially your sex errors!—they'd be horrified, wouldn't they?

C-60: Yes.

T-61: You have the same silly horror! Because *they* think you ought to be a sexless angel, you think you ought to be.

C-62: *(Silence)*

T-63: You've accepted their idiotic judgments—the same judgments that have driven your father to drink and made your mother utterly miser-able. They both have been miserable all your life. That's what perfec-tionism leads to. A beautiful object lesson there! Anybody who is perfectionistic tends to become disturbed, unhappy—ultimately often crazy. The gospel of perfection!

C-64: That's what I have to work on. Because I don't want to get like they are.

T-65: No, but you are partly like they are already—we had better change that. It isn't a matter of getting—you've already got! Let's face it. You don't do the same kind of behavior as they do, but you hate yourself when you don't. You make the mistakes; they don't make them. But then you say, "I'm no good! How could I have done this? This is ter-rible! I'm not Florence Nightingale. I go to bed with guys. I do bad things. I make blunders. How awful!" That's the same philosophy that they have, isn't it? And it's an impossible philosophy, because we'd re-ally literally have to be angels to live up to it. There *are* no angels! Not even your parents!

I make a mistake when I tell Martha that she believes she is worthless largely because her parents and her society teach her to believe this. I fail to note that practically all humans seem to be born with a tendency to believe this sort of drivel; that they must be pretty perfect and are no good if they are not; and that therefore their parents and their society are easily able to con-vince them that this is "true."

Clinically, however, I felt when I talked to Martha that she was already prejudiced against her parents' views and that she might therefore see the per-niciousness of her own ideas if I emphasized how similar they were to those of her parents. As a rational emotive behavior therapist, I am a frank propagan-dist, since I deliberately use appeals that I think will work with a given client. But I only propagandize in accordance with what appears to be the empiri-cal reality that some people do define themselves as worthless slobs. I do not propagandize only to win Martha's approval, but to dramatically (emotively) bring to her attention the realities of life.

Rational emotive behavior therapists are sometimes accused of foisting on their clients their own prejudiced views of the world. Actually, they base their views on the facts of human existence and the usual nature of people. And they teach individuals with disturbances to look at these facts and to realistically accept and work with them. They may teach through dramatic or emotive methods in order to put a point over more effectively, taking into consideration that clients generally hold their wrong-headed views in a highly emotionalized, not easily uprootable manner.

C-66: *(Pause)* I guess that's this great fear of failure. That might have been what was keeping me from concentrating on writing, which I really want to do. I'm afraid that I might make a mistake, you know.

T-67: Yes, that's the other grim tragedy. Two things happen if you have a terrible, grim fear of failure. One is, as you just said, you get anxious, unhappy, ashamed. Two, you don't live; you don't do the things you want to do. Because if you did them, you might make a mistake, an error, be a poor writer—and wouldn't that be awful, according to your definition? So you just don't do things. That's your parents again. How could they be happy, when they haven't done anything? And you have been following the same general pattern. You haven't taken it to their extremes as yet, but it's the same bullshit, no matter how you slice it. And in your case you're afraid to write; because if you wrote, you'd commit yourself. And if you committed yourself, how horrible *that* would be!

C-68: I've done a lot of thinking since the last time I saw you. And I've gone at the typewriter with a fresh burst of enthusiasm. I'm really anxious to get to my writing—I want to get home from work so I can write. Nothing big has happened, but I feel as though if I concentrate on it and keep feeling this way, all I have to do is to keep working at it.

T-69: And one of two things will happen. Either you'll become a good writer, with enough work and practice; or you'll prove that you're not—which would be a good thing, too. It would be far better to prove you're not a good writer by working at it than not to write. Because if you don't write, you may go on for the rest of your life hating yourself; while if you really work solidly day after day, and you just haven't got it in this area, that's tough. So you won't be a writer—you'll be something else. It would be better to learn by that experience.

C-70: That's right. Because—I don't know—I felt so different, sitting at the typewriter and working at it, that it got to be enjoyable.

T-71: It will!

C-72: But it was painful before.

T-73: It was painful because you were *making* it painful by saying, "My God! Look what would happen if I failed! How awful!" Well, anything would become painful if you kept saying that.

C-74: Another thing that bothers me, I guess—it's the whole pattern of behavior; the way everything has been in my life. It's a sort of—"Go ahead and do it now, and then something will come along and take care of it." Like my parents always said, "We'll go ahead and do this, even though we don't have the money for it, and it'll come from somewhere."

T-75: Right: "In God we trust!" . . .

C-84: And when I tell myself, "Don't be silly; you can't do it, so don't," I'm tempted to go ahead and do it anyway.

T-85:   Yes, because you're telling yourself stronger and louder: "It'll take care of itself. Fate will intervene in my behalf. The Lord will provide!"

C-86:   And I get mad at myself for doing it—

T-87:   That's illegitimate! Why not say, "Let's stop the crap!" instead of getting mad at yourself? How will getting mad at yourself help?

C-88:   It doesn't. It just causes more tension.

T-89:   That's exactly right. It doesn't do any good whatsoever. Let's cut out all the self-blame. That's doesn't mean cut out all criticism. Say, "Yes, I am doing this wrongly, so how do I not do it wrongly?"—instead of: "I am doing it wrongly; what a louse I am! I'm no good; I deserve to be punished!"

I persist at showing Martha that she can take chances, do things badly, and still not condemn herself. At every possible turn, I get back to her underlying philosophies concerning (a) failing and defining herself as a worthless individual and (b) unrealistically relying on the world or fate to take care of difficult situations. She consistently describes her feelings, but I bring her back to the ideas behind them. Then she seems to accept my interpretations and to seriously consider working against her disturbance-creating ideas. My persistence and determination may importantly induce her to tentatively accept my explanations and to use them herself.

C-90:   When I am particularly worried about anything, I have very strange dreams. I have dreams that I can't describe, but I have them several times a week.

T-91:   There's nothing unusual about that. They're probably anxiety dreams. All the dreams say—if you told me what they are, I could show you right away—the same kind of things you're saying to yourself during the day. They're doing it in a vague and more abstract way. But that's all they are, just repetitious of the crap you're telling yourself during the day. In dreams, our brain is not as efficient as it is when we're awake; and therefore it uses symbols, vague representations, indirectness, and so on. But the dreams tell us the same crap we think during the day.

C-92:   I had a dream last week that disturbed me. I dreamed that I ran off somewhere with my boss, and his wife found us in bed; and I was so upset over that—I really was. Because I never consciously thought of my boss in a sexual way.

T-93:   That doesn't mean that that's what the dream represented, that you thought of your boss in a sexual way. There's a more obvious explanation of the dream. All the dream is really saying is: You did the wrong thing and got found out.

C-94:   I never thought of that.

T-95:   That's all it was saying, probably. And what's one of the wrongest things you can do in our society? Have intercourse with your boss and have his wife find out! That's all. It probably has little to do with sex at all; and you're probably not going around unconsciously lusting after your boss.

C-96:   No, I don't think I am.

T-97:   No. But it would be the wrong move, if you did have sex with him; it might, of course, jeopardize your job. So that's all you're saying in your dream: if I do the wrong thing, I'm no goddamned good; I may lose my job; I may get terribly penalized; and so on. That's what you say all day, isn't it? Why should you not translate it into dreams at night? It's the same crap!

In REBT, dreams are not overemphasized and are often used only to a small extent; for, as I say to Martha, they are hardly the royal road to the unconscious (as Freud believed), but seem to be rather distorted and muddled representations of the same kind of thinking and feeling that the individual tends to do during his waking life. Since they are experienced in symbolic, vague, and ambiguous ways, and since they can easily be misinterpreted (according to whatever biases the individual therapist happens to hold), the REBT practitioner would rather stick with the client's conscious thoughts, feelings, and behaviors and with the unconscious (or unaware) thoughts and feelings that can be deduced from them. Dreams are rather redundant material, and can consume a great deal of therapeutic time if they are taken too seriously. Moreover, long-winded dream analysis can easily (and dramatically!) distract the client from what he'd better do most of all: look at his philosophies of life and work hard at changing them.

The beauty of the REBT approach is that no matter what the client seems to be upset about, the therapist can quickly demonstrate that there is no good reason for her upsetness. Thus, if Martha's dream represents (a) her lusting after her boss, (b) her being out of control, or (c) any other kind of mistake, REBT theory holds that she cannot be a rotter and that she therefore need not be terribly anxious, guilty, angry, or depressed. She creates her disturbed feelings, not from the dream events, nor from her foolish motives that may be revealed in these events, nor from the happenings in her real life, nor from anything *except* her own attitudes about these events, motives, or happenings. And I, as her therapist, am concerned much more with her attitudes than with things transpiring in her waking or sleeping life. So if REBT is consistently followed, *any* emotional problem may be tracked down to its philosophic sources (or the ways in which the individual blames herself, others, or the world); and these philosophies may then be challenged, attacked, changed, and uprooted.

C-192: I guess the main thing is to keep in mind that a lot of the thoughts I have—whenever I get a thought like that, I'd better challenge it.

T-193: That's right, to see that it is invalid. First you start with the feeling—the upset. Then you know, on theoretical grounds, that you have an invalid thought, because you don't get negative feelings without first having some silly thought. Then you look for the thought—which is pretty obvious most of the time. You're invariably blaming yourself or saying that something is horrible when it isn't. Then you say, "Why is this horrible? Why would it be dreadful if such-and-such a thing happened?" Challenge it; question it; counter it. That's the process. And if you go through that process, your thoughts can't persist. Because they're *your* irrational thoughts now. They're no longer your parents' ideas. You have internalized them.

C-194: *(Long pause)* I guess it has to be done.

T-195: Yes. And you will get immense benefit from doing it—as you've already been deriving this week. It felt good when you acted that way, didn't it?

C-196: Since I have been back at the typewriter again, I've been thinking differently. I can see myself falling back, as I used to be able to do, into a clear pattern of thought. I mean, I'm not just thinking in symbols and metaphors, but am able to describe things incisively, or at least have descriptive impressions of things.

T-197: Yes. That's because you're letting yourself go—you're not pouncing on yourself so much.

C-198: Yes, you're right. Not that I've done very much in this last week, but I do feel like I'm loosening up more.

T-199: That's very good progress in one week's time! All you have to do is keep that up—and go a little further.

C-200: And another thing I've done: I haven't called up my father because I felt I had to. And he hasn't called me—so that means something.

T-201: Fine! When would you like to make the next appointment?

Martha's apparent progress represents a common occurrence in REBT. After one or two active-directive sessions, clients frequently report that something they thought they were never able to do before is now in their repertoire. This does not mean that they are truly "cured" of their emotional disturbances. But it often does seem to mean that they are well on the way to resolving at least one or two major aspects of these disturbances.

Even if clients such as Martha are quickly helped, this hardly means that all or most individuals who try REBT encounters are similarly relieved; many of them, of course, are not. I assume, however, that a certain large minority of people can almost immediately profit by the REBT approach; and I assume that a given individual with whom I am talking may be one of this minority. If my assumption proves to be correct, fine! If it does not, I am prepared, if necessary, to doggedly continue with the approach for as many sessions as are desirable—until the client finally begins to see that she is causing her own upsets, that she can observe the specific meanings and beliefs by which she causes them, that she can vigorously and consistently dispute and challenge these beliefs, and that she can thereby become considerably less disturbed.

THIRD SESSION

The third session with Martha was uneventful. Because she was afflicted with some expensive physical ailments and had financial difficulties, she decided to discontinue therapy for a time.

SEGMENTS FROM
THE FOURTH SESSION

The fourth session with Martha took place nine months after the third session. She had expected to come back to therapy sooner than she actually did, but she was able to get along nicely and didn't feel impelled to return until she had a specific problem to discuss. She now comes with this problem—her relations with men.

T-1:   How are things with you?

C-2:   Pretty well, I would say. I've been hearing good things about you from some of the people I sent to see you. From Matt, in particular. He thinks that you've helped him immensely.

T-3:   I'm glad that he thinks so.

C-4:   And I see that you're making yourself comfortable, as usual. That's the way I found you last time: shoes off, feet up.

T-5:   Yes; that's the way I usually am.

C-6:   I came to you back in January because I needed some help in writing; and also I didn't know how to handle my parents.

T-7:   Yes.

C-8:   Well, I think I solved those two problems fairly well. I get along very well with my parents now. Not because I'm giving in to them at all. I've sort of established myself as a human being, apart from them completely. And I also found some other work. I was working, as I told you, for an advertising agency. But it didn't have any interest for me at the time. I was terribly bored, and I felt I could write on my own. But I was afraid. Then I got an idea for a novel, and a publisher has taken an option on it, and I've been working on it ever since. It will be published in the spring by the same publisher who has been having such success recently with several young novelists.

T-9:   I see. That's fine!

C-10:   So that's all working out very well. But there's something that is bothering me, that I thought you could help me with. I've been thinking of getting married. I've been thinking of marriage in general, first of all. But before that—maybe I'm not quite sure that I really know how to love anybody. Not that I consider that there's a formula. But I've always, in a way, been somewhat afraid of men. The other thing is that there is someone in particular who would like to marry me. And— maybe I'd better tell you how this all happened.

T-11:   Sure.

C-12:   In trying to analyze it—in trying to figure it out—I guess it all started to go back to my father. My father was a nice guy, but he has been alcoholic since I was twelve; and he has been getting worse since I last saw you. But I was absolutely adoring of my father when I was a little girl. And then I realized he was a human being, and he fell off his pedestal. Now I don't know how much can be attributed to that, but I don't think I ever trusted a man. I guess I was afraid that if I devoted myself to that person completely, sooner or later he would walk out on me. And this has always terrified me, no matter what kind of associations I've had. I always have to keep one step ahead of them.

T-13:   All right; it *would* terrify you if you keep saying to yourself, "They'll find out how worthless I am and leave me!"

C-14:   I guess you're right.

T-15:   And if you get rid of that fear—and as you said yourself, a couple of minutes ago, it is a fear—then you can be pretty sure that you'll love someone. I don't know *whom* you'll love—this person you're talking about, who wants to marry you, or anybody else—but I'm sure you have the *capacity* to love if you're not absorbed in, "Oh, my God! What a louse I am! When is he going to find it out?" See? . . .

C-40:   Another thing that I seem to do: every time I get interested in someone, I find myself looking at other men.

T-41:   Yes, that's possible. But it's also possible that if you think of one man in terms of marrying him and you still get interested in other men, you may not be so sure as yet, in terms of your experience, that it should be the first one. And therefore you'd like to try others. So some of what you feel may be normal, and some of it may be your fear of getting involved. The basic problem still is getting you to be unfearful—to realize yourself that you don't have to be afraid of anything. . . .

C-42:   Well, I would like to overcome this. I don't want to be afraid of them—that they might leave me.

T-43:   The basic thing they can do, as you said before, is reject you. Now, let's suppose that they do. Let's suppose that you went with this guy, and you really let yourself go with him, and he finally did reject you, for whatever his reasons might be. What could you conclude should this happen?

C-44:   I could always suppose that he was the one who had shortcomings, rather than me.

T-45:   But let's suppose he doesn't have serious shortcomings, and he rejects you. Let's suppose he's perfect and then he spurns you. Now what does that prove?

C-46:   I don't know.

T-47:   All it proves is that he doesn't like you for some deficiencies. It proves, assuming that he's objective about your deficiencies, that you have certain defects. But does having these defects prove that you're worthless? Or that you're thoroughly inadequate, that you're no good?

C-48:   It doesn't.

T-49:   That's exactly right! And yet that's what you automatically think every single time: that it means something bad about you. That's what your parents believe: that if you are deficient and somebody finds it out, that proves that you're worthless, as a total human. Isn't that their philosophy?

C-50:   I guess so.

T-51:   They've told you that in so many words, so many times—as you told me they did awhile ago. When they found out something about you that they didn't like—such as your not running to their beck and call—you were not just a daughter who didn't like them that much (which is all that was evident); no, you were a louse—no good! They called you every name under the sun. They tried to make you guilty, you told me. Over the phone, they'd call you several times—and so on. Isn't that right? They assume that when someone is deficient in their eyes, that person is a slob. That's their philosophy: that unless you're an angel, you are no good.

C-52:   I guess I just carried it with me. I let myself carry it with me.

T-53:   That's right. You've let yourself carry it with you—which is normal enough. Most people do. But look at the results! If it had good results, if it really made you happy, we might say, "Go carry it!" But the result is the normal result—or the abnormal result, in your case. You can't give to a man because you're always worrying, "How worthless I am! And how soon will he see it? And before he sees it, maybe I'd better do something to get rid of him." Which is your logical conclusion from an irrational premise, the premise being that if people do find your deficiencies and therefore reject you, you're totally no good. Actually, there are *two* premises here. One, that they'll find your deficiencies and therefore will reject you—which is quite an assumption! Two, that if they do reject you, you're no damned good. These are two completely irrational premises. They're not supported by any evidence.

I try to show Martha that it is not her boyfriend but her own attitudes about herself that are upsetting her, and that no matter how defective she is, and no matter how badly her boyfriend (or anyone else) rejects her, she can still fully accept herself and try to better her relationships. Although I am therefore ruthless about insisting that she acknowledge her deficiencies, I am (in a typical REBT manner) highly supportive about the possibility of her unconditionally accepting herself. In REBT, the therapist generally does not give warm, personal affection (since there is the always existing danger that the client will, in getting it, wrongly think he is "good" *because* the therapist or group cares for him). Instead, the rational emotive behavior therapist (and group) tries to give unconditional acceptance, that is, complete tolerance and lack of condemnation of the client no matter what his or her faults are. I think an incisive reading of these sessions with Martha will show that I am rarely loving or warm to her but that I frequently show full acceptance of her.

C-56: How do I go about convincing myself that this is wrong?

T-57: The first thing you'd better do before you convince yourself that this is wrong is to convince yourself—that is, fully admit to yourself—that you very strongly have this belief. You can't very well tackle a belief and change it unless you fully admit that you have it. After seeing this, the second thing is to see the degree—which is enormous and intense—to which you have it. You can at first do this by inference—by observing your behavior and asking yourself what ideas lie behind it. For your behavior itself is not necessarily fearful. It may take the form of your *feeling* in a state of panic, or it may be defensive.

C-58: Well, my behavior is mostly defensive.

T-59: All right. Then we have to start with your defensive behavior. Look at it, question it, challenge it, and see—by inference, at first—that it could only be this way if you *were* fearful. For why would you be defensive if you were not, underneath, also afraid of something? If we can get you to see how many times a day you're unduly restricted, defensive—and therefore fearing—until you see the real frequency and intensity of your fears, then at least we get you to see what the cancer really is. You can't really understand the cancer without seeing the depths of it. Okay, we have the first step, then, which is to make you see fully what the depths of your cancerous ideation are. Then, as you begin to see this, the second step is to get you to calmly assess it. The first cancer is your defense and your fear behind it. The second cancer is—and this is the reason why so many people *are* defensive—if you admit to yourself, "My God! What a terribly fearful person I am!" you will then tend to blame yourself for that. In other words, you say on level number one, "My heavens, I'm a wrongdoing person, am therefore terribly worthless, and I'd better not let anyone know this." So you become defensive because your real philosophy is: "What a worthless slob I am because I'm imperfect; I have deficiencies; I have faults." So the first level is to make yourself fearful because of your feelings of worthlessness—the philosophy that human beings who are deficient are no damned good. Then, as a derivative of that first level, you come to the second level: "Because I'm deficient, because I'm fearful, because I'm neurotic, I'm a louse and am worthless for *that* reason. So I'd better deny that I'm really that fearful *(a)* because people will find out about it and hate me and *(b)* because I'll use my fear to prove to myself what a louse I am."

So first we have to get you to admit the fact that you're fearful, defensive, and so on—that you are a perfectionist who tends to bring on feelings of worthlessness. Then we have to get you to see that by admitting your fear and defensiveness you're not a louse for having these traits; and to get you to see that simply because you have a *feeling* you're worthless doesn't mean that you really *are*. So we have to get you to *(a)* admit that you feel like a skunk; *(b)* objectively perceive—and not blamefully perceive—that you believe you're one; and *(c)* (which is really just an extension of *b*) start tackling your concept of being a skunk. . . .

C-72:   But actually, your parents bring you up that way. Because you are naughty, you stand in a corner; you don't get your supper; you get spanked; or someone says to you, "That wasn't very nice; that wasn't very good!"

T-73:   That's right. They don't only spank you—that wouldn't be so bad, because then they would just penalize you—but they also say, "You're no good!" And the attitude they take in doing the spanking is an angry attitude; and the whole implication of the anger is that you're worthless. People do this in order to train you when you're a child; and it's a very effective method of training. But look at the enormous harm it does! Incidentally, one of the main reasons we would want you to undo your self-blaming tendencies is that if you do get married and have children, you will tend to do the same kind of thing to them that was done to you—unless you see very clearly what was done to you and what you're doing now to continue it.

C-74:   And also, I'm absolutely terrified of being somebody's mother.

T-75:   Yes, that's right. Just look how incompetent you might be, and how you might screw it up! And wouldn't *that* be awful!

C-76:   You know, I've been asking myself that a hundred thousand times.

T-77:   All right; but those are the times we have to clip. Let's just take that sentence, "Suppose I was somebody's mother and brought my child up badly." That's what you're saying. How are you *ending* the sentence?

C-78:   Wouldn't that be awful! Wouldn't I be terrible!

T-79:   That's right. Now is that a logical conclusion to make from the observed facts? Let's suppose the facts were true—that you did bring up a child badly. Let's suppose that. Would it still follow that you'd be a worthless slob?

C-80:   No, it wouldn't. Because I'd be defining—that's what it is—I'd be defining *worthless* in terms of whatever it is I lack, whatever it is that I do badly in.

T-81:   That's right. The equation you'd be making is: my deficiency equals my worthlessness. That's exactly the equation—and it's a definition. Now is it a *true* definition?

C-82:   No.

T-83:   It's a true or an accurate definition if you *make* it true—if you *insist* that it's true.

C-84:   But it's not necessarily a correct one.

T-85:   That's right. And what happens when you make that definition?

C-86:   Then you feel worthless, because you define yourself as worthless.

T-87:   Yes, pragmatically, you defeat yourself. If it were a definition that led to good results, that might be fine. But *does* it lead to that?

C-88: No. Because you tend to look at everything negatively, rather than—I hate to say positively, because it sounds like 'positive thinking," and that's not it.

T-89: Yes, let's say it makes you look at things negatively rather than looking at them without prejudice.

C-90: Yes, without prejudice.

From responses T-77 to T-89, I resort to a questioning dialogue, instead of my previous use of straight lecturing and explaining. I keep asking Martha various questions about what she's telling herself, what results she is thereby getting, and whether the things she is saying to herself and the definitions she is setting up about her behavior are really accurate. She shows, by her answers, that she is following what I have previously explained and that she can probably use this material in her future living. . . .

T-95: . . . a child will lots of times define himself as a blackguard on his own. Because if he fails and does so lots of times—as he inevitably will—even if Mommy didn't call him a slob, he would probably tend to think he is worthless. It's sort of a normal, natural conclusion for a young child, who can't think straight because of his youth, to say, "Because I failed at A, B, C, and D, I'm bound to fail at X, Y, and Z; and therefore I'm thoroughly incompetent at everything." That's what we call overgeneralization; and human beings, especially young children, tend to overgeneralize. Now, unfortunately, we also help them to do this, in our society—in fact, in most societies. But they might well do it without social help, though probably to a lesser degree. Anyway, it behooves us to help them to think in a less overgeneralized manner. We'd better take the child who tends to overgeneralize and calmly show him, a thousand times if necessary, "Look, dear, because you did A, B, C, and D mistakenly, that doesn't mean—"

C-96: "—that you're going to do X, Y, and Z wrongly."

T-97: That's right! "And even if you do A, B, C, and D badly, and also do X, Y, and Z wrongly, that doesn't mean that you're a louse. It means, objectively, that you have deficiencies. So you're not Leonardo da Vinci. Tough!" But we don't teach them anything of the kind.

C-98: No. "You have to excel in everything. If you don't, that's bad!"

T-99: "That's terrible!" We don't even say it's bad. Because it is, of course, objectively bad; it's inconvenient; it's a nuisance when you fail; and you will get certain poor results if you keep failing. But it doesn't say anything about you personally, as a *human being*, except that you're the kind of a creature who often fails. It doesn't say that you're a worm—unless you define it so.

C-100: Well, I think I'll know what to look for.

T-101: Yes. It will take a little practice. It won't take very long, I'm sure, in your case, because you see the outlines, and I think you're very able to do this kind of thinking, which is highly important. Many people deliberately shy away from doing it, so they never see it. They're hopeless because, in a sense, they don't *want* to see it; they want the world to change, or others to change, rather than wanting to change themselves. But you want to see it, and you have seen a large hunk of it already, in dealing recently with your parents. Considering the short length of time that I saw you and that you've been working on it, you've done remarkably well. Now there's no reason why you can't see the bigger hunk of it—which applies to you much more than to your relations with your father and mother.

So you go off and look for these things we've been talking about. As I said, make a list, if you're not going to remember the things that come up during the week that you bother yourself about. Make a list of the major times when you feel upset, or when you believe you acted defensively instead of feeling overtly upset. Look for these things; come in, and we'll talk about them. I'll check what you find, just as I'd check your lessons if I were teaching you how to play the piano. You'll then be able to see your own blockings more clearly. There's no reason why not.

I continue to be encouraging to show Martha that she has been able to make good progress so far and that she should be able to continue to do so. But I stress that she well may not be able to do this entirely on her own at the present time and that therefore it would be best if she kept coming in to see me, to check her own impressions of what is bothering her and to make sure that she works concertedly against her internalized philosophies that lead her astray.

C-102: Because I know I need this right now. I mean I can feel the need for it. Logically, I know that my hang-up with relating to males is a big stumbling block; and this is something I have to overcome.

T-103: Yes. What I would advise you to do is to see me every week or so for therapy, or every other week or so; and also, if possible, join one of my therapy groups for awhile, where you'll see and relate to others who have similar problems to yours. You may get some insight into some of the things you're doing by watching them and showing them how to solve some of their difficulties. That's another helpful way, because we're often just too close to ourselves. But if we see the same kind of behavior in someone else, we say, "Ah, I do that, too!"

C-104: When do the groups meet? . . .

The client came for one more individual session and several group sessions of therapy, and then felt that she was doing very well and that she could manage things on her own. She returned, over the years, for other sessions from time to time, mainly to discuss the problems of her parents, her husband, her children, or other close associates. She continues to get along remarkably well. She is still in touch with me at intervals, largely to refer her friends and relatives for therapy sessions. She has reality (rather than emotional) problems with her parents; she is happily married and has two lively and seemingly little-disturbed children; she gets along well with her husband, in spite of his personal hang-ups; and she keeps writing successful books and taking great satisfaction in her work. She is hardly free from all disturbances, since she still has a tendency to become overwrought about people treating her unfairly. But she seems almost fully to accept herself, and most of her original problems are solved or managed. She still marvels at, and keeps telling her new acquaintances about, the relatively few sessions of REBT that helped her to look at, understand, and change her basic anxiety-creating and hostility-inciting philosophy of life.

Editors' Introduction

This case illustrates an important behavioral technique, covert sensitiza-
tion, applied to a serious clinical problem, pedophilia.

    We selected the case because it illustrates how behavior therapists have em-
braced the use of cognitions as therapeutic tools. In addition, the case was writ-
ten by Dr. David Barlow, arguably the most important figure in contemporary
behavior therapy. Dr. Barlow has been an outspoken and eloquent advocate
for the use of empirically supported treatment methodologies.

    Careful reading of this case will dispel the myth that behavior therapists
are indifferent to relationship variables, as well as the false belief that be-
havioral methods are applied in a lockstep manner without consideration
for personality factors and family dynamics. We quickly see that Dr.
Barlow is a sensitive therapist who tailors his treatment to the unique needs
of his patient, and the case provides a glimpse of the genuine concern this
therapist has for this very troubled minister.

    It will be useful for students to think about how practitioners from the
other therapeutic approaches represented in Current Psychotherapies
would have conceptualized the etiology and maintenance of this particular
problem, and to speculate about how the treatment—and outcome—might
have differed.

COVERT SENSITIZATION
FOR PARAPHILIA

David H. Barlow

CASE BACKGROUND

At the time of presentation, Reverend X was a 51-year-old married minister from the Midwest. He had three grown children, two females and a male, the youngest of whom was his 19-year-old daughter. He was tall and quite serious and although cooperative, did not volunteer a great deal of information at the initial interview. He came to my office after referral by a prominent psychiatrist in another state for assessment and possible treatment of heterosexual pedophilic behavior.

Reverend X reported that he had been touching and caressing girls between the ages of 10 and 16 for more than 20 years. He estimated at this time that there were probably more than 50 girls with whom he had had some interaction. Most typically this interaction was restricted to hugging or caressing their breasts. On occasion, he would also touch their genitals. He did not expose himself to girls nor did he ask them to touch him in any way. Generally, he reported achieving a partial erection during this type of contact but never ejaculated during one of these encounters. He did not report this to be primarily an erotic experience but rather continued to suggest that the emphasis was on an exchange of affection. In fact, during the initial interview

From *Covert Conditioning Casebook,* First Edition, by J. R. Cautela, A. J. Kearney, L. Ascher, A. Kearney, and M. Kleinman and 17 others. © 1993. Reprinted with permission of Wadsworth, a division of Thomson Learning.

he reported feeling little remorse about his activities for this reason, although he was deeply concerned over the effect of being "found out" on his family and his career.

Some 12 years before he presented for treatment, his activities were discovered for the first time and he was forced to leave his church in another state in the Midwest, but the matter was kept relatively quiet and he was able to take up a new position in a different state, a position he retained until just prior to treatment. Although he sought treatment and agreed to refrain from any physical interaction with young girls in his new church, he was soon.as active as ever. This behavior continued on until several months before presenting for treatment.

According to Reverend X, in most of the cases the young girls responded positively to his advances and did not seem offended or frightened. In several instances this type of activity would continue with the girl for several months and it was with these girls that genital touching occurred.

During these years, although responsible administratively and spiritually for the entire parish, he took particular interest in activities involving young adolescent girls, such as the local Girl Scout troop. In addition to this activity, Reverend X, who was particularly attracted to small breasts characteristic of young adolescent girls, would masturbate once or twice a week to pictures of girls with these features, which he found in what he referred to as "nudist magazines." In fact, he subscribed to a rather extensive series of pedophilic pornographic magazines, which, much to the embarrassment of himself and his family, continued to arrive at his old rectory for months after his discovery only to be received by the new occupants.

Several months before presenting for treatment he was confronted by the parents of an 11-year-old Girl Scout who were hearing "strange stories" about physical touching from their daughter and wanted to discuss them. His behavior was presented as a misunderstanding and the incident died down until the parents of another young girl with similar experiences mentioned them to the parents of the first girl. The story spread like wildfire and quickly led to outrage and dismissal from the parish by the bishop and suspension as a minister with strong recommendations to seek treatment.

Reverend X grew up a rather inhibited teenager with few lasting social contacts with girls. When he married at age 26, he engaged in sexual intercourse for the first time. He had begun dating at approximately age 22 and on only one occasion before marriage had he engaged in even light petting. Masturbatory fantasies in high school were centered on developing breasts.

After discovery 12 years ago at his previous parish, he was the client in a number of long-term psychotherapeutic relationships. He reported that none of these had had the slightest effect whatsoever on his sexual arousal patterns. At least one of his previous therapists had taken the approach that there must be something wrong within his marital relationship. This only angered him and was disconfirmed by his wife, who reported a normal and satisfying sexual and marital relationship.

Despite the incident, his relationship with his family remained excellent and his wife was extremely supportive, determined to stick by him through "thick and thin." His children were also quite supportive but seemed to largely dismiss the incidents or deny that they were anything but exaggerations and innuendos. He had never approached any of his children sexually.

ASSESSMENT AND BEHAVIOR ANALYSIS

The most striking aspect of the presentation of Reverend X alluded to previously and also mentioned by his referring psychiatrist was the absence of any remorse. Reverend X himself also commented on his relative absence of remorse and seemed puzzled by it since he had at least an intellectual appreciation of the seriousness of his acts. It became clear that before attempting formal intervention with covert sensitization it would be necessary to deal with his motivation to change, which would be likely to affect his compliance with covert sensitization procedures. Thus it became necessary to strip away some of the rationalizations that were interfering with his motivation for treatment.

The primary rationalization commonly found in pedophiles is the notion that they are somehow providing love and affection to children that is beneficial to them and that this affection may be restricted or absent from other sources. Indeed, this rationalization was clearly present in Reverend X, who considered his behavior to be primarily affectionate despite the occasional genital contact and masturbatory activity to "nudist magazines." The client was instructed to make a list of various specific rationalizations. He began working on these rationalizations at home. He was also asked to contemplate how his contacts were received by the girls and whether or not he was oblivious to any negative cues. It became apparent that he had established a strong "boundary" between "proper and improper" pedophilic behavior. For example, intercourse with a child or coercion was as repugnant to him as it would be to the average person. But fondling breasts and genitals was affectionate. Evidence for rationalization was present in the following reports or observations: (1) he reported that most children were very responsive to his advances; (2) his description of many of his episodes was objectified by his use of third person speech; (3) he was very indignant over the angry manner with which most of his congregation responded to him after discovery, thinking they were somehow ungrateful for all of his years of service to the parish (this included his bishop, whom he accused of not providing appropriate support); and (4) he had established boundaries between "good and bad" pedophilic behavior, as mentioned earlier.

In an attempt to break down some of these barriers, two scenarios were presented to him for consideration. First, he was asked how he would react if he discovered that one of his daughters had been fondled or molested by a strange adult male. Initially he digressed into problems of hypothetical questions but then replied that he had never considered that possibility and had probably blocked it out. In fact, in the remainder of the session he refused to consider the topic despite subsequent attempts to introduce it. In regard to the reaction of his parishioners, he was asked what his reaction would be if it was discovered that his bishop had been raping women in the back alleys of the city for several years on Saturday night. He was able to admit that his behavior was at least as repugnant as the hypothetical behavior of his bishop and that it would seem quite shocking indeed.

Thinking about these issues in and between the first several sessions sensitized Reverend X to several facets of his problem, and he was able to recognize, at least at a rational level, the horror that his behavior evoked in others and by inference, the repugnant nature of the behavior itself. Nevertheless, he was now requested in sessions to imagine that his daughter was being molested and to picture it as vividly as possible. He was instructed to feel it emotionally and then report his reactions. Second, he was asked to imagine a similar situation in which he was engaging in genital contact with his most recent victim with all of the parishioners watching.

During this time he was also given materials to read on the consequences of sexual abuse of children. In fact, he reported that he had been familiar with some of these materials before but had read them in a more abstract intellectual manner. During the next several weeks he reported that his masturbatory fantasies began to incorporate images of nameless, faceless people watching him and that his fantasies became a bit fuzzy, much like static on a television set.

By approximately the fourth session the patient clearly began to experience some of the horror and aversiveness of his behavior and actually demonstrated some negative affect and a few tears. This was a marked change from previous sessions characterized by little or no affect of any kind while discussing his behavior. Masturbation of any kind stopped. At this point steps preliminary to implementing covert sensitization were begun.

Detailed descriptions of his behavior and preliminary explorations of the most aversive consequences he could imagine allowed a behavior analysis prior to implementing formal covert sensitization. Self-monitoring revealed infrequent pedophilic fantasies at this time. The decreased frequency of his fantasies most likely related to the punishing effect of his recent discovery. Nevertheless, his pattern of pedophilic behavior was fairly consistent. Typically he would playfully approach a young girl who happened to be alone in a room at the church recreation center or perhaps in his car if he were driving her somewhere. He would then put his arms on her or around her and gradually move his hands to the breast area or, on occasion, the genital area. He would be very careful to ascertain if the girl would be likely to be responsive beforehand and if she remained responsive during the encounter. If there was any sign of resisting or lack of responsiveness he would quickly desist or revert to a wrestling or playing type of activity that did not involve breast or genital contact. On rare occasions the same behavior might occur during the summer while swimming in a nearby lake.

In addition to these rather restricted behavioral patterns, the client would experience a number of urges upon seeing young girls in various locations. These urges would range from a full-blown sexual thought sequence while watching a young girl to what he would call a "glimpse." During a glimpse he would not be aware of any frank sexual thoughts but would notice himself glancing at a young girl who was not directly in his line of sight and therefore represented someone who probably would not attract his attention if she were not the appropriate age and sex.

Since no behavior was occurring at this time and since fantasies (sexual thoughts in the absence of young girls) were also absent, self-monitoring was restricted to "urges" such as those described above. This "urge" once again was defined as a sexual thought, image, or impulse upon seeing a young adolescent girl. The client recorded all sexual urges on a self-monitoring record that he carried with him at all times. The record was divided into daily segments in which the patient could total the number of occurrences of full-blown urges or "glimpses" each day. The patient was instructed to record these urges or glimpses as soon as possible after their occurrence. Physiological assessment of sexual arousal patterns was also conducted using penile strain gauge measures. This assessment revealed continued marked responsiveness to pedophilic stimuli.

One further assessment procedure necessary before beginning covert sensitization is a determination of the worst possible consequences of the behavior in the patient's own mind. Reverend X reported, consistent with his reaction during the first several sessions of treatment, that being observed engaging in this behavior provoked a particularly strong negative emotional reaction in him. He also displayed some sensitivity to images of nausea and vomiting, which comprise a common set of aversive scenes in covert sensitization. In cases where nausea and vomiting are not particularly aversive, scenes of blood and injury or scenes of snakes or spiders crawling on one's skin can be very effective. With this information the patient was ready to begin covert sensitization trials.

TREATMENT PROGRAM

Prior to my initiating covert sensitization, I presented Reverend X with the following therapeutic rationale:

> We will now initiate a procedure with the purpose of directly reducing remaining arousal to young girls using a technique called covert sensitization. This procedure involves having you imagine sexual scenes with young girls similar to those interactions you have actually experienced or masturbate to, and to pair an aversive image with that scene. This procedure has been successfully employed with individuals with similar problems in the past and we have every reason to believe that it will be very helpful in your case.

The purpose of covert sensitization is to neutralize what has become a very automatic uncontrollable sexual arousal to young girls. This will be accomplished by repeatedly imagining a very unpleasant scene in association with your typically sexually arousing scenes. It is very important that you imagine, as vividly as possible, all of the scenes that I present. In addition, this procedure is very useful because you will be learning a skill that you can apply to situations where in the past you would have become aroused. That is, if you find yourself becoming aroused by young girls you can utilize your aversive images in a self-control fashion and very quickly eliminate the arousal. Since this is basically a skill that you are learning, it is also very important that you do a fair amount of homework between sessions.

Initially, I will be presenting vivid descriptions of sexually arousing scenes based on everything we have talked about thus far. I want you to make yourself comfortable, close your eyes, and imagine the scene as if you are actually there. It is very important that you "live" the scene. You should feel, hear, and sense every part of the image. You should not see yourself in the scene but should actually be there. We will also develop some aversive scenes along the lines we have already discussed to be associated with the arousing scenes.

As noted, Reverend X had identified being caught in the act and observed by his family and close friends as perhaps the most aversive naturally occurring event he could think of. In addition, some preliminary exploration revealed a sensitivity to nausea and vomiting. Therefore, these two aversive scenes were used throughout covert sensitization trials.

Sit back in the chair and get as relaxed as possible. Close your eyes and concentrate on what I'm saying. Imagine yourself in the recreation room of the church. Notice the furniture . . . the walls . . . and the feelings of being in the room. Standing to one side is Joan, a 13-year-old girl. As she comes toward you, you notice the color of her hair . . . the clothes she is wearing . . . and the way she is walking. She comes over and sits by you. She is being flirtatious and very cute. You touch her playfully and begin to get aroused. She is asking you questions about sex education and you begin to touch her. You can feel your hands on her smooth skin . . . on her dress . . . and on her breasts under her shirt.

As you become more and more aroused, you begin taking off her clothes. You can feel your fingers on her dress as you slip it off. You begin touching arms . . . her back and her breasts . . . Now your hands are on her thighs and her buttocks. As you get more excited, you put your hand between her legs. She begins rubbing your penis. You're noticing how good it feels. You are stroking her thighs and genitals and getting very aroused.

You hear a scream! As you turn around you see your two daughters and your wife. They see you there—naked and molesting that little girl. They begin to cry. They are sobbing hysterically. Your wife falls to her knees and holds her head in her hands. She is saying "I hate you, I hate you!" You start to go over to hold her, but she is afraid of you and runs away. You start to panic and lose control. You want to kill yourself and end it all. You can see what you have done to yourself.

The aversive scenes were presented in great detail in order to elicit arousal and to facilitate the imagery process. Initially, they were presented late in the chain of behavior. As treatment progressed, the aversive scenes were introduced earlier in the arousing sequence.

In addition to these scenes where Reverend X was caught by his family, other images involving nausea and vomiting were used. In these images as he would begin genital contact with young girls he would feel himself becoming more and more nauseous . . . feel the vomit working its way up into his throat and begin swallowing hard to attempt to keep it down. At that point he would start gagging uncontrollably until vomit and mucus began spilling out of his mouth and nose all over his clothes and the clothes of the young girl. In this particular case I embellished the scene by having him continue to vomit all over the lap of the young girl until the girl's flesh would actually begin to rot before his eyes and worms and maggots would begin crawling around in it. These embellishments are not effective with everyone but were very effective with Reverend X. During the scenes he would become visibly tense, rise in his chair, and be quite drained by the end of the session. During vomiting scenes patients on occasion will bring in a fresh shirt for fear that they might actually vomit during the sessions. This illustrates once again that there is no limit to the vividness of the scenes, and some dramatic presentations on the part of the therapist, at least initially, can be very helpful if the patient is able to process them in such a way that they are effective.

In the example presented earlier, the patient progressed rather far in the chain of sexual behaviors before the aversive scene was introduced. In general, as treatment progresses, the aversive scenes are introduced earlier in the arousing sequence. In this fashion, aversive scenes are paired with the very early parts of the chain, often the first glimpse, by the end of treatment. It is this early pairing that is rehearsed in a self-control fashion.

In this particular case these scenes were presented in two different formats. In the first format, referred to as "punishment," the sexually arousing scene was presented and resulted in the aversive scenes mentioned earlier. In the second format, described as "escape," the patient would begin the sexually arousing scene, contemplate briefly the aversive consequences, and then turn and flee the situation as quickly as possible, feeling greatly relieved and relaxed as he got farther away from the situation.

For Reverend X a typical session involved presenting five of the scenes, either three punishment and two escape or vice versa. The location of the scenes would be varied to conform to the typical locations that were relevant for this particular patient. The two aversive scenes would also be alternated in a random fashion or sometimes integrated or combined.

When it was clear that the patient could imagine these images vividly and was fully processing the information, he was asked to go through the trial himself in the presence of the therapist. Methods for overcoming difficulties in achieving clear images were discussed and practiced. The self-administered practices within sessions were interspersed with therapist-conducted trials. After several sessions, when it was dear that the patient could self-administer the procedure as effectively as the therapist, homework assignments were prescribed. The patient monitored the intensity of his self-administered sessions on a scale of 0 to 100, where 0 equaled no intensity whatsoever and 100 represented an intensity as vivid as real life. Initially, his practice sessions were rated in the 10% to 50% range. As time went on the practice sessions were more consistently rated in the 50% to 70% range, which was judged to be sufficiently intense to produce the desired effects. Initially sessions were prescribed once a day in which he would be asked to conduct three trials (imagine three scenes). After several weeks this was cut back to two practices a week to maximize the intensity. Scenes were varied slightly by the patient to prevent habituation.

During this time self-monitoring revealed occasional urges and glimpses but still no fantasies or masturbatory activity. In fact, the patient had cut back on masturbatory activity shortly after his apprehension and ceased altogether just before treatment began, as noted earlier. Nevertheless, occasional interviews with his wife, who remained extremely supportive, revealed some increase in sexual activity in their relationship, averaging two to three times per week. This relationship was described by both as improved and entirely satisfactory.

At this time the final phase of covert sensitization was introduced. In this phase the patient used the aversive images in vivo in a self-control fashion whenever an urge or even a glimpse occurred. This information was also noted on self-monitoring forms such that any urge or glimpse would be immediately consequated by an aversive image. While he found this somewhat difficult at first, Reverend X reported increasing facility in carrying out his part of the treatment and noted a gradually decreasing number of urges and glimpses.

RESULTS

Rather early in the course of treatment a reaction to Reverend X's behavior on the part of his community threatened to disrupt progress. Although he had moved out of the rectory and away from the church, some of his family remained in his hometown. On occasion he would return to town from his temporary residence, which was convenient to my office, to assist with some practical matters concerning an upcoming move that he and his wife were planning. He would also see a few old friends. During this period a very ugly reaction to his earlier apprehension occurred in the community. Rumors circulated describing very exaggerated accounts of his behavior as well as the fact that he was living in another state simply to wait out the statute of limitations and avoid criminal charges. It was also rumored that he had stopped seeking treatment and had a cavalier attitude toward his problem. This community reaction, which also affected his family, had a serious impact on therapy. A brief but deep state of depression retarded progress and forced a temporary cessation of covert sensitization sessions while the implications of the community reaction were discussed. In fact, Reverend X was deeply distressed by the incident, not only because of the vicious allegations, but also because it became clear that he still harbored some illusions that the community, which had showed deep support and respect for him during his years of service, would somehow welcome him back with open arms once his treatment was completed. Only when he fully appreciated that this was not going to happen and began to make realistic plans about permanently relocating was he able to continue on with therapy.

Four months after treatment began, pedophilic urges had dropped to zero and remained there. At this time Reverend X and his wife permanently relocated to another state, where he obtained work in a local hardware store. He would continue to commute approximately five hours each way for remaining treatment sessions such that he would have one long session every two weeks. Six months after treatment began, a full assessment revealed an excellent response. Treatment was terminated with plans for the first follow-up session to occur one month later and then at decreasing intervals after that as indicated.

Periodic follow-ups were conducted during the ensuing 18 months. A full evaluation at that time, including penile plethysmography, revealed no return of pedophilic arousal patterns. This pattern of results was supported by lengthy interviews with Reverend X as well as independent and separate interviews with his wife. Both individuals reported a satisfactory adaptation to their new location, where Reverend X had worked steadily and productively for the same employer and had been asked to take on additional supervisory responsibilities. The marital relationship, if anything, had continued to improve during the past year. He had begun to engage in extensive volunteer activity in his community.

DISCUSSION

Covert sensitization has proven very effective for paraphilic patterns of arousal, as noted earlier. Nevertheless, there were several aspects of this case that undoubtedly facilitated treatment. Reverend X received deep and sustaining support from his family not only during the initial crisis but also throughout treatment. This support extended to at least some of his old friends in his community who were aware of his problem and, increasingly, friends that he met in his new community, who, of course, were not aware of his problem. In view of the stigma so often attached to sexual offenders and the outright desertion by even close family and friends that often occurs, this support was undoubtedly very valuable to Reverend X.

In addition, throughout this period he maintained his deeply religious attitude and convictions. He attended service regularly and continued to express a desire to resume the provision of some service to the church, even if not on a full-time basis. Nevertheless, despite several inquiries to the church hierarchy, he received no response to his request and began to give up hope of resuming any vestiges of a career that had been at the very center of his existence and had provided deep meaning to his life for some 25 years.

More than two years following this contact and nearly four years after beginning treatment, another follow-up visit confirmed no return of pedophilic arousal patterns whatsoever. Reverend X continued to do extremely well in his new job and was now second-in-command of a small chain of hardware stores. He continued to be active in his community. The church continued to ignore his occasional letters asking for clarification of his status, and he had given up all hope of any return to even part-time duties. Nevertheless, he still hoped against hope that some day the church that he had served for so long might at least lift the suspension and allow him to occasionally conduct religious services for his immediate family. Beyond that his thoughts centered on his day-to-day life in his new community and the distant plan of retirement with his wife somewhere in the South in another 10 or 15 years.

Editors' Introduction

Aaron Beck, the leading figure in cognitive therapy, is an authority on suicide and depression. In the case that follows, the reader has an opportunity to see how Beck works with a depressed, professional woman.

The cognitive approach to therapy is precise, straightforward, and methodological. Beck lays out a sort of road map for therapy in the introduction to the case and then illustrates how the actual therapy sessions link to the therapy plan. Like Ellis, he challenges his patient's irrational beliefs, but he does so in a more probing, Socratic manner consistent with the philosophy of collaborative empiricism that forms the foundation of Cognitive Therapy. This case nicely illustrates the sometimes subtle differences between Cognitive Therapy, Rational Emotive Behavior Therapy, and Cognitive Behavior Therapy.

AN INTERVIEW WITH A DEPRESSED AND SUICIDAL PATIENT

Aaron T. Beck

Perhaps the most critical challenge to the adequacy of cognitive therapy is its efficacy in dealing with the acutely suicidal patient. In such cases the therapist often has to shift gears and assume a very active role in attempting to penetrate the barrier of hopelessness and resignation. Since intervention may be decisive in saving the patient's life, the therapist has to attempt to accomplish a number of immediate goals either concurrently or in rapid sequence: establish a working relationship with the patient, assess the severity of the depression and suicidal wish, obtain an overview of the patient's life situation, pinpoint the patient's "reasons" for wanting to commit suicide, determine the patient's capacity for self-objectivity, and ferret out some entry point for stepping into the patient's phenomenological world to introduce elements of reality.

Such a venture, as illustrated in the following interview, is taxing and demands all the qualities of a "good therapist"—genuine warmth, acceptance, and empathetic understanding—as well as the application of the appropriate strategies drawn from the system of cognitive therapy.

The patient was a 40-year-old clinical psychologist who had recently been left by her boyfriend. She had a history of intermittent depressions since the age of 12 years, had received many courses of psychotherapy,

Excerpt from Aaron T. Beck et al., *Cognitive Therapy of Depression* (pp. 225–243). Published in 1979 by Guilford Publications, Inc. Reprinted by permission of the author.

antidepressant drugs, electroconvulsive therapy, and hospitalizations. The patient had been seen by the author five times over a period of 7 or 8 months. At the time of this interview, it was obvious that she was depressed and, as indicated by her previous episodes, probably suicidal.

In the first part of the interview, the main thrust was to *ask appropriate questions* in order to make a clinical assessment and also to try to elucidate the major psychological problems. The therapist, first of all, had to make an assessment as to how depressed and how suicidal the patient was. He also had to assess her expectations regarding being helped by the interview (T-1;T-8) in order to determine how much leverage he had. During this period of time, in order to keep the dialogue going, he also had to repeat the patient's statements.

It was apparent from the emergence of suicidal wishes that this was the salient clinical problem and that her hopelessness (T-7) would be the most appropriate point for intervention.

Several points could be made regarding the first part of the interview. The therapist accepted the seriousness of the patient's desire to die but treated it as a topic for further examination, a problem to be discussed. "We can discuss the advantages and disadvantages" (T-11). She responded to this statement with some amusement (a favorable sign). The therapist also tried to test the patient's ability to look at herself and her problems with objectivity. He also attempted to test the rigidity of her irrational ideas and her acceptance of his wish to help her (T-13–T-20).

In the first part of the interview the therapist was not able to make much headway because of the patient's strongly held belief that things could not possibly work out well for her. She had decided that suicide was the only solution, and she resented attempts to "get her to change her mind."

In the next part of the interview, the therapist attempted to isolate the participating factor in her present depression and suicidal ideation, namely, the breakup with her boyfriend. It becomes clear as the therapist tries to explore the significance of the breakup that the meaning to the patient is, "I have nothing" (P-23). The therapist then selects, "*I have nothing*" as a target and attempts to elicit from the patient information contradictory to this conclusion. He probes for a previous period of time when she did *not* believe "I have nothing" and also was not having a relationship with a man. He then proceeds (T-26) to probe for other goals and objects that are important to her; he seeks concrete sources of satisfaction (T-24–T-33). The therapist's attempt to establish that the patient does, indeed, "have something" is parried by the patient's tendency to discount any positive features in her life (P-32).

Finally, the patient does join forces with the therapist, and it is apparent in the latter part of the interview that she is willing to separate herself from her problems and consider ways of solving them. The therapist then moves to a consideration of the basic assumption underlying her hopelessness, namely, "I cannot be happy without a man." By pointing out disconfirming past experiences, he tries to demonstrate the error of this assumption. He also attempts to explain the value of shifting to the assumption, "I can make myself happy." He points out that it is more realistic for her to regard herself as the active agent in seeking out sources of satisfaction than as an inert receptacle dependent for nourishment on the whims of others.

The taped interview, which was edited down from 60 minutes to 35 minutes for practical reasons, is presented verbatim. (The only changes made were to protect the identity of the patient.) The interview is divided into five parts.

PART 1. QUESTIONING TO ELICIT VITAL INFORMATION

1. How depressed is the patient? How suicidal?
2. Attitude about coming to appointment (expectancy about therapy).
3. Emergence of suicidal wishes: immediate critical problem.
4. Attempt to find the best point for therapeutic intervention: hopelessness—negative attitude toward future (P-7).
5. Accept seriousness of patient's desire to die but treat it as a topic for further examination—"Discuss advantages and disadvantages" (T-11).
6. Test ability to look at herself—objectivity; test rigidity of her irrational ideas; test responsiveness to therapist (T-13–T-20).

PART 2. BROADENING PATIENT'S PERSPECTIVE

1. Isolate the precipitating factor—breakup with boyfriend; reduce use of questioning.
2. Determine meaning to patient of the breakup.
3. Immediate psychological problem: "I have nothing."
4. Question the conclusion, "I have nothing."
5. Probe for other objects that are important to her: concrete sources of satisfaction (T-24–T-33).
6. Shore up reality-testing and positive self-concept (T-35–T-37).

PART 3. "ALTERNATIVE THERAPY"

1. Therapist very active in order to engage patient's interest in understanding and dealing with her problem. Induce patient to examine options (T-38). "Eliminate" suicide as an option.
2. Undermine patient's all-or-nothing thinking by getting her to regard herself, her future, and her experiences in quantitative probabilities (T-45).

3. Feedback: important information as to success of interview. Look for (a) affect shift, (b) positive statements about herself, (c) consensus with patient regarding solution of problem (P-47).

PART 4. OBTAINING MORE ACCURATE DATA

1. More therapeutic collaboration: discussion about therapeutic techniques and rationale.

2. Testing her conclusions about "no satisfaction," indirectly disproving her conclusion.

3. Patient's spontaneous statement, "Can I tell you something positive?"

4. Periodic attempts to evoke a mirth response.

PART 5. CLOSURE

Reinforce independence (T-106), self-help, optimism.

Therapist (T-1): Well, how have you been feeling since I talked to you last? . . .
Patient (P-1): Bad.

T-2:   You've been feeling bad . . . well, tell me about it?

P-2:   It started this weekend . . . I just feel like everything is an effort. There's just completely no point to do anything.

T-3:   So, there are two problems; everything is an effort, and you believe there's no point to doing anything.

P-3:   It's because there's no point to doing anything that makes everything too hard to do.

T-4:   *(Repeating her words to maintain interchange. Also to acknowledge her feelings.)* Because there's no point and everything feels like an effort . . . And when you were coming down here today, were you feeling the same way?

P-4:   Well, it doesn't seem as bad when I am working. It's bad on weekends and especially on holidays. I sort of expected that it would happen.

T-5:   *(Eliciting expectancy regarding session)* You expected to have a hard time on holidays . . . And when you left your office to come over here, how were you feeling then?

P-5:   Kind of the same way. I feel that I can do everything that I have to do, but I don't *want* to.

T-6:   You don't want to do the things you have to.

P-6:   I don't want to do anything.

T-7:   Right . . . and what kind of feeling did you have? Feel low?

P-7:   *(Hopelessness to be target)* I feel that there's no hope for me. I feel my future . . . that everything is futile, that there's no hope.

T-8:   And what idea did you have about today's interview?

P-8:   I thought that it would probably help as it has always happened in the past . . . that I would feel better—temporarily. But that makes it worse because then I know that I am going to feel bad again.

T-9:   That makes it worse in terms of how you feel?

P-9:   Yes.

T-10:   And the reason is that it builds you up and then you get let down again?

P-10:   *(Immediate problem—suicide risk)* I feel like it's interminable, it will just go this way forever, and I am not getting any better . . . I don't feel any less inclined to kill myself than I ever did in my life . . . In fact, if anything, *I feel like I'm coming closer to it.*

T-11:   Perhaps we should talk about that a little bit because we haven't talked about the advantages and disadvantages of killing yourself.

P-11:   *(Smiles)* You make everything so logical.

T-12:   *(Testing therapeutic alliance)* Is that bad? Remember you once wrote something . . . that reason is your greatest ally. Have you become allergic to reason?

P-12:   But I can't try anymore.

T-13:   Does it take an effort to be reasonable?

P-13:   *(Typical "automatic thoughts")* I know I am being unreasonable; the thoughts seem so real to me . . . it does take an effort to try to change them.

T-14:   Now, if it came easy to you—to change the thoughts, do you think that they would last as long?

P-14:   No . . . see, I don't say that this wouldn't work with other people. I don't try to say that, but I don't feel that it can work with me.

T-15:   So, do you have any evidence that it did work with you?

P-15:   It works for specific periods of time, and that's like the Real Me comes through.

T-16:   Now, is there anything unusual that happened that might have upse the apple cart?

P-16:   You mean this weekend?

T-17:   Not necessarily this weekend. As you know, you felt you were making good progress in therapy and you decided that you were going to be like the Cowardly Lion Who Found His Heart. What happened after that?

P-17:   *(Agitated, bows head)* It's too hard . . . it would be easier to die.

T-18:   *(Attempts to restore objectivity. Injects perspective by recalling previous mastery experience.)* At the moment, it would be easier to die—as you say. But, let's go back to the history. You're losing sight and losing perspective. Remember when we talked and made a tape of that interview and you liked it. You wrote a letter the next day and you said that you felt you had your Heart and it wasn't any great effort to reach that particular point. Now, you went along reasonably well until you got involved. Correct? Then you got involved with Jim. Is that correct? And then very predictably when your relationship ended, you felt terribly let down. Now, what do you conclude from that?

P-18: *(Anguish, rejects therapist's venture)* My conclusion is that I am always going to have to be alone because I can't stay in a relationship with a man.

T-19: All right, that's one possible explanation, What other possible explanations are there?

P-19: That's the only explanation.

T-20: Is it possible you just weren't *ready* to get deeply involved and then let down?

P-20A: But, I feel like I'll never be ready. *(Weeps)*

P-20B: I have never given up on him, even when I couldn't see him for a year at a time. He was always in my mind, all the time. So how can I think now that I can just dismiss him.

T-21: This was never final until now. There was always the hope that . . .

P-21: There wasn't, and he told me very clearly that he could not get involved with me.

T-22: Right, but before January, it was very quiescent. You weren't terribly involved with him. It started up in January again. He did show serious interest in you.

P-22: For the first time in four years.

T-23: *(Attempts to restore perspective)* All right, so that's when you got involved again. Prior to January, you weren't involved, weren't thinking of him every minute and you weren't in the situation you are in now, and you were happy at times. You wrote that letter to me that you were happy, right? Okay. So that was back in January, you were happy and you did not have Jim. Now comes May, and you're unhappy because you have just broken up with him. Now, why do you still have to be unhappy, say, in July, August, or September?

P-23: *(Presents specific target belief)* I have nothing.

T-24: You weren't unhappy in January, were you?

P-24: At first I was, that's why I called.

T-25: All right, how about December? December you weren't unhappy. What did you have in December? You had something that made you happy.

P-25: I was seeing other men. That made me happy.

T-26: There are other things in your life besides men that you said you liked very much.

P-26: Yes and I . . .

T-27: *(Aims at target beliefs. Shows she had and has something.)* Well, there were other things you say were important that are not important right now. Is that correct? What were the things that were important to you back in December, November, and October?

P-27: Everything was important.

T-28: Everything was important. And what were those things?

P-28: It's hard to even think of anything that I cared about.

T-29: Okay, now how about your job?

P-29: My job.

T-30: Your job was important. Did you feel that you were accomplishing something on the job?

P-30: Most of the time I did.

T-31: *(Still aiming)* Most of the time, you felt you were accomplishing something on the job. And what about now? Do you feel you are accomplishing on the job *now*?

P-31: *(Discounts positive)* Not as much as I could.

T-32: *(Reintroduces positive)* You're not accomplishing as much as you could but even when you are "off," I understand that you do as well or better than many of the other workers. Is that not correct?

P-32: *(Disqualifies positive statement)* I can't understand why you say that. How do you know that? Because I told you that. How do you know that's true?

T-33: I'm willing to take your word for it.

P-33: From somebody who is irrational.

T-34: *(Presents positive evidence of satisfactions and achievements.)* Well, I think that somebody who is as irrationally down on herself as you, is very unlikely to say something positive *about herself* unless the positive thing is so strong that it is unmistakable to anybody... In any event, you do get some satisfaction out of the job right now and you do feel you are doing a reasonably good job, although you are not doing as well as you would like to, but as well as you are capable. You're still doing a reasonably good job. You can see for yourself. Your clients' plans are improving? Are they being helped? Does anyone say they are appreciative of your efforts?

P-34: Yes.

T-35: They do tell you? Yet you are saying you are so irrational that I can't believe anything you say. Do you say, "You're just a dumb client.. no judgment at all," to your clients?

P-35: I wouldn't say that about somebody.

T-36: Well, do you think it about yourself?

P-36: Yes.

T-37: *(Points out inconsistency. Underscores her capacity for rationality. Fortifies her professional role.)* So, you trust the word of your clients, but you won't trust your own word. You won't think of your clients as being irrational, and yet, you think of you—when you are the client—as being irrational. How can you be rational when you are the therapist and irrational when you are the patient?

P-37: I set different standards for myself than what I set for anybody else in the world.

P-37B: Suppose I'll never get over it?

T-38: *(Changes the options—consider nonsuicidal solutions. Sweat it out or fight to solve problem.)* Suppose you'll never get over it? Well, we don't know whether you'll never get over it or not ... so there're two things you can do. One is, you can take it passively and see, and you might find that you will get over it, since almost everybody gets over grief reactions. Or, you can attack the problem aggressively and actively build up a solid basis for yourself. In other words, you can capitalize on the chance...

P-38:   *(Thinks of finding another man.)* I feel desperate. I feel that I have to find somebody right now—right away.

T-39:   All right, now if you found somebody right away, what would happen?

P-39:   The same thing would happen again.

T-40:   *(Omits suicide as one of the options.)* Now, remember when we talked about Jim and you said back in January you decided that you would take that chance and you'd chance being involved, with the possibility that something would come of it positively. Now, you have two choices at this time. You can either stick it out now and try to weather the storm with the idea that you are going to keep fighting it, or you can get involved with somebody else and not have the opportunity for this elegant solution. Now, which way do you want to go?

P-40:   *(Compulsion to get involved with somebody.)* I don't want to, but I feel driven. I don't know why I keep fighting that, but I do. I'm not involved with anybody now and I don't want to be, but I feel a compulsion.

T-41:   That's right, because you're hurting very badly. Isn't that correct? If you weren't hurting you wouldn't feel the compulsion.

P-41:   But I haven't done anything yet.

T-42:   *(Emphasizes ideal option. Also turning disadvantage into advantage.)* Well, you know it's your decision. If you do seek somebody else, nobody is going to fault you on it. But I'm trying to show that there's an opportunity here. There's an unusual opportunity that you may never have again—that is to go it alone... to work your way out of the depression.

P-42:   That's what I'll be doing the rest of my life... that's what worries me.

T-43:   You really just put yourself in a "no-win" situation. You just acknowledged that if you get involved with another man, probably you would feel better.

P-43:   Temporarily, but then, I'd go through the same thing.

T-44:   I understand that. So now, you have an opportunity to not have to be dependent on another guy, but you have to pay a price. There's pain now for gain later. Now are you willing to pay the price?

P-44:   I'm afraid that if I don't involve myself with somebody right away... I know that's dichotomous thinking... I think if I don't get immediately involved, that I will never have anybody.

T-45:   That's all-or-nothing thinking.

P-45:   I know.

T-46:   *(Seeking a consensus on nonsuicidal option.)* That's all-or-nothing thinking. Now, if you going to do it on the basis of all-or-nothing thinking, that's not very sensible. if you are going to do it on the basis of, "The pain is so great that I just don't want to stick it out anymore," all right. Then you take your aspirin temporarily and you'll just have to work it out at a later date. The thing is—do you want to stick it out right now? Now, what's the point of sticking it out now?

P-46: I don't know.

T-47: You don't really believe this.

P-47: *(Reaching a consensus.)* Theoretically, I know I could prove to myself that I could, in fact, be happy without a man, so that if I were to have a relationship with a man in the future, I would go into it not feeling desperate, and I would probably eliminate a lot of anxiety and depression that have in the past been connected to this relationship.

T-48: So, at least you agree, theoretically, on a logical basis this could happen. If you try to stick it out ... Now, what do you think is the probability that this could happen?

P-48: For me?

T-49: For you.

P-49: For another person I'd say the probability is excellent.

T-50: For one of your clients?

P-50: Yeah.

T-51: For the average depressed person that comes to the Mood Clinic ... most of whom have been depressed seven years or more. You would still give them a high probability.

P-51 Listen, I've been depressed all of my life. I thought of killing myself when I was 14 years old.

T-52: *(Undermining absolutistic thinking by suggesting probabilities.)* Well, many of the other people that have come here too have felt this way. Some of the people that have come here are quite young and so have not had time to be depressed very long ... Okay, back to this. Hypothetically, this could happen. This could happen with almost anybody else, this could happen with anybody else. But you don't think it can happen to you. Right ... It can't happen to you. But what is the possibility ... (you know, when we talked about the possibility with Jim, we thought it was probably five in a hundred that a good thing could come from it) ... that you could weather the storm and come out a stronger person and be less dependent on men than you had been before?

P-52: I'd say that the possibility was minimal.

T-53: All right, now is it minimal like 1 in a hundred, one in a million ... ?

P-53: Well, maybe a 10% chance.

T-54: 10% chance. So, you have one chance in ten of emerging from this stronger.

P-54: *(More perspective; disqualifies evidence.)* Do you know why I say that . . . I say that on the basis of having gone through that whole summer without a man and being happy ... and then getting to the point where I am now. That's not progress.

T-55: *(Using data base.)* I'd say that is evidence. That summer is very powerful evidence.

P-55: *(Discredits data.)* Well, look where I am right now.

T-56: The thing is, you did very well that summer and proved as far as any scientist is concerned that you could function on your own. But you didn't prove it to your own self. You wiped out that experience as soon as you got involved with a man. That experience of independence became a nullity in your mind after that summer.

P-56:   (*Mood shift. A good sign.*) Is that what happened?

T-57:   Of course.When I talked to you the first time I saw you, you said "I cannot be happy without a man." We went over that for about 35 or 40 minutes until I finally said, "Has there ever been a time when you didn't have a man?" And you said, "My God, that time when I went to graduate school." You know, suddenly a beam of light comes in. You almost sold me on the idea that you couldn't function without a man. But that's *evidence*. I mean, if I told you I couldn't walk across the room, and you were able to demonstrate to me that I could walk across the room, would you buy my notion that I could not walk across the room? You know, there is an objective reality here. I'm not giving you information that isn't valid. There are people . . .

P-57:   I would say, how could you negate that if it didn't happen?

T-58:   What?

P-58:   (*Asks for explanation. A good sign.*) I'd say what's wrong with my mind, having once happened, how can I negate it?

T-59:   (*Alliance with patient's rationality.*) Because it's human nature, unfortunately, to negate experiences that are not consistent with the prevailing attitude. And that is what attitude therapy is all about. You have a very strong attitude, and anything that is inconsistent with that attitude stirs up cognitive dissonance. I'm sure you have heard of that, and people don't like to have cognitive dissonance. So, they throw out anything that's not consistent with their prevailing belief.

P-59:   (*Consensus gels.*) I understand that.

T-60:   (*Optimistic sally.*) You have a prevailing belief. It just happens, fortunately, that that prevailing belief is wrong. Isn't that marvelous? To have a prevailing belief that makes you unhappy, and it happens to be wrong! But it's going to take a lot of effort and demonstration to indicate to you, to convince you that it is wrong. And why is that?

P-60;   I don't know.

T-61:   (*Since patient is now collaborating, he shifts to didactic strategy. Purpose is to strengthen patient's rationality.*) Do you want to know now why? Because you've always had it. Why? First of all, this belief came on at a very early age. We're not going into your childhood, but obviously, you made a suicide attempt or thought about it when you were young. It's a belief that was in there at a very young age. It was very deeply implanted at a very young age, because you were so vulnerable then. And it's been repeated how many times since then in your own head?

P-61:   A million times.

T-62:   A million times. So do you expect that five hours of talking with me is going to reverse in itself something that has been going a million times in the past?

P-62:   Like I said, and you agreed, my reason was my ally. Doesn't my intelligence enter into it? Why can't I make my intelligence help?

T-63: Yeah, that's the reason intelligence comes into it, but that's exactly what I'm trying to get you to do. To use your intelligence.

P-63: There's nothing wrong with my intelligence. I know that.

T-64: I understand that. Intelligence is fine, but intelligence has to have tools, just as you may have the physical strength to lift up a chair, but if you don't believe at the time that you have the strength to do it, you're not going to try. You're going to say, "It's pointless." On the other hand, to give you a stronger example, you may have the physical strength to lift a heavy boulder, but in order to really lift it, you might have to use a crowbar. So, it's a matter of having the correct tool. It isn't simply a matter of having naked, raw intelligence, it's a matter of using the right tools. A person who has intelligence cannot solve a problem in calculus, can he?

P-64: If she knows how to. *(Smiles)*

T-65: *(Reinforces confidence in maturity.)* All right. Okay. You need to have the formulas, that's what you're coming in here for. If you weren't intelligent, you wouldn't be able to understand the formulas, and you know very well you understand the formulas. Not only that, but you use them on your own clients with much more confidence than you use them on yourself.

P-65: *(Self-praise, confirms therapist's statement.)* You wouldn't believe me if you heard me tell things to people. You'd think I was a different person. Because I can be so optimistic about other people. I was encouraging a therapist yesterday who was about to give up on a client. I said, "You can't do that." I said, "You haven't tried everything yet," and I wouldn't let her give up.

T-66: All right, so you didn't even have a chance to use the tools this weekend because you had the structure set in your mind, and then due to some accidental factor you were unable to do it. But you concluded on the weekend that the tools don't work since "I am so incapable that I can't use the tools." It wasn't even a test was it? Now for the next weekend . . .

P-66: *(Agrees.)* . . . It wasn't a true test . . .

T-67: No, it wasn't even a fair test of what you could do or what the tools could do. Now for weekends, what you want to do is prepare yourself for the Fourth of July. You prepare for the weekends by having the structure written down, and you have to have some backup plans in case it gets loused up. You know you really do have a number of things in your network that can bring you satisfaction. *What are some of the things you have gotten satisfaction from last week?*

P-67: I took Margaret to the movies.

T-68: What did you see?

P-68: It was a comedy.

T-69: What?

P-69: A comedy.

T-70: That's a good idea. What did you see?

P-70: (*Smiles*) It was called *Mother, Jugs and Speed*.

T-71: Yeah, I saw that.

P-71: Did you see that?

T-72: Yeah, I saw that on Friday.

P-72: (*Smiles*) I liked it.

T-73: It was pretty good. A lot of action in that. So you enjoyed that. Do you think you could still enjoy a good movie?

P-73: I can. If I get distracted, I'm all right.

T-74: So what's wrong with that?

P-74: Because then what happens . . . while I'm distracted the pain is building up and then the impact is greater when it hits me. Like last night I had two friends over for dinner. That was fine. While they're there . . . I'm deliberately planning all these activities to keep myself busy . . . and while they were there I was fine. But when they left . . .

T-75: That's beautiful.

P-75: The result was that the impact was greater because all this pain had accumulated . . .

T-76: We don't know because you didn't run a control, but there is no doubt there is a letdown after you've had satisfactory experience . . . so that what you have to do is set up a mechanism for handling the letdown. See what you did is you downed yourself, you knocked yourself and said, "Well . . . it's worse now than if I hadn't had them at all." Rather than just taking it phenomenologically: "They were here and I felt good when they were here, then I felt let down afterward." So then obviously the thing to pinpoint is what? The letdown afterward. So what time did they leave?

P-76: About 9.

T-77: And what time do you ordinarily go to bed?

P-77: About 10.

T-78: So you just had one hour to plan on.

P-78: To feel bad . . .

T-79: All right, one hour to feel bad. That's one way to look at it. That's not so bad, is it? It's only one hour.

P-79: But then I feel so bad during the hour. That's when I think that I want to die.

T-80: All right, what's so bad about feeling bad? You know what we've done with some of the people? And it's really worked. We've assigned them. We've said, "Now we want to give you one hour a day in which to feel bad." Have I told you about that? "I want you to feel just as bad as you can," and in fact sometimes we even rehearse it in the session. I don't have time today but maybe another time.

P-80: It's time-limited.

T-81: (*Alliance with patient as a fellow therapist.*) Yeah, and we have the people—I'd say, "Why don't you feel as bad as you can—just think of a situation, the most horribly devastating, emotionally depleting situation you can. Why don't you feel as bad as you possibly can?" And they really can do it during a session. They go out and after that they can't feel bad again even though they may even want to. It's as though they've depleted themselves of the thing and they also get a certain degree of objectivity toward it.

P-81: *(Helping out.)* It has to be done in a controlled . . .

T-82: It has to be done in a structured situation.

P-82: It has to be controlled.

T-83: That's true. It has to—that's why I say, "Do it in here, first."

P-83: Yes.

T-84: Then, I can pull them out of it . . . You need to have a safety valve.

P-84: If you do it at home . . . you might . . .

T-85: Right, the therapist has to structure it in a particular way. I'm just saying that one hour of badness a day is not necessarily antitherapeutic. And so it doesn't mean you have to kill yourself because you have one bad hour. What you want to do is to think of this as "my one bad hour for today." That's one way of looking at it. And then you go to sleep at 10 o'clock and it's over. You've had one bad hour out of 12. That's not so terrible. Well, you told yourself during that time something like this. "See, I've had a pretty good day and now I've had this bad hour and it means I'm sick, I'm full of holes, my ego is . . ."

P-85: See I'm thinking, "It never ends."

T-86: For one hour, but yeah, but that's not even true because you thought that you couldn't have any good times in the past, and yet as recently as yesterday you had a good day.

P-86: But what gives it momentum is that thought that it's not going to end.

T-87: Maybe the thought's incorrect. How do you know the thought is incorrect?

P-87: I don't know.

T-88: *(Retrospective hypothesis-testing.)* Well, let's operationalize it. What does it mean, "It's not going to end?" Does that mean that you're never going to feel good again in your whole life? Or does that mean that you're going to have an unremitting, unrelenting, inexorable sadness day in, day out, hour after hour, minute after minute. I understand that is your belief. That's a hypothesis for the moment. Well, let's test the hypothesis retrospectively. Now you have that thought: "This is never going to end." You had that thought when? Yesterday at 9 a.m.

P-88: Yes.

T-89: Now that means that if that hypothesis is correct, every minute since you awoke this morning, you should have had unending, unrelenting, unremitting, inevitable, inexorable sadness and unhappiness.

P-89: *(Refutes hypothesis.)* That's not true.

T-90: It's incorrect.

P-90: Well, you see, when I wake up in the morning, even before I'm fully awake the first thing that comes to my mind inevitably is that I don't want to get up. That I have nothing that I want to live for. And that's no way to start the day.

T-91:   That's the way a person who has a depression starts the day. That's the perfectly appropriate way to start the day if you're feeling depressed.

P-91:   Even before you're awake?

T-92:   Of course. When people are asleep they even have bad dreams. You've read the article on dreams. Even their dreams are bad. So how do you expect them to wake up feeling good after they have had a whole night of bad dreams? And what happens in depression as the day goes on? They tend to get better. You know why? Because they get a better feel of reality—reality starts getting into their beliefs.

P-92:   Is that what it is?

T-93:   Of course.

P-93:   I always thought it was because the day was getting over and I could go to sleep again.

T-94:   Go to sleep to have more bad dreams? The reality encroaches and it disproves this negative belief.

P-94:   That's why it's diurnal.

T-95:   Of course, and we have already disproven the negative belief, haven't we? You had that very strong belief last night—strong enough to make you want to commit suicide—that this would be unremitting, unrelenting, inevitable, and inexorable.

P-95:   (Cheerful) Can I tell you something very positive I did this morning?

T-96:   (Kidding) No, I hate to hear positive things. I'm allergic. Okay. I'll tolerate it. (Laughs)

P-96:   (Recalls rational self instruction.) I got that thought before I was even awake, and I said, "Will you stop it, just give yourself a chance and stop telling yourself things like that."

T-97:   So what's wrong with saying that?

P-97:   I know. I thought that was a very positive thing to do. (Laughs)

T-98:   (Underscores statement.) That's terrific. Well, say it again so I can remember.

P-98:   I said, "Stop it and give yourself a chance."

T-99:   (More hopeful prediction. Self-sufficiency.) When you had your friends over, you found intrinsic meaning there. This was in the context of *no man* . . . Now when the pain of the breakup has washed off completely, do you think you're going to be capable of finding all these goodies, yourself, under your own power, and attaching the true meaning to them?

P-99:   I suppose if the pain is less . . .

T-100: Well, the pain's less right now.

P-100: Does it matter?

T-101: Yeah.

P-101: But that doesn't mean it won't continue.

T-102: Well, in the course of time, you know, it's human nature that people get over painful episodes. You've been over painful episodes in the past.

P-102: Suppose I keep on missing him forever.

T-103: What?

P-103: Suppose I keep on missing him forever?

T-104: There's no reason to expect you to miss him forever. That isn't the way people are constructed. People are constructed to forget after a while and then get involved in other things. You had them before.

P-104: You spoke of a man who missed a mother for 25 years.

T-105: (*Emphasizes self-sufficiency.*) Well, I don't know...this may have been one little hang-up he had, but, I don't know that case... In general, that isn't the way people function. They get over lost love. All right? And one of the ways we can speed the process is by you, yourself, attaching meaning to things that are in your environment that you are capable of responding to... You demonstrated that...

P-105: Not by trying to replace a lost love right away?

T-106: (*Reinforcing independence.*) Replace it? What you're trying to do is find another instrument to happiness. He's become your mechanism for reaching happiness. That's what's bad about the whole man hang-up. It is that you are interposing some other unreliable entity between you and happiness. And all you have to do is to move this entity out of the way, and there's nothing to prevent you from getting happiness. But you want to keep pulling it back in. I say, leave it out there for a while, and then you'll see. Just in the past week you found that when you didn't have a man, you were able to find happiness without a man. And if you leave the man out of the picture for a long enough period of time, you'll see that you don't need him. Then if you want to bring him in as one of the many things that can bring satisfaction, that's fine, you can do that. But if you see him as the *only* conduit between you and happiness, then you are right back to where you were before.

P-106: Is it an erroneous thing to think that if I get to the point where I really believe that I don't need him, that I won't want him?

T-107: Oh, you're talking about him. I think it will just...

P-107: Any man...a ny man?

T-108: (*Undermines regressive dependency.*) ... Well, you might still want him, like you might like to go to a movie, or read a good book, or have your friends over for dinner. You know, you still have to have relationships with your friends. But if they didn't come over for dinner last night it wouldn't plunge you into a deep despondency. I'm not underestimating the satisfaction that one gets from other people... but it's not a necessity... It's something that you, yourself, can relate to on a one-to-one basis ... but one does, as one individual to another. You're relating to a man the way a child does to a parent, or the way a drug addict does to his drugs. He sees the drug as the mechanism for achieving happiness. And you know you can't achieve happiness artificially. And you have been using men in an artificial way. As though they are going to bring you happiness ... rather than they are simply one of the things external to yourself by which you, yourself, can bring yourself happiness. *You* must bring *you* happiness.

P-108: I can ... I've been focusing on dependency.

T-109: *(Emphasizing available pleasures.)* Well, you've done it. You've brought yourself happiness by going to the movies, by working with your clients, by having friends over for dinner, by getting up in the morning and doing things with your daughter. You have brought you happiness . . . but you can't depend on somebody else to bring you happiness the way a little girl depends on a parent. It doesn't work. I'm not opposed to it . . . I have no religious objection to it . . . It just doesn't work. Pragmatically, it is a very unwise way to conduct one's life. And in some utopian society after this, children will be trained not to depend on others as the mechanism for happiness. In fact, you can even demonstrate that to your daughter . . . through your own behavior, she can find that out.

P-109: She's a very independent child.

T-110: *(Probing for adverse reaction to interview.)* Well, she's already found that out. Okay, now do you have any questions? Anything that we discussed today? Is there anything that I said today that rubbed you the wrong way?

P-110: You said it would be damaging . . . not damaging . . . but you think it would deprive me of more opportunity to test this out if I were to go to another man.

T-111: Well, it's an unusual opportunity . . .

P-111: It's not so unusual, because I might get involved with somebody else.

T-112: *(Turning disadvantage into advantage.)* Well, yes, but this is like the worst—you said this is the worst—depression you felt for a long time. It's a very *unusual* opportunity to be able to demonstrate how you were able to pull yourself from the very deepest depths of depression onto a very solid independent position. You may not have that opportunity again, really, and it would be such a very sharp contrast. Now, you don't have to do it, but I'm saying it's really a very rich chance, and it does mean possibly a lot of gain. I don't want to make any self-fulfilling hypotheses, but you've got to expect the pain and not get discouraged by it. What are you going to say to yourself . . . if you feel the pain tonight? Suppose you feel pain after you leave the interview today, what are you going to say to yourself?

P-112: "Present pain for future gain."

T-113: Now where are you now on the hopelessness scale?

P-113: Down to 15%.

T-114: It's down to 15% from 95%, but you have to remember that the pain is handled in a structured way, the way I told you about the people who make themselves feel sad during that one period. It has to be structured. If you can structure your pain, this pain is something that's going to build you up in the future, and, indeed it will. But if you see yourself as just being victimized by these forces you have no control over, . . . you're just helpless in terms of the internal things and external things . . . . then you are going to feel terrible . . . And what you have to do is convert yourself from somebody who feels helpless, right? . . . And you are the only person who can do it . . . I can't make you strong and independent . . . I can show you the way, but if you do it, you haven't done it by taking anything from me; you've done it by drawing on resources within yourself.

P-114: How does it follow then that I feel stronger when I have a man? If things are going . . .

T-115: *(Counteracts assumption about getting strength from another person. Empirical test.)* You mean you make yourself feel strong because you yourself think, "Well, I've got this man that's a pillar of strength, and since I have him to lean on, therefore, I feel strong." But, actually, nobody else can give you strength. That's a fallacy that you feel stronger having a man, but you can't trust your feelings. What you're doing is just probably drawing on your own strength. You have the definition in your mind. "I'm stronger if I have a man." But the converse of that is very dangerous . . . which is, "I am weak if I don't have a man . . ." What you have to do, if you want to get over this is to disprove the converse, "I am weak if I don't have a man." Now, are you willing to subject that to the acid test? Then you will know. Okay, well suppose you give me a call tomorrow and let me know how you're going and then we can go over some of the other assignments.

It was apparent by the end of the interview that the acute suicidal crisis had passed. The patient felt substantially better, was more optimistic, and had decided to confront and solve her problems. She subsequently became involved in cognitive therapy on a more regular basis and worked with one of the junior staff in identifying and coping with her intrapersonal and interpersonal problems.

This interview is typical of our crisis intervention strategies but is a departure from the more systematic approach used during the less dramatic phases of the patient's depression. We generally attempt to adhere to the principle of collaborative empiricism in our routine interviews and deviate from standard procedures for a limited period of time only. Once the crisis is over, the therapist returns to a less intrusive and less active role and structures the interview in such a way that the patient assumes a greater responsibility for clarifying and devising possible solutions to problems.

Editors' Introduction

Irvin Yalom, a novelist and until recently a practicing Stanford psychiatrist, is the author of the seminal work Existential Psychotherapy *as well as a classic textbook on* The Theory and Practice of Group Psychotherapy. *Following the 1994 death of Rollo May (Yalom's former therapist), Yalom became the primary spokesperson for Existential Psychotherapy. Yalom and May co-authored the chapter on Existential Psychotherapy in* Current Psychotherapies.

This provocative case study, taken from Yalom's book Love's Executioner, *illustrates the problem all therapists confront as they attempt to cope with countertransference. Yalom is quite open about his revulsion and antipathy for obese people, and this case helps students appreciate how even very experienced therapists continue to grow professionally and personally as a result of their experiences as therapists.*

The case also illustrates how clients paradoxically cling to the superficial in therapy while avoiding the difficult issues that lie at the heart of the existential approach. Yalom's patient was only able to make progress with her obesity when she began to seriously address her anxiety about death. Analysis of death, isolation, freedom, and meaninglessness—the core existential issues—define this particular approach to psychotherapy.

Yalom uses this case to discuss the issue of touch in therapy and the advantages to setting limits to the duration of therapy. The case also includes two examples of the way in which an existential therapist is likely to use dreams in therapy. It will be useful for students to contrast this particular approach with the other schools of psychotherapy presented in Current Psychotherapies, *and to debate the ethics of agreeing to work with clients whose appearance or behavior one initially finds repugnant.*

FAT LADY

Irvin D. Yalom

The world's finest tennis players train five hours a day to eliminate weaknesses in their game. Zen masters endlessly aspire to quiescence of the mind, the ballerina to consummate balance; and the priest forever examines his conscience. Every profession has within it a realm of possibility wherein the practitioner may seek perfection. For the psychotherapist that realm, that inexhaustible curriculum of self-improvement from which one never graduates, is referred to in the trade as countertransference. Where *transference* refers to feelings that the patient erroneously attaches ("transfers") to the therapist but that in fact originated out of earlier relationships, *countertransference* is the reverse—similar irrational feelings the therapist has toward the patient. Sometimes countertransference is dramatic and makes deep therapy impossible: imagine a Jew treating a Nazi, or a woman who has once been sexually assaulted treating a rapist. But, in milder form, countertransference insinuates itself into every course of psychotherapy.

The day Betty entered my office, the instant I saw her steering her ponderous two-hundred-fifty-pound, five-foot-two-inch frame toward my trim, high-tech office chair, I knew that a great trial of countertransference was in store for me.

I have always been repelled by fat women. I find them disgusting: their absurd sidewise waddle, their absence of body contour—breasts, laps, buttocks, shoulders, jawlines, cheekbones, *everything*, everything I like to see in a woman, obscured in an avalanche of flesh. And I hate their clothes—the shapeless, baggy dresses or, worse, the stiff elephantine blue jeans with the barrel thighs. How dare they impose that body on the rest of us?

The origins of these sorry feelings? I had never thought to inquire. So deep do they run that I never considered them prejudice. But were an explanation demanded of me, I suppose I could point to the family of fat, controlling women, including—featuring—my mother, who peopled my early life. Obesity, endemic in my family, was a part of what I had to leave behind when I, a driven, ambitious, first-generation American-born, decided to shake forever from my feet the dust of the Russian shtetl.

I can take other guesses. I have always admired, perhaps more than many men, the woman's body. No, not just admired: I have elevated, idealized, ecstacized it to a level and a goal that exceeds all reason. Do I resent the fat woman for her desecration of my desire, for bloating and profaning each lovely feature that I cherish? For stripping away my sweet illusion and revealing its base of flesh—flesh on the rampage?

I grew up in racially segregated Washington, D.C., the only son of the only white family in the midst of a black neighborhood. In the streets, the black attacked me for my whiteness, and in school, the white attacked me for my Jewishness. But there was always fatness, the fat kids, the big asses, the butts of jokes, those last chosen for athletic teams, those unable to run the circle of the athletic track. I needed someone to hate, too. Maybe that was where I learned it.

Of course, I am not alone in my bias. Cultural reinforcement is everywhere. Who ever has a kind word for the fat lady? But my contempt surpasses all cultural norms. Early in my career, I worked in a maximum security prison where the *least* heinous offense committed by any of my patients was a simple, single murder. Yet I had little difficulty accepting those patients, attempting to understand them, and finding ways to be supportive.

But when I see a fat lady eat, I move down a couple of rungs on the ladder of human understanding. I want to tear the food away. To push her face into the ice cream. "Stop stuffing yourself! Haven't you had enough, for Chrissakes?" I'd like to wire her jaws shut!

Poor Betty—thank God, thank God—knew none of this as she innocently continued her course toward my chair, slowly lowered her body, arranged her folds and, with her feet not quite reaching the floor, looked up at me expectantly.

Now why, thought I, do her feet not reach the ground? She's not that short. She sat high in the chair, as though she were sitting in her own lap. Could it be that her thighs and buttocks are so inflated that her feet have to go farther to reach the floor? I quickly swept this conundrum from my mind—after all, this person had come to seek help from me. A moment later, I found myself thinking of the little fat woman cartoon figure in the movie *Mary Poppins*—the one who sings "Supercalifragilisticexpialido-cious"—for that was who Betty reminded me of. With an effort I swept that away as well. And so it went: the entire hour with her was an exercise of my sweeping from my mind one derogatory thought after another in order to offer her my full attention. I fantasized Mickey Mouse, the sor-cerer's apprentice in *Fantasia*, sweeping away my distracting thoughts until I had to sweep away that image, too, in order to attend to Betty.

As usual, I began to orient myself with demographic questions. Betty in-formed me that she was twenty-seven and single, that she worked in public relations for a large New York-based retail chain which, three months ago, had transferred her to California for eighteen months to assist in the opening of a new franchise.

She had grown up, an only child, on a small, poor ranch in Texas where her mother has lived alone since her father's death fifteen years ago. Betty was a good student, attended the state university, went to work for a de-partment store in Texas, and after two years was transferred to the central office in New York. Always overweight, she became markedly obese in late adolescence. Aside from two or three brief periods when she lost forty to fifty pounds on crash diets, she had hovered between two hundred and two hundred fifty since she was twenty-one.

I got down to business and asked my standard opening question: "What ails?"

"Everything," Betty replied. Nothing was going right in her life. In fact, she said, she had no life. She worked sixty hours a week, had no friends, no social life, no activities in California. Her life, such as it was, she said, was in New York, but to request a transfer now would doom her career, which was already in jeopardy because of her unpopularity with co-workers. Her com-pany had originally trained her, along with eight other novices, in a three-month intensive course. Betty was preoccupied that she was neither performing nor progressing through promotions as well as her eight classmates. She lived in a furnished suburban apartment doing nothing, she said, but working and eating and chalking off the days till her eighteen months were up.

A psychiatrist in New York, Dr. Farber, whom she saw for approximate-ly four months, had treated her with antidepressant medication. Though she continued to take it, it had not helped her: she was deeply depressed, cried every evening, wished she were dead, slept fitfully, and always awoke by four or five A.M. She moped around the house and on Sundays, her day off, never dressed and spent the day eating sweets in front of the television set. The week before, she had phoned Dr. Farber, who gave her my name and suggested she call for a consultation.

"Tell me more about what you're struggling with in your life," I asked.

"My eating is out of control," Betty said, chuckling, and added, "You could say my eating is always out of control, but now it is *really* out of control. I've gained around twenty pounds in the past three months, and I can't get into most of my clothes."

That surprised me, her clothes seeming so formless, so infinitely expandable, that I couldn't imagine them being outdistanced.

"Other reasons why you decided to come in just now?"

"I saw a medical doctor last week for headaches, and he told me that my blood pressure is dangerously high, around 220 over 110, and that I've got to begin to lose weight. He seemed upset. I don't know how seriously to take him—everyone in California is such a health nut. He wears jeans and running shoes in his office."

She uttered all these things in a gay chatty tone, as though she were talking about someone else, or as though she and I were college sophomores swapping stories in a dorm some rainy Sunday afternoon. She tried to poke me into joining the fun. She told jokes. She had a gift for imitating accents and mimicked her laid-back Marin County physician, her Chinese customers, and her Midwestern boss. She must have laughed twenty times during the session, her high spirits apparently in no way dampened by my stern refusal to be coerced into laughing with her.

I always take very seriously the business of entering into a treatment contract with a patient. Once I accept someone for treatment, I commit myself to stand by that person: to spend all the time and all the energy that proves necessary for the patient's improvement; and most of all, to relate to the patient in an intimate, authentic manner.

But could I relate to Betty? To be frank, she revolted me. It was an effort for me to locate her face, so layered and swathed in flesh as it was. Her silly commentary was equally offputting. By the end of our first hour, I felt irritated and bored. Could I be intimate with her? I could scarcely think of a single person with whom I *less* wished to be intimate. But this was *my* problem, not Betty's. It was time, after twenty-five years of practice, for me to change. Betty represented the ultimate countertransference challenge—and, for that very reason, I offered then and there to be her therapist.

Surely no one can be critical of a therapist striving to improve his technique. But what, I wondered uneasily, about the rights of the patient? Is there not a difference between a therapist scrubbing away unseemly countertransference stains and a dancer or a Zen master striving for perfection in each of those disciplines? It is one thing to improve one's backhand service return but quite another to sharpen one's skills at the expense of some fragile, troubled person.

These thoughts all occurred to me but I found them dismissible. It was true that Betty offered an opportunity to improve my personal skills as a therapist. It was, however, also true that my future patients would benefit from whatever growth I would attain. Besides, human service professionals have always practiced on the living patient. There is no alternative. How could medical education, to take one example, survive without student clinical clerkships? Furthermore, I have always found that responsible neophyte therapists who convey their sense of curiosity and enthusiasm often form excellent therapeutic relationships and can be as effective as a seasoned professional.

It's the relationship that heals, the relationship that heals, the relationship that heals—my professional rosary. I say that often to students. And say other things as well, about the way to relate to a patient—positive unconditional regard, nonjudgmental acceptance, authentic engagement, empathic understanding. How was I going to be able to heal Betty through our relationship? How authentic, empathic, or accepting could I be? How honest? How would I respond when she asked about my feelings toward her? It was my hope that I would change as Betty and I progressed in her (our) therapy. For the time being, it seemed to me that Betty's social interactions were so primitive and superficial that no penetrating therapist-patient relationship analysis would be necessary.

I had secretly hoped that her appearance would be offset in some way by her interpersonal characteristics—that is, by the sheer vivacity or mental agility I have found in a few fat women—but that, alas, was not to be. The better I knew her, the more boring and superficial she seemed.

During the first few sessions, Betty described, in endless detail, problems she encountered at work with customers, co-workers, and bosses. She often, despite my inner groans, described some particularly banal conversation by playing several of the roles—I've always hated that. She described, again in tedious detail, all the attractive men at work and the minute, pathetic machinations she'd go through to exchange a few sentences with them. She resisted every effort on my part to dip beneath the surface.

Not only was our initial, tentative "cocktail chatter" indefinitely prolonged, but I had a strong sense that, even when we got past this stage, we would remain fused to the surface of things—that as long Betty and I met, we were doomed to talk about pounds, diets, petty work grievances, and the reasons she did not join an aerobics class. Good Lord, what had I gotten myself into?

Every one of my notes of these early sessions contains phrases such as: "Another boring session"; "Looked at the clock about every three minutes today"; "The most boring patient I have ever seen"; "Almost fell asleep today—had to sit up in my chair to stay awake"; "Almost fell off my chair today."

While I was considering shifting to a hard, uncomfortable chair, it suddenly occurred to me that when I was in therapy with Rollo May, he used to sit in a straight-backed wooden chair. He said he had a bad back, but I knew him well for many years afterward and never heard him mention back trouble. Could it be that he found *me*——?

Betty mentioned that she hadn't liked Dr. Farber because he often fell asleep during their hour. Now I knew why! When I spoke to Dr. Farber on the phone, he did not mention his naps, of course, but he did volunteer that Betty had not been able to learn how to use therapy. It was not hard to understand why he had started her on medication; we psychiatrists so often resort to that when we cannot get anything going in therapy.

Where to start? How to start? I struggled to find some handhold. It was pointless to begin by addressing her weight. Betty made it clear immediately that she hoped therapy would help her get to the point where she could seriously consider weight reduction, but she was a long way from that at this time. "When I'm this depressed, eating is the only thing that keeps me going."

But when I focused on her depression, she presented a persuasive case that depression was an appropriate response to her life situation. Who wouldn't feel depressed holed up in a small furnished apartment in an impersonal California suburb for eighteen months, torn away from one's real life—one's home, social activities, friends?

So I then attempted to help her work on her life situation, but I could make little headway. She had plenty of daunting explanations. She didn't make friends easily, she pointed out: no obese woman does. (On that point I needed no persuasion.) People in California had their own tight cliques and did not welcome strangers. Her only social contacts were at work, where most of her co-workers resented her supervisory role. Besides, like all Californians, they were jocks—into surfing and skydiving. Could I see her doing that? I swept away a fantasy of her slowly sinking on a surfboard and acknowledged she had a point—those did not seem to be her sports.

What other options were there? she asked. The singles world is impossible for obese people. To prove that point, she described a desperation date she had had the month before—her only date in years. She answered an ad in the personal section of *The Bay Guardian*, a local newspaper. Although most of the ads placed by men explicitly specified a "slim" woman, one did not. She called and arranged to go out to dinner with a man named George, who asked her to wear a rose in her hair and to meet him in the bar of a local restaurant.

His face fell, she reported, when he first caught sight of her, but, to his everlasting credit, he acknowledged that he was indeed George and then behaved like a gentleman throughout dinner. Though Betty never again heard from George, she often thought about him. On several other such attempts in the past, she had been stood up by men who probably spotted her from afar and left without speaking to her.

In some desperation, I stretched for ways to be helpful to Betty. Perhaps (in an effort to conceal my negative feelings) I tried too hard, and I made the beginner's mistake of suggesting other options. Had she considered the Sierra Club? No, she lacked the stamina for hiking. Or Overeaters Anonymous, which might provide a social network. No, she hated groups. Other suggestions met a similar fate. There had to be some other way.

The first step in all therapeutic change is responsibility assumption. If one feels in no way responsible for one's predicament, then how can one change it? That was precisely the situation with Betty: she completely externalized the problem. It was not *her* doing: it was the work transfer, or the sterile California culture, or the absence of cultural events, or the jock social scene, or society's miserable attitude toward obese people. Despite my best efforts, Betty denied any personal contribution to her unhappy life situation.

Oh yes, she could, on an intellectual level, agree that, if she stopped eating and lost weight, the world might treat her differently. But that was too far removed from her, too long term, and her eating seemed too much out of her control. Besides she marshaled other responsibility-absolving arguments: the genetic component (there was considerable obesity on both sides of her family); and the new research demonstrating physiological abnormalities in the obese, ranging from lower basal metabolic rates to a preset, programmed, relatively uninfluencible body weight. No, that would not work. Ultimately I would have to help her assume responsibility for her appearance—but saw no leverage for achieving that at this time. I had to start with something more immediate. I knew a way.

The psychotherapist's single most valuable practical tool is the "process" focus. Think of *process* as opposed to *content*. In a conversation, the content consists of the actual words uttered, the substantive issues discussed; the process, however, is *how* the content is expressed and especially what this mode of expression reveals about the relationship between the participating individuals.

What I had to do was to get away from the content—to stop, for example, attempting to provide simplistic solutions to Betty—and to focus on process—on how we were relating to each other. And there was one outstanding characteristic of our relationship—*boredom*. And that is precisely where countertransference complicates things: I had to be clear about how much of the boredom was *my* problem, about how bored I would be with *any* fat woman.

So I proceeded cautiously—too cautiously. My negative feelings slowed me down. I was too afraid of making my aversion visible. I would never have waited so long with a patient I liked more. I spurred myself to get moving. If I were going to be helpful to Betty, I had to sort out, to trust, and to act upon my feelings.

The truth was that this was a very boring lady, and I needed to confront her with that in some acceptable way. She could deny responsibility for anything else—the absence of friends in her current life, the tough singles scene, the horrors of suburbia—but I was *not* going to let her deny responsibility for boring me.

I dared not utter the word *boring*—far too vague and too pejorative. I needed to be precise and constructive. I asked myself what, exactly, was boring about Betty, and identified two obvious characteristics. First of all, she never revealed anything intimate about herself. Second, there was her damned giggling, her forced gaiety, her reluctance to be appropriately serious.

It would be difficult to make her aware of these characteristics without hurting her. I decided upon a general strategy: my basic position would be that I wanted to get closer to her but that her behavioral traits got in the way. I thought it would be difficult for her to take offense with any criticism of her behavior when framed in that context. She could only be pleased at my wanting to know her better. I decided to start with her lack of self-revelation and, toward the end of a particularly soporific session, took the plunge.

"Betty, I'll explain later why I'm asking you this, but I'd like you to try something new today. Would you give yourself a score from one to ten on how much revealing about yourself you've done during our hour together today? Consider ten to be the most significant revealing you can imagine and one to be the type of revealing you might do, let's say, with strangers in a line at the movies."

A mistake. Betty spent several minutes explaining why she wouldn't go to the movies alone. She imagined people pitied her for having no friends. She sensed their dread that she might crowd them by sitting next to them. She saw the curiosity, the bemusement in their faces as they watched to see whether she could squeeze into a single narrow movie seat. When she began to digress further—extending the discussion to airline seats and how seated passengers' faces grew white with fear when she started down the aisle searching for her seat—I interrupted her, repeated my request, and defined "one" as "casual conversation at work."

Betty responded by giving herself a "ten." I was astonished (I had expected a "two" or "three") and told her so. She defended her rating on the basis that she had told me things she had never shared before: that, for example, she had once stolen a magazine from a drugstore and was fearful about going alone to a restaurant or to the movies.

We repeated that same scenario several times. Betty insisted she was taking huge risks, yet, as I said to her, "Betty, you rate yourself 'ten,' yet it didn't *feel* that way to me. It didn't feel that you were taking a real risk with me."

"I have never told anybody else these things. Not Dr. Farber, for example."

"How do you feel telling me these things?"

"I feel fine doing it."

"Can you use other words than *fine*? It must be scary or liberating to say these things for the first time!"

"I feel O.K. doing it. I know you're listening professionally. It's O.K. I feel O.K. I don't know what you want."

"How can you be so sure I'm listening professionally? You have no doubts?"

Careful, careful! I couldn't promise more honesty than I was willing to give. There was no way that she could deal with my revelation of negative feelings. Betty denied any doubts—and at this point told me about Dr. Farber's falling asleep on her and added that I seemed much more interested than he.

What *did* I want from her? From *her* standpoint she was revealing much. I had to be sure I really knew. What was there about her revealing that left me unmoved? It struck me that she was always revealing something that occurred elsewhere—another time, another place. She was incapable, or unwilling, to reveal herself in the immediate present that we two were sharing. Hence, her evasive response of "O.K." or "Fine" whenever I asked about her here-and-now feelings.

That was the first important discovery I made about Betty: she was desperately isolated, and she survived this isolation only by virtue of the sustaining myth that her intimate life was being lived elsewhere. Her friends, her circle of acquaintances, were not here, but elsewhere, in New York, in Texas, in the past. In fact, everything of importance was elsewhere. It was at this time that I first began to suspect that for Betty there was no "here" there.

Another thing: if she was revealing more of herself to me than to anyone before, then what was the nature of her close relationships? Betty responded that she had a reputation for being easy to talk to. She and I, she said, were in the same business: she was everyone's therapist. She added that she had a lot of friends, but no one knew *her*. Her trademark was that she listened well and was entertaining. She hated the thought, but the stereotype was true: she was the jolly fat woman.

This led naturally into the other primary reason I found Betty so boring: she was acting in bad faith with me—in our face-to-face talks she was never real, she was all pretense and false gaiety.

"I'm really interested in what you said about being, or rather pretending to be, jolly. I think you are determined, absolutely committed, to be jolly with me."

"Hmmm, interesting theory, Dr. Watson."

"You've done this since our first meeting. You tell me about a life that is full of despair, but you do it in a bouncy 'aren't-we-having-a-good-time?' way."

"That's the way I am."

"When you stay jolly like that, I lose sight of how much pain you're having."

"That's better than wallowing in it."

"But you come here for help. Why is it so necessary for you to entertain me?"

Betty flushed. She seemed staggered by my confrontation and retreated by sinking into her body. Wiping her brow with a tiny handkerchief, she stalled for time.

"Zee suspect takes zee fifth."

"Betty, I'm going to be persistent today. What would happen if you stopped trying to entertain me?"

"I don't see anything wrong with having some fun. Why take everything so . . . so . . . I don't know—You're always so serious. Besides, this is me, this is the way I am. I'm not sure I know what you're talking about. What do you mean by my entertaining you?"

"Betty, this is important, the most important stuff we've gotten into so far. But you're right. First, you've got to know exactly what I mean. Would it be O.K. with you if, from now on in our future sessions, I interrupt and point out when you're entertaining me—the moment it occurs?"

Betty agreed—she could hardly refuse me; and I now had at my disposal an enormously liberating device. I was now permitted to interrupt her instantaneously (reminding her, of course, of our new agreement) whenever she giggled, adopted a silly accent, or attempted to amuse me or to make light of things in any distracting way.

Within three or four sessions, her "entertaining" behavior disappeared as she, for the first time, began to speak of her life with the seriousness it deserved. She reflected that she had to be entertaining to keep others interested in her. I commented that, in this office, the opposite was true: the more she tried to entertain me, the more distant and less interested I felt.

But Betty said she didn't know how else to be: I was asking her to dump her entire social repertoire. Reveal herself? If she were to reveal herself, what would she show? There was nothing there inside. She was empty. (The word *empty* was to arise more and more frequently as therapy proceeded. Psychological "emptiness" is a common concept in the treatment of those with eating disorders.)

I supported her as much as possible at this point. *Now*, I pointed out to Betty, she was taking risks. *Now* she was up to eight or nine on the revealing scale. Could she feel the difference? She got the point quickly. She said she felt frightened, like jumping out of a plane without a parachute.

I was less bored now. I looked at the clock less frequently and once in a while checked the time during Betty's hour not, as before, to count the number of minutes I had yet to endure, but to see whether sufficient time remained to open up a new issue.

Nor was it necessary to sweep from my mind derogatory thoughts about her appearance. I no longer noticed her body and, instead, looked into her eyes. In fact, I noted with surprise the first stirrings of empathy within me. When Betty told me about going to a western bar where two rednecks sidled up behind her and mocked her by mooing like a cow, I felt outraged for her and told her so.

My new feelings toward Betty caused me to recall, and to be ashamed of, my initial response to her. I cringed when I reflected on all the other obese women whom I had related to in an intolerant and dehumanized fashion.

These changes all signified that we were making progress: we were successfully addressing Betty's isolation and her hunger for closeness. I hoped to show her that another person could know her fully and still care for her.

Betty now felt definitely engaged in therapy. She thought about our discussions between sessions, had long imaginary conversations with me during the week, looked forward to our meetings, and felt angry and disappointed when business travel caused her to miss meetings.

But at the same time she became unaccountably more distressed and reported more sadness and more anxiety. I pounced at the opportunity to understand this development. Whenever the patient begins to develop symptoms in respect to the relationship with the therapist, therapy has really begun, and inquiry into these symptoms will open the path to the central issues.

Her anxiety had to do with her fear of getting too dependent or addicted to therapy. Our sessions had become the most important thing in her life. She didn't know what would happen to her if she didn't have her weekly "fix." It seemed to me she was still resisting closeness by referring to a "fix" rather than to me, and I gradually confronted her on that point.

"Betty, what's the danger in letting me matter to you?"

"I'm not sure. lt feels scary, like I'll need you too much. I'm not sure you'll be there for me. I'm going to have to leave California in a year, remember."

"A year's a long time. So you avoid me now because you won't always have me?"

"I know it doesn't make sense. But I do the same thing with California. I like New York and I don't want to like California. I'm afraid that, if I form friends here and start to like it, I might not want to leave. The other thing is that I start to feel, 'Why bother?' I'm here for such a short time. Who wants temporary friendships?"

"The problem with that attitude is you end up with an unpeopled life. Maybe that's part of the reason you feel empty inside. One way or another, every relationship must end. There's no such thing as a lifetime guarantee. It's like refusing to enjoy watching the sun rise because you hate to see it set."

"It sounds crazy when you put it like that, but that's what I do. When I meet a new person whom I like, I start right away to imagine what it will be like to say goodbye to them."

I knew this was an important issue, and that we would return to it. Otto Rank described this life stance with a wonderful phrase: "Refusing the loan of life in order to avoid the debt of death."

Betty now entered into a depression which was short-lived and had a curious, paradoxical twist. She was enlivened by the closeness and the openness of our interaction; but, rather than allow herself the enjoyment of that feeling, she was saddened by the realization that her life heretofore had been so devoid of intimacy.

I was reminded of another patient I had treated the year before, a forty-four-year-old excessively responsible, conscientious physician. One evening in the midst of a marital dispute, she uncharacteristically drank too much, went out of control, threw plates against the wall, and narrowly missed her husband with a lemon pie. When I saw her two days later, she seemed guilty and depressed. In an effort to console her, I tried to suggest that losing control is not always a catastrophe. But she interrupted and told me I had misunderstood: she felt no guilt but was instead overcome with regret that she had waited until she was forty-four to relinquish her controls and let some real feelings out.

Despite her two hundred and fifty pounds, Betty and I had rarely discussed her eating and her weight. She had often talked about epic (and invariably unproductive) struggles she had had with her mother and with other friends who tried to help her control her eating. I was determined to avoid that role; instead, I placed my faith in the assumption that, if I could help remove the obstacles that lay in her path, Betty would, on her own, take the initiative to care for her body.

So far, by addressing her isolation, I had already cleared away major obstacles: Betty's depression had lifted; and, having established a social life for herself, she no longer regarded food as her sole source of satisfaction. But it was not until she stumbled upon an extraordinary revelation about the dangers of losing weight that she could make the decision to begin her diet. It came about in this way.

When she had been in therapy for a few months, I decided that her progress would be accelerated if she worked in a therapy group as well as in individual therapy. For one thing, I was certain it would be wise to establish a supportive community to help sustain her in the difficult diet days yet to come. Furthermore, a therapy group would provide Betty an opportunity to explore the interpersonal issues we had opened up in our therapy—the concealment, the need to entertain, the feeling she had nothing to offer. Though Betty was very frightened and initially resisted my suggestion, she gamely agreed and entered a therapy group led by two psychiatric residents.

One of her first group meetings happened to be a highly unusual session in which Carlos, also in individual therapy with me (see "If Rape Were Legal . . . "), informed the group of his incurable cancer. Betty's father had died of cancer when she was twelve, and since then she had been terrified of the disease. In college she had initially elected a premedical curriculum but gave it up for fear of being in contact with cancer patients.

Over the next few weeks, the contact with Carlos generated so much anxiety in Betty that I had to see her in several emergency sessions and had difficulty persuading her to continue in the group. She developed distressing physical symptoms—including headaches (her father died of brain cancer), backaches, and shortness of breath—and was tormented with the obsessive thought that she, too, had cancer. Since she was phobic about seeing doctors (because of her shame about her body, she rarely permitted a physical exam and had never had a pelvic exam), it was hard to reassure her about her health.

Witnessing Carlos's alarming weight loss reminded Betty of how, over a twelve-month period, she had watched her father shrink from an obese man to a skeleton wrapped in great folds of spare skin. Though she acknowledged that it was an irrational thought, Betty realized that since her father's death she had believed that weight loss would make her susceptible to cancer.

She had strong feelings about hair loss as well. When she first joined the group, Carlos (who had lost his hair as a result of chemotherapy) was wearing a toupee, but the day he informed the group about his cancer, he came bald to the meeting. Betty was horrified, and visions of her father's baldness— he had been shaven for his brain surgery—returned to her. She remembered also how frightened she had been when, on previous strenuous diets, she herself had suffered considerable hair loss.

These disturbing feelings had vastly compounded Betty's weight problems. Not only did food represent her sole form of gratification, not only was it a method of assuaging her feeling of emptiness, not only did thinness evoke the pain of her father's death, but she felt, unconsciously, that losing weight would result in *her* death.

Gradually Betty's acute anxiety subsided. She had never before talked openly about these issues: perhaps the sheer catharsis helped; perhaps it was useful for her to recognize the magical nature of her thinking; perhaps some of her horrifying thoughts were simply desensitized by talking about them in the daylight in a calm, rational manner.

During this time, Carlos was particularly helpful. Betty's parents had, until the very end, denied the seriousness of her father's illness. Such massive denial always plays havoc with the survivors, and Betty had neither been prepared for his death nor had the opportunity to say goodbye. But Carlos modeled a very different approach to his fate: he was courageous, rational, and open with his feelings about his illness and his approaching death. Furthermore, he was especially kind to Betty—perhaps it was that he knew she was my patient, perhaps that she came along when he was in a generous ("everybody has got a heart") state of mind, perhaps simply that he always had a fondness for fat women (which, I regret to say, I had always considered further proof of his perversity).

Betty must have felt that the obstructions to losing weight had been sufficiently removed because she gave unmistakable evidence that a major campaign was about to be launched. I was astonished by the scope and complexity of the preparatory arrangements.

First, she enrolled in an eating-disorder program at the clinic where I worked and completed their demanding protocol, which included a complex physical workup (she still refused a pelvic exam) and a battery of psychological tests. She then cleared her apartment of food—every can, every package, every bottle. She made plans for alternative social activities: she pointed out to me that eliminating lunches and dinners puts a crimp into one's social calendar. To my surprise, she joined a square-dancing group (this lady's got guts, I thought) and a weekly bowling league—her father had often taken her bowling when she was a child, she explained. She bought a used stationary bicycle and set it up in front of her TV set. She then said her goodbyes to old friends—her last Granny Goose Hawaiian-style potato chip, her last Mrs. Fields chocolate chip cookie, and, toughest of all, her last honey-glazed doughnut.

There was considerable internal preparation as well, which Betty found difficult to describe other than to say she was "gathering inner resolve" and waiting for the right moment to commence the diet. I grew impatient and amused myself with a vision of an enormous Japanese sumo wrestler pacing, posturing, and grunting himself into readiness.

Suddenly she was off! She went on a liquid Optifast diet, ate no solid food, bicycled forty minutes every morning, walked three miles every afternoon, and bowled and square-danced once a week. Her fatty casing began to disintegrate. She began to shed bulk. Great chunks of overhanging flesh broke off and were washed away. Soon the pounds flowed off in rivulets—two, three, four, sometimes five pounds a week.

Betty started each hour with a progress report: ten pounds lost, then twenty, twenty-five, thirty. She was down to two hundred forty pounds, then two hundred thirty, and two hundred twenty. It seemed astonishingly fast and easy. I was delighted for her and commended her strongly each week on her efforts. But in those first weeks I was also aware of an uncharitable voice within me, a voice saying, "Good God, if she's losing it that fast, think of how much food she must have been putting away!"

The weeks passed, the campaign continued. After three months, she weighed in at two hundred ten. Then two hundred, a fifty-pound loss! Then, one hundred ninety. The opposition stiffened. Sometimes she came into my office in tears after a week without food and no compensating weight loss. Every pound put up a fight, but Betty stayed on the diet.

Those were ghastly months. She hated everything. Her life was a torment—the disgusting liquid food, the stationary bicycle, the hunger pangs, the diabolic McDonald's hamburger ads on television, and the smells, the ubiquitous smells: popcorn in the movies, pizza in the bowling alley, croissants in the shopping center, crab at Fisherman's Wharf. Was there nowhere in the world an odor-free place?

Every day was a bad day. Nothing in her life gave her pleasure. Others in the eating-disorder clinic's weight-reduction group gave up—but Betty hung tough. My respect for her grew.

I like to eat, too. Often I look forward all day to a special meal; and, when the craving strikes, no obstacle can block my way to the dim sum restaurant or the gelato stand. But as Betty's ordeal continued, I began to feel guilty eating—as though I were acting in bad faith toward her. Whenever I sat down to eat pizza or pasta al pesto or enchiladas con salsa verde or German-chocolate-cake ice cream, or any other special treat I knew Betty liked, I thought of her. I shuddered when I thought of her dining, can opener in hand, on Optifast liquid. Sometimes I passed up seconds in her honor.

It happened that, during this period, I passed the upper weight limit I allow myself, and went on a three-week diet. Since my diets consist primarily of eliminating ice cream and French fries, I could hardly say to Betty that I was joining hands with her in a sympathy fast. Nonetheless, during these three weeks I felt her deprivation more keenly. I was moved now when she told me how she cried herself to sleep. I ached for her when she described the starving child within her howling, "Feed me! Feed me!"

One hundred eighty. One hundred seventy. An eighty-pound weight loss! Betty's mood now fluctuated wildly, and I grew increasingly concerned for her. She had occasional brief periods of pride and exhilaration (especially when she went shopping for slimmer clothing), but mainly she experienced such deep despondency that it was all she could do to get herself to work each morning.

At times she grew irritable and raised several old grievances with me. Had I referred her to a therapy group as a way of dumping her or, at least, sharing the load and getting her partly off my hands? Why had I not asked her more about her eating habits? After all, eating was her life. Love her, love her eating. (Careful, careful, she's getting close.) Why had I agreed with her when she listed the reasons that medical school was not possible for her (her age, lack of stamina, laziness, having taken few of the prerequisite courses, and lack of funds)? She viewed, she told me now, my suggestion about a possible career in nursing as a putdown, and accused me of saying, "The girl's not smart enough for medical school—so let her be a nurse!"

At times, she was petulant and regressed. Once, for example, when I inquired about why she had become inactive in her therapy group, she simply glared and refused to answer. When I pressed her to say exactly what was on her mind, she said in a singsong child's voice, "If I can't have a cookie, I won't do anything for you."

During one of her depressed periods, she had a vivid dream.

> I was in a place like Mecca where people go to commit suicide legally. I was with a close friend but I don't remember who. She was going to commit suicide by jumping down a deep tunnel. I promised her I'd retrieve her body but, later, I realized that to do this I'd have to crawl down this terrible tunnel with all sorts of dead and decaying bodies around and I didn't think I could do it.

In associating to this dream Betty said that, earlier the day of the dream, she had been thinking that she had shed a whole body: she had lost eighty pounds, and there was a woman in her office who weighed only eighty pounds. At the time she had imagined granting an autopsy and holding a funeral for the "body" she had shed. This macabre thought, Betty suspected, was echoed in the dream image of retrieving her friend's dead body from the tunnel.

The imagery and depth of the dream brought home to me how far she had come. It was hard to remember the giggling, superficial woman of a few months before. Betty had my full attention for every minute of every session now. Who could have imagined that, out of that woman whose vacuous chatter had so bored me and her previous psychiatrist, this thoughtful, spontaneous, and sensitive person could have emerged?

One hundred sixty-five. Another kind of emergence was taking place. One day in my office I looked over at Betty and noticed, for the first time, that she had a lap. I looked again. Had it always been there? Maybe I was paying more attention to her now. I didn't think so: her body contour, from chin to toes, had always been smoothly globular. A couple of weeks later, I saw definite signs of a breast, two breasts. A week later, a jawline, then a chin, an elbow. It was all there—there had been a person, a handsome woman, buried in there all the time.

Others, especially men, had noticed the change, and now touched and poked her during conversations. A man at the office walked her out to her car. Her hairdresser, gratuitously, gave her a scalp massage. She was certain her boss was eyeing her breasts.

One day Betty announced, "one hundred fifty-nine," and added that this was "virgin territory"—that is, she hadn't weighed in the one hundred fifties since high school. Though my response—asking whether she worried about entering "nonvirgin territory"—was a sorry joke, it nonetheless initiated an important discussion about sex.

Though she had an active sexual fantasy life, she had never had any physical contact with a man—not a hug, not a kiss, not even a lascivious grab. She had always craved sex and was angry that society's attitude toward the obese sentenced her to sexual frustration. Only now, when she was approaching a weight when sexual invitations might materialize, only now when her dreams teemed with menacing male figures (a masked doctor plunging a large hypodermic needle into her abdomen, a leering man peeling the scab off a large abdominal wound), did she recognize that she was very frightened of sex.

These discussions released a flood of painful memories about a lifetime of rejection by males. She had never been asked on a date and never attended a school dance or party. She played the confidante role very well and had helped many friends plan their weddings. They were just about all married off now, and she could no longer conceal from herself that she would forever play the role of the unchosen observer.

We soon moved from sex into the deeper waters of her basic sexual identity. Betty had heard that her father had really wanted a son and been silently disappointed when she was born. One night she had two dreams about a lost twin brother. In one dream she and he wore identification badges and kept switching them with each other. She finished him off in another dream: he squeezed into a crowded elevator into which she couldn't fit (because of her size). Then the elevator crashed, killing all the passengers, and she was left sifting through his remains.

In another dream, her father gave her a horse called "She's a Lady." She had always wanted a horse from him, and in the dream not only was that childhood wish fulfilled but her father officially christened her a lady.

Our discussions about sexual practice and her sexual identity generated so much anxiety and such an agonizing sense of emptiness that, on several occasions, she binged on cookies and doughnuts. By now Betty was permitted some solid food—one diet TV dinner a day—but found this more difficult to follow than the liquid-only diet.

Looming ahead was an important symbolic marker—the loss of the one-hundredth pound. This specific goal, never to be attained, had powerful sexual connotations. For one thing Carlos had, months before, only half jokingly told Betty he was going to take her to Hawaii for a weekend when she had lost a hundred pounds. Furthermore, as part of her pre-diet mental preparation, Betty had vowed herself that when she lost a hundred pounds she was going to contact George, the man whose personal ad she had answered, to surprise him with her new body and reward his gentlemanly behavior with her sexual favors.

In an effort to reduce her anxiety, I urged moderation and suggested she approach sex with less drastic steps: for example, by spending time talking to men; by educating herself about such topics as sexual anatomy, sexual mechanics, and masturbation. I recommended reading material and urged her to visit a female gynecologist and to explore these issues with her girlfriends and her therapy group.

Throughout this period of rapid weight loss, another extraordinary phenomenon was taking place. Betty experienced emotional flashbacks and would spend much of a therapy hour tearfully discussing startlingly vivid memories, such as the day she left Texas to move to New York, or her college graduation, or her anger at her mother for being too timid and fearful to attend her high school graduation.

At first it seemed that these flashbacks, as well as the accompanying extreme mood swings, were chaotic, random occurrences; but after several weeks, Betty realized that they were following a coherent pattern: as she lost weight she *re-experienced the major traumatic or unresolved events of her life that had occurred when she was at a particular weight.* Thus her descent from two hundred fifty pounds set her spinning backward in time through the emotionally charged events of her life: leaving Texas for New York (210 pounds), her college graduation (190 pounds), her decision to drop the premed curriculum (and to give up the dream of discovering the cure for the cancer that killed her father) (180 pounds), her loneliness at her high school graduation—her envy of other daughters and fathers, her inability to get a date for the senior prom (170 pounds), her junior high graduation and how much she missed her father at that graduation (155 pounds). What a wonderful proof of the unconscious realm! Betty's body had remembered what her mind had long forgotten.

Memories of her father permeated these flashbacks. The closer we looked, the more apparent it was that everything led back to him, to his death, and to the one hundred fifty pounds Betty weighed at that time. The closer she approached that weight, the more depressed she grew and the more her mind swarmed with feelings and recollections of her father.

Soon we spent entire sessions talking about her father. The time had come to unearth everything. I plunged her into reminiscence and encouraged her to express everything she could remember about his illness, his dying, his appearance in the hospital the last time she saw him, the details of his funeral, the clothes she wore, the minister's speech, the people who attended.

Betty and I had talked about her father before but never with such intensity and depth. She felt her loss as never before and, over a two-week period, wept almost continuously. We met thrice weekly during this time, and I attempted to help her understand the source of her tears. In part she cried because of her loss, but in large part because she considered her father's life to have been such a tragedy: he never obtained the education he wanted (or that she wanted for him), and he died just before he retired and never enjoyed the years of leisure for which he had longed. Yet, as I pointed out to her, her description of his life's activities—his large extended family, his wide social circle, his daily bull sessions with friends, his love of the land, his youth in the navy, his afternoons fishing—was a picture of a full life in which her father was immersed in a community of people who knew and loved him.

When I urged her to compare his life with her own, she realized that some of her grief was misplaced: it was her own life, not her father's, that was tragically unfulfilled. How much of her grief, then, was for all her unrealized hopes? This question was particularly painful for Betty who, by that time, had visited a gynecologist and been told that she had an endocrine disorder that would make it impossible for her to have children.

I felt cruel during these weeks because of the pain our therapy was uncovering. Every session was an ordeal, and Betty often left my office badly shaken. She began to have acute panic attacks and many disturbing dreams, and, as she put it, she died at least three times a night. She could not remember the dreams except for two recurrent ones that had begun in adolescence, shortly after her father's death. In one dream, she lay paralyzed in a small closet which was being bricked up. In the other, she was lying in a hospital bed with a candle, which represented her soul, burning at the head of the bed. She knew that when the flame went out she would die, and she felt helpless as she watched it get smaller and smaller.

Discussing her father's death obviously evoked fears of her own death. I asked Betty to talk about her first experiences and early conceptions of death. Living on a ranch, she was no stranger to death. She watched her mother kill chickens and heard the squeal of hogs being slaughtered. Betty was extremely unsettled by her grandfather's death when she was nine. According to her mother (Betty told me she had no recollection of this), she was reassured by her parents that only old people die, but then she pestered them for weeks by chanting she didn't want to grow old and by repeatedly asking her parents how old they were. But it was not until shortly after her father died that Betty grasped the truth about the inevitability of her own death. She remembered the precise moment.

"It was a couple days after the funeral, I was still taking off from school. The teacher said I should return when I felt ready. I could have gone back earlier, but it didn't seem right to go back so soon. I was worried that people wouldn't think I was sad enough. I was walking in the fields behind the house. It was cold out—I could see my breath, and it was hard to walk because the earth was clumped and the plow ridges were frozen. I was thinking of my father lying beneath the ground and how cold he must have been, and I suddenly heard a voice from above saying to me, 'You're next!'"

Betty stopped and looked at me. "You think I'm crazy?"

"No, I told you before, you don't have the knack for it."

She smiled. "I've never told that story to anyone. In fact I'd forgotten it, forgotten it for years until this week."

"I feel good you're willing to trust me with it. It sounds important. Say some more about being 'next.'"

"It's like my father was no longer there to protect me. In a way he stood between me and the grave. Without him there, I was next in line." Betty hunched up her shoulders and shuddered. "Can you believe I still feel spooky when I think about this?"

"Your mother? Where was she in all this?"

"Like I've told you before—way, way in the background. She cooked and she fed me—-she was real good at that—but she was weak—I was the one protecting her. Can you believe a Texan who can't drive? I started driving at twelve when my father got sick, because she was afraid to learn."

"So there was no one shielding you?"

"That's when I started having nightmares. That dream about the candle— I must have had it twenty times."

"That dream makes me think of what you said before about your fear of losing weight, about having to stay heavy to avoid dying of cancer like your father. If the candle flame stays fat, you live."

"Maybe, but sounds farfetched."

Another good example, I thought, of the pointlessness of the therapist rushing in with an interpretation, even a good one like this. Patients, like everyone else, profit most from a truth they, themselves, discover.

Betty continued, "And somewhere in that year I got the idea I was going to die before I was thirty. You know, I think I still believe that."

These discussions undermined her denial of death. Betty began to feel unsafe. She was always on guard against injury—when driving, bicycling, crossing the street. She became preoccupied with the capriciousness of death. "It could come at any instant," she said, "when I least expect it." For years her father had saved money and planned a family trip to Europe only to develop a brain tumor shortly before the departure date. She, I, anyone, can be struck down at any time. How does anyone, how do *I*, cope with that thought?

Now committed to being entirely "present" with Betty, I tried not to flinch from any of her questions. I told her of my own difficulties in coming to terms with death; that, though the fact of death cannot be altered, one's attitude toward it can be vastly influenced. From both my personal and my professional experience, I have come to believe that the fear of death is always greatest in those who feel that they have not lived their life fully. A good working formula is: the more unlived life, or unrealized potential, the greater one's death anxiety.

My hunch was, I told Betty, that when she entered more fully into life, she would lose her terror of death—some, not all of it. (We are all stuck with some anxiousness about death. It's the price of admission to self-awareness.)

At other times Betty expressed anger at my forcing her to think about morbid topics. "Why think about death? We can't do anything about it!" I tried to help her understand that, though the *fact* of death destroys us, the *idea* of death can save us. In other words, our awareness of death can throw a different perspective on life and incite us to rearrange our priorities. Carlos had learned that lesson—it was what he meant on his deathbed when he talked about his life having been saved.

It seemed to me that an important lesson Betty could learn from an awareness of death was that life had to be lived *now*; it could not be indefinitely postponed. It was not difficult to lay out before her the ways she avoided life: her reluctance to engage others (because she dreaded separation); her overeating and obesity, which had resulted in her being left out of so much life; her avoidance of the present moment by slipping quickly into the past or the future. It was also not difficult to argue that it was within her power to change these patterns—in fact she had already begun: consider how she was engaging me that very day!

I encouraged her to plunge into her grief, I wanted her to explore and express every facet of it. Again and again, I asked the same question: "Who, what, are you grieving for?"

Betty responded, "I think I'm grieving for love. My daddy was the only man who ever held me in his arms. He was the only man, the only person, who told me he loved me. I'm not sure that will come my way again."

I knew we were entering an area where once I would never have dared to go. It was hard to remember that less than a year before it had been difficult for me even to look at Betty. Today I felt positively tender toward her. I stretched to find a way to respond, but still it was less than I wanted to give.

"Betty, being loved is not sheer chance or fate. You can influence it—more than you think. You are much more available for love now than you were a few months ago. I can see, I can feel the difference. You look better, you relate better, you are so much more approachable and available now."

Betty was more open with her positive feelings toward me and shared long daydreams in which she became a physician or a psychologist and she and I worked together side by side on a research project. Her wish that I could have been her father led us into one final aspect of her grief that had always caused her much torment. Alongside her love for her father, she also had negative feelings: she felt ashamed of him, of his appearance (he was extremely obese), of his lack of ambition and education, of his ignorance of social amenities. As she said this, Betty broke down and sobbed. It was so hard to talk about this, she said, because she was so ashamed of being ashamed of her own father.

As I searched for a reply, I remembered something my first analyst, Olive Smith, said to me over thirty years before. (I remember it well, I think, because it was the only remotely personal—and the most helpful—thing she said in my six hundred hours with her.) I had been badly shaken by having expressed some monstrous feelings about my mother, and Olive Smith leaned over the couch and said gently, "That just seems to be the way we're built."

I cherished those words; and now, thirty years later, I passed along the gift and said them to Betty. The decades had eroded none of their restorative powers: she exhaled deeply, calmed herself, and sat back in her chair. I added that I knew personally how difficult it is for highly educated adults to relate to uneducated blue-collar parents.

Betty's year-and-a-half assignment in California was now drawing to a close. She did not want to stop therapy and asked her company to extend her time in California. When that failed, she considered searching for a job in California but ultimately decided to return to New York.

What a time to stop—in the midst of work on important issues and with Betty still camped outside the one-hundred-fifty-pound roadblock! At first I thought that the timing could not have been worse. Yet, in a more reflective moment, I realized that Betty may have plunged so deeply into therapy *because of*, not despite, our limited time frame. There is a long tradition in psychotherapy going back to Carl Rogers and, before him, to Otto Rank, which understood that a pre-set termination date often increases the efficiency of therapy. Had Betty not known that her time in therapy was limited, she might, for example, have taken far longer to achieve the inner resolve she needed to begin her weight loss.

Besides, it was by no means clear that we could have gone much further. In our last months of therapy, Betty seemed interested more in resolving the issues we had already opened than in uncovering new ones. When I recommended that she continue therapy in New York and offered her the name of a suitable therapist, she was noncommittal, stating that she wasn't sure whether she would continue, that maybe she had done enough.

There were other signs as well that Betty might go no further. Though not bingeing, she was no longer dieting. We agreed to concentrate on maintaining her new weight of one hundred sixty and, to that end, Betty bought a whole new wardrobe.

A dream illuminated this juncture in therapy:

> I dreamed that the painters were supposed to paint the outside trim on my house. They were soon all over the house. There was a man at every window with a spray gun. I got dressed quickly and tried to stop them. They were painting the whole outside of the house. There were wisps of smoke coming up all over the house from between the floorboards. I saw a painter with a stocking over his face spraying inside the house. I told him I just wanted the trim painted. He said he had orders to paint everything, inside and out. "What is the smoke?" I asked. He said it was bacteria and added they had been in the kitchen culturing deadly bacteria. I got scared and kept saying over and over, "I only wanted the trim painted."

At the onset of therapy, Betty had indeed wanted only the trim painted but had been drawn inexorably into reconstructive work on the deep interior of her house. Moreover, the painter-therapist had sprayed death—her father's death, her own death—into her house. Now she was saying she had gone far enough; it was time to stop.

As we neared our final session, I felt a mounting relief and exhilaration— as though I had gotten away with something. One of the axioms of psychotherapy is that the important feelings one has for another *always* get communicated through one channel or another—if not verbally, then nonverbally. For as long as I can remember, I have taught my students that if something big in a relationship is not being talked about (by either patient or therapist), then nothing else of importance will be discussed either.

Yet I had started therapy with intense negative feelings about Betty—feelings I had never discussed with her and that she had never recognized. Nevertheless, without doubt, we had discussed important issues. Without doubt, we had made progress in therapy. Had I disproven the catechism? Are there no "absolutes" in psychotherapy?

Our final three hours were devoted to work on Betty's distress at our impending separation. What she had feared at the very onset of treatment had come to pass: she had allowed herself to feel deeply about me and was now going to lose me. What was the point of having trusted me at all? It was as she had said at first: "No involvement, no separation."

I was not dismayed by the re-emergence of these old feelings. First, as termination approaches, patients are bound to regress temporarily. (*There* is an absolute.) Second, issues are never resolved once and for all in therapy. Instead, therapist and patient inevitably return again and again to adjust and to reinforce the learning—indeed, for this very reason, psychotherapy has often been dubbed "cyclotherapy."

I attempted to address Betty's despair, and her belief that once she left me all our work would come to naught, by reminding her that her growth resided neither in me nor in any outside object, but was a part of her, a part she would take with her. If, for example, she was able to trust and to reveal herself to me more than to anyone previously, then she contained within herself that experience as well as the ability to do it again. To drive my point home, I attempted, in our final session, to use myself as an example.

"It's the same with me, Betty. I'll miss our meetings. But I'm changed as a result of knowing you—"

She had been crying, her eyes downcast, but at my words she stopped sobbing and looked toward me, expectantly.

"And, even though we won't meet again, I'll still retain that change."

"What change?"

"Well, as I mentioned to you, I hadn't had much professional experience with . . . er . . . with the problem of obesity—" I noted Betty's eyes drop with disappointment and silently berated myself for being so impersonal.

"Well, what I mean is that I hadn't worked before with heavy patients, and I've gotten a new appreciation for the problems of—" I could see from her expression that she was sinking even deeper into disappointment. "What I mean is that my attitude about obesity has changed a lot. When we started I personally didn't feel comfortable with obese people—"

In unusually feisty terms, Betty interrupted me. "Ho! ho! ho! 'Didn't feel comfortable'—that's putting it mildly. Do you know that for the first six months you hardly ever looked at me? And in a whole year and a half you've never—not once—touched me? Not even for a handshake!"

My heart sank. My God, she's right! I *have* never touched her. I simply hadn't realized it. And I guess I didn't look at her very often, either. I hadn't expected her to notice!

I stammered, "You know, psychiatrists don't ordinarily touch their—"

"Let me interrupt you before you tell any more fibs and your nose gets longer and longer like Pinocchio." Betty seemed amused at my squirming. "I'll give you a hint. Remember, I'm in the same group with Carlos and we often chat after the group about you."

Uh-oh, I knew I was cornered now. I hadn't anticipated this. Carlos, with his incurable cancer, was so isolated and felt so shunned that I had decided to support him by going out of my way to touch him. I shook his hand before and after each hour and usually put my hand on his shoulder as he left the office. Once, when he learned about the spread of his cancer to his brain, I held him in my arms while he wept.

I didn't know what to say. I couldn't point out to Betty that Carlos was a special case, that he needed it, God knows she had needed it, too. I felt myself flushing. I saw I had no choice but to own up.

"Well, you're pointing out one of my blind spots! It is true—or, rather, was true—that, when we first began to meet, I was put off by your body."

"I know. I know. It wasn't too subtle."

"Tell me, Betty, knowing this—seeing that I didn't look at you or was uncomfortable with you—why did you stay? Why didn't you stop seeing me and find someone else? Plenty of other shrinks around." (Nothing like a question to get off the hot seat!)

"Well, I can think of at least two reasons. First, remember that I'm used to it. It's not like I expect anything more. Everyone treats me that way. People hate my looks. No one *ever* touches me. That's why I was surprised, remember, when my hairdresser massaged my scalp. And, even though you wouldn't look at me, you at least seemed interested in what I had to say—no, no, that's not right—you were interested in what I *could* or *might* say if I stopped being so jolly. Actually, that was helpful. Also, you didn't fall asleep. That was an improvement on Dr. Farber."

"You said there were two reasons."

"The second reason is that I could understand how you felt. You and I are very much alike—in one way, at least. Remember when you were pushing me to go to Overeaters Anonymous? To meet other obese people—make some friends, get some dates?"

"Yeah, I remember. You said you hated groups."

"Well, that's true. I do hate groups. But it wasn't the whole truth. The *real* reason is that I can't stand fat people. They turn my stomach. I don't want to be seen with them. So how can I get down on you for feeling the same way?"

We were both on the edge of our chairs when the clock said we had to finish. Our exchange had taken my breath away, and I hated to end. I didn't want to stop seeing Betty. I wanted to keep on talking to her, to keep on knowing her.

We got up to leave, and I offered her my hand, both hands.

"Oh no! Oh no, I want a hug! That's the only way you can redeem yourself."

When we embraced, I was surprised to find that I could get my arms all the way around her.

Editors' Introduction

Frederick S. Perls, known to all during his lifetime and after as "Fritz," was a genuine maverick, a man on the go, a lonely seeker, a genius. As was the case with many—and possibly all—other innovators in psychotherapy, the therapeutic system that he called "Gestalt Therapy" was in a sense an extension of himself. Fritz Perls was unconventional, emotional, and he existed in the moment—so too his system of therapy.

Perls was obsessed with time, particularly the here-and-now. He believed that the therapist had to go directly to the heart of the problem, confront it and even exaggerate it, and show that the therapist was always in control of both the problem and the situation.

The selection we present is the best short account of how Perls and Gestalt operate, but only longer readings will give the full flavor of this remarkable person and his methodology.

THE CASE OF JANE

Frederick S. Perls

The following transcripts are taken from audiotape recordings made at a Gestalt Therapy workshop....

Fritz: Now, I want you all to talk to your dreams, and let the dreams talk back—not the content, but as if the dreams were a thing. "Dreams, you are frightening me," "I don't want to know about you," or something, and let the dreams answer back. *(All talk to their dreams for several minutes)* ...

So, now I would like each one of you to play the role of their dreams, such as, "I only seldom come to you, and then only in little bits and pieces," or however you experience your dreams. I want you to *be* that dream. Reverse the role, so that you are the dream, and talk to the whole group, as if you were the dream talking to yourself.

Neville: I fool you, don't I, because I'm full of important facts about you, and I won't allow you to remember me. That annoys the hell out of you, doesn't it? Confuses you, and I get a big kick out of it when I depress you, and watch you kind of sink deeper and deeper as the day goes along. You wouldn't have any difficulty remembering me if you just concentrated on me a little. So I play hide-and-seek

Perls, F. S. (1969). *Gestalt Therapy Verbatim* (pp. 217–272). Lafayette. CA: Real People Press.

with you, and I kind of enjoy your discomfort with it. I fool you all. I play games with you and then elude you, so that I confuse you all . . . I make you see a different me, don't I? . . .

Glenn: I don't come on very clear, very often, because you don't seem to understand me very well. I would put on many spectaculars, if you paid more attention, but as it is, you pay little attention to me and I do kind of a shoddy job for you.

Raymond: I'm sneaky. You know I'm here but I won't let you know what's going on.

Blair: I'm going to mystify you. I'm going to be symbolic, impenetrable . . . keep you confused . . . unclear.

Bob: I'm all enclosed in mist, like that mountain over there. Even if the mist left, you'd have a hard time getting things out of me.

Frank: You shouldn't be ashamed of me. You should come out and meet me more. I feel that I can help you. I'd like to meet you more.

Lily: I can see, and hear, and feel and talk, and touch, and do everything you want to do.

Jane: I'm merry, exciting, interesting, I'm going to really turn you on, and then when we get to the end, I'm going to turn you off. And you're not going to get to see the end. And then you'll go around pouting all day, because you didn't get to the end.

Sally: It's not us that disturb your sleep. If we could find a chance when you would listen to us, and then after this, we'd be clear, like lightning, it's very shocking. We're going to shock you, but you'll shake it off in a little while, and when you wake up, going about the chores of the day you'll take us with you. But if we keep doing this, over and over again, finally, you'll find that nothing goes right. You'll try to hide from all your faults, all your fears, but we will be there to upset you.

Abe: Be good enough to yourself to remember that we've given you some very fine moments, often of meaning, sometimes power. Recently we've given you horror—frightening horror, and also recently you've turned away from us.

Jan: I don't think you really want to remember me, or know me. I don't feel you want to enjoy me. Every time I do let myself get close to you, you always say, "Well, I'm too tired to write you down or pay attention to you. Maybe in the morning I'll do it." I feel you're still trying to avoid me.

Fergus: I'm very weird. I'm the only honest, the only spontaneous part of you, the only free part of you.

Tony: I feel very sorry for you.

Nancy: I'm not going to give you the pleasure of knowing me, or the enjoyment of feeling grown up.

Daniel: You know that I'm made of all kinds of bits and pieces left unfinished during the day, and it's better that I have them, than just forget about them. Besides, sometimes I'm very beautiful and very meaningful, and you know that I'm doing much good for you, especially when you look at me carefully.

Steve: I am a multicolored cloak that sweeps down and carries you off, gives you power.

Clair: You're just playing games, and I am really all. And you can wait for me forever.

Dick: You're very much aware of my existence, but most of the time you ignore me.

Teddy: I am a very creative, interesting situation. Plots, juxtapositions, that you'd never think of in your waking life. I'm much more creative, I'm much more frightening, and I appear to you not as pictures. You know what's going on when I'm there; afterwards you forget. But I'm not in movies; I'm a kind of knowing. You would like to see me in pictures but I don't appear.

June: I am going to make you *miserable*, I am going to *destroy* you, I am going to *encompass* you, and push you *under*, and make you feel as if you can't breathe. And I'm going to *stay* here and *sit* on you! ...

Fritz: Well, possibly you noticed something very interesting for quite a few of you, how the dream as such symbolizes your hidden self. I would like you to work with that in the groups, to more and more act out *being* that thing that you just imagined was a dream. I don't know how much those who have played their dreams realize how much of themselves came through, but I'm pretty sure that most of you can easily recognize that this is the part of you that you don't like to bring forth. If you take *literally* what I asked you to do, to play your dream as if the dream was a person, these instructions would be complete nonsense. How can you be your dream? And then as you express it, finally it became so real. You really felt this is the person here. Sometimes there is a surprise, if this person had managed to wear his mask with grace and confidence. For instance, you noticed how much came out of June. I don't know how many of you have seen this tremendous destructive power of hers. It came out very clearly. Very beautiful.

JANE 1

Jane: Ah, in my dream I'm going home to visit my mother and my family ... and I'm dr—I'm driving from Big Sur to—to my mother's house ...

Fritz: What's going on right now?

J: It's really scary up here. I didn't know it would be half as scary. [*This workshop session was held in a large room, with another seminar group of thirty people observing.*]

F: Close your eyes ... and stay with your scariness ... How do you experience scariness?

J: Shakiness in my upper chest, *(Sighs)* fluttering in my breathing. Ah, my—

my right leg is shaking. My left leg—now my left leg's shaking. If I keep my eyes closed long enough my arms are going to start shaking.

F: At what moment did this scariness come up?

J: I looked out there. *(Laughter)*

F: So look again. Talk to those people there. "You make me scared" or whatever.

J: Well, it's not so bad now. I'm picking and choosing.

F: So whom do you pick and choose?

J: Oh, Mary Ellen, and Alison. John. I skipped over a whole bunch of faces.

F: Now let's call your father and mother into the audience.

J: I wouldn't look at them.

F: Say this to them.

J: Ah, wherever you're sitting I'm not going to look at you . . . because I don't—You want me to explain it? Oh, no. *(Laughter)* OK, I'm not going to look at you, Mom and Dad.

F: What do you experience when you *don't* look at them?

J: More anxiety. When I tell you the dream it's like—it's just the same.

F: OK, tell me the dream.

J: OK, I'm going home to see my mother and father, and I'm anxious the whole time when I'm driving home. And I—there's a long flight of steps up to the house—there's about sixty steps. And in the dream I get more and more afraid each step I take. So I open the door and the house is very dark. And I call to my mother—Oh, I notice that all the cars are there, so they're home. I call to my mother and there's no answer. I call to my father and there's no answer. I call the children and there's no answer. So I—it's a very, very big house and so I go from room to room to look for them and I—I get into the bedroom and my mother and father are in bed but they're, they're just, they're not my—they're skeletons. They don't have any skin. They're not, they don't talk . . . they don't say anything. And I shake—This dream happens over and over and lately I've gotten brave enough to shake them. But . . .

F: In the dream you can play the part . . . What happens when you shake them?

J: Ah, nothing. I mean I—I just feel a skeleton—a skeleton. And I yell really loud in the dream to them both. I tell them to wake up. And they don't wake up. They're just skeletons.

F: Good. Let's start all over again. You're entering the house, yah?

J: OK. I'm entering the house and I first—I first walk into the kitchen and it's very dark, and it doesn't smell like I remember it. It smells musty, like it hadn't been cleaned in a long time. And I don't hear any noises. It's usually very noisy—a lot of children noises. And I don't hear any noises. Then I go to what used to be my bedroom, and there's nobody there, and everything is clean. Everything is neat and everything is untouched.

F: Let's have an encounter between the kitchen of your dream and your bedroom.

J: The kitchen and the bedroom. OK. I'm the kitchen, and—I don't smell the way I usually smell. I usually smell of food. I usually smell of people.

And now I smell of dust and cobwebs. I'm usually not very neat but now I'm very, very neat. Everything is put away. Nobody's inside of me.

F: Now play the bedroom.

J: Bedroom . . . I'm very—I'm neat. . . . I don't know how to encounter the kitchen.

F: Just boast about what you are.

J: Well, I'm as neat as you are. I'm very neat, too. But I smell bad like you do, and I don't smell like perfume, and I don't smell like people. I just smell like dust. Only there's no dust on my floor. I'm very neat and I'm very clean. But I don't smell good and I don't feel good like I usually feel. And I know when Jane comes inside of me she feels bad when I'm so neat and there's no one inside of me. And she comes inside of me like she comes inside of you in the dream. And she's very scared. And we're very—I'm very hollow. I'm very hollow. When you make a sound inside of me it echoes. That's how it feels in the dream.

F: Now be the kitchen again . . .

J: I'm very hollow, too—I, ooh . . .

F: Yah? What happened?

J: I feel empty.

F: You feel the emptiness now. /J: Yeah./ Stay with the emptiness.

J: OK, I . . . don't feel it there now. Wait. I lost it. I'm very, you know, I—

F: Stay with what you experience now.

J: I have the anxious feeling again.

F: When you become the kitchen. Yah?

J: Yeah. I'm the kitchen . . . And there's no fresh air inside of me. There's no good—I'm supposed to be encountering the bedroom. Hmmm. Ohhh . . .

F: Just tell all this to the bedroom.

J: I'm as musty as you are. And it's very incongruous because I'm very clean and spotless. And Jane's mother usually doesn't keep me so neat. She's usually too busy to keep me so neat. Something's wrong with me. I'm not getting the kind of attention that I usually get. I'm dead. I'm a dead kitchen.

F: Say this again.

J: I'm dead. /F: Again./ I'm dead.

F: How do you experience being dead? . . .

J: Well, it doesn't feel bad . . .

F: Now stay as you are and be aware of your right and left hand. What are they doing?

J: My right hand is shaking and it's stretched out. And the left hand is clenched very tight and my fingernails are pushing into the palm of my hand.

F: What does your right hand want to do?

J: It's OK the way it is. I think it wants not to shake.

F: Besides this, anything else? Does it want to stop? To reach? I can't read your right hand. Continue the movement. (*Jane makes reaching move-*

ments with right hand.) You want to reach out. Good. And what does your left hand want to do? . . .

J: My left hand wants to hold back. It's holding tight. My right hand feels good.

F: So change. Let the left hand do now what the right hand does, and vice versa. Reach out with your left hand.

J: No   My left hand doesn't want to reach out.

F: What's the difficulty in reaching out with your left hand?

J: It feels much different, and my right hand isn't clenched: it's limp. I can *do* it. I can *do* it, yet—

F: This would be artificial. /J: Yeah./ Now reach out with your left hand again . . . *(Softly)* Reach out to me . . . *(Jane reaches out . . . sighs.)* . . . Now what happened?

J: It started to shake . . . and I stopped it.

F: Now have an encounter between your right hand and left hand as it was originally, "I am holding back and you are reaching out."

J: I'm the right hand and I'm reaching out. I'm free. I'm very relaxed, and even when I shake, it doesn't feel bad. I'm shaking now and I don't feel bad . . . Ah, I'm the left hand and I don't reach out. I make a fist. And now my fingernails are long so when I do it I hurt myself when I make a fist . . . Ohh . . .

F: Yah, what happened?

J: I hurt myself.

F: I want to tell you something that is usually the case. I don't know whether it will be the case with you. The right hand is usually the male part of a person and the left side is the female part. The right side is the aggressive, active, outgoing part and the left side is the sensitive, receptive, open part. Now try this on for size to see if it might fit with you.

J: OK. The loudmouth can come out, you know. /F: Yah./ But the soft part is . . . not so easy . . .

F: OK. Enter the house once more and have an encounter with what you encounter—namely, silence.

J: Encounter with silence. /F: Silence, yah./ Be the silence?

F: No, no. You enter the house and all that you meet is silence. Right?

J: Yes. You annoy me. The silence annoys me. I don't like it.

F: Say this to silence.

J: I am. He's sitting right there. You annoy me. I don't like you. I don't hear much in you and when I do, I don't like it.

F: What does silence answer?

J: Well, I have never had a chance to come around much because when you were young there were many children around you all the time and your parents are both loud, and you're loud, and you really don't know much about me. And I think maybe you're afraid of me. Could you be afraid of me?

   Now let's try that one. Yeah. I don't feel afraid now, but I could be afraid of you.

F: So enter the house once more and again meet silence. Go back to the dream.

J: OK. I'm in the house and it's very silent and I don't like it. I don't like that it's quiet. I want to hear noises, I want to hear noises in the kitchen and noises in the bedroom and I want to hear children, *(Voice begins to break.)* I want to hear my mother and father laughing and talking, I—

F: Say this to them.

J: I want to hear you, laughing and talking. I want to hear the children. I miss you. *(Begins to cry.)* I can't let go of you . . . I want to hear you. I want to hear you . . . and I want to hear you.

F: OK, let's now reverse the dream. Let them talk. Resurrect them.

J: Resurrect them. /F: Yah./ I have them there.

F: You say you try to shake them. They are only skeletons. /J: *(Fearfully)* Ohhh./ I want you to be successful.

J: You want me to encounter—I'm confused. *(Has stopped crying.)*

F: You are in the bedroom. Right? /J: Yeah./ Your parents are skeletons./J: Uh-huh./Skeletons usually don't talk. At best they shake and rattle. /J: Yeah./ I want you to resurrect them.

J: To make them alive.

F: Make them alive. So far you say you would blot them out. That's what you're doing in the dream.

J: I shake them in the dream. I take them and I shake them.

F: Talk to them.

J: Wake up! /F: Again./
(Loudly) Wake up! /F: Again./
(Loudly) Wake up! /F: Again./
(Loudly) Wake up! . . . And . . . *(Loudly, almost crying)* You can't hear me! Why can't you hear me? . . . *(Sighs)* And they don't answer. They don't say anything.

F: Come. Be phony. Invent them. Resurrect them. Let's have a phony game.

J: OK. We don't know why we can't hear you. We don't know. We don't know that we even don't want to hear you. We're just skeletons. Or are we still? No . . . We don't know why we can't hear you. We don't know why we're like this. We don't know why you found us like this. *(Crying)* Maybe if you never went away, maybe if you never went away, this wouldn't have happened. It feels right. That's what they would say. That's what they would say.

F: OK. Take your seat again . . .

J: I feel like I want to tell you that I went away too soon and I really can't go all the way away. *(Almost crying)*

F: Tell them that you still need them.

J: I still need you.

F: Tell them in more detail what you need.

J: I still need my mother to hold me.

F: Tell this to her.

J: I still need you to hold me. *(Crying)* I want to be a little girl, sometimes— forget the "sometimes."

F: You're not talking to her yet.

J: *(Sobbing)* OK. Mother, Mother, you think I'm very grown up ... And I think I'm very grown up. But there's a part of me that isn't away from you and I can't, I can't let go of.

F: You see how this is a continuation of our last session? You started out as the toughy, the brazen girl, and the softness came out? Now you begin to accept that you have soft needs ... So be your mother.

J: *(Diffidently)* Well, you know you can come back any time you want, Jane. But it's not going to be quite the same because I have other little girls to take care of. I have your sisters to take care of and they're little girls, and you're a big girl and you can take care of yourself now. And I'm glad you're so grown up. I'm glad you're so smart ... Anyway, I don't know how to talk to you any more. I mean I know—I respect you but I don't understand you half the time ... *(Sobbing)* and, and ...

F: What happened right now? What happened when you stopped?

J: I felt a pain in my stomach. I felt frustrated.

F: Tell Jane that.

J: Jane, I—*(Crying)* I have a pain in my stomach. I feel frustrated; because I don't understand you because you do such funny things; because you went away when you were so young and you never really came back. And you ran away from me and I loved you and I wanted you to come back and you wouldn't come back. And now you want to come back and it's too late.

F: Play Jane again.

J: *(Not crying)* But I still need you. I want to sit on your lap. Nobody else can give me what you have. I still need a mother. *(Crying)* ... I can't believe it. I just can't believe what I'm saying. I mean I can agree with what I'm saying but—

F: OK, let's interrupt. You woke up anyhow. Go back to the group. How do you experience us? Can you tell the group that you need a mother?

J: Hmm. *(Laughter) (Jane laughs.)* I can tell you, Fritz. Ah, no, there's too many.

F: All right, now let's see whether we can't get these things together. Now have an encounter between your baby dependence and brazenness. / J: OK./ Those are your two poles.

J: *(As brazenness)* You really are a punk. You sound just like a punk. You've been around. You've been around for a long time. You've learned a lot of things. You know how to be on your own. What the fuck's the matter with you? What are you crying about?

Well. I like to be helpless sometimes, Jane, and I know you don't like it. I know you don't put up with it very often. But sometimes it just comes out. Like I can't work with Fritz without it coming out. I can hide it ... for a long time, but ... if you don't own up to me I'm gonna really, I'm gonna keep coming out and maybe you'll never grow up.

F: Say this again.

J: I'm gonna keep coming out and maybe you'll never grow up.

F: Say it very spitefully.

J: I'm gonna *keep* coming out and maybe you'll *never* grow up . . .

F: OK, be the brazenness again.

J: *(Sighs)* Well I've tried stomping on you and hiding you and shoving you in corners and making everybody believe that you don't exist. What more do you want me to do with you? What do you want from me? . . .
    I want you to listen to me . . .

F: Is brazen Jane willing to listen?

J: I just started to listen . . . OK, I'm gonna give you a chance. I feel like if I give you a chance . . . *(Right hand makes a threatening fist.)*

F: Yah? Yah?—No no no, don't—don't hide it. Come out. You don't give her a chance, you give her a threat.

J: Yeah, I know. That's what I do.

F: Yah, yah . . . Give her both. Give her a threat and give her a chance.

J: OK. I'll give you a chance. *(Right hand beckons.)*

F: Ahah, this means, "Come to me."

J: Yeah. Let's get together. Let's try to get together and see what we can do . . . But I'm warning you, *(Laughter)* if you keep making a fool of me the way you do, Jane, with your crying and your dependency . . . you're never gonna let me grow up. *(Thoughtfully)* I'm never gonna let you—Hm. *(Laughter)* Well.

F: Be the other Jane again.

J: Well, I don't want to grow up—this part of—I don't want to grow up. I want to stay the way I am.

F: Say this again.

J: I want to stay the way I am.

F: "I don't want to grow up."

J: I don't wanna grow up. /F: Again./
    I don't wanna grow up. /F: Louder./
    I don't wanna grow up. /F: Louder./
    I don't wanna grow up. *(Voice begins to break.)* /F: Louder./
    I don't wanna grow up!

F: Say it with your whole body.

J: *(Crying)* I don't *wanna* grow up! I don't wanna grow up. I'm tired of growing up. *(Crying)* It's too *fucking hard!* . . . *(Sighs)*

F: Now be brazen Jane again.

J: Sure it's hard. I know it's hard. I can do it. I can do anything. I go around proving it all the time. What's the matter with you? You're always behind me. You have to catch up with me . . . Come and catch up with me . . .
    OK, I'll catch up with you, Jane, but you have to help me.

F: Tell her how she can help you.

J: You have to allow me to exist without threatening me, without punishing me.

F: Say this again.

J: *(Almost crying)* You have to allow me to exist without threatening me and punishing me.

F: Can you say this without tears?

J: (*Calmly*) You have to allow me to exist without threatening me, and without punishing me.

F: Say this also to the group—the same sentence . . .

J: You have to allow me to exist without threatening me and without punishing me.

F: Say this also to Raymond [her fiancé].

J: (*Crying*) You have to allow me to exist without threatening me . . . you know that . . .

F: Got it?

J: Yes . . .

F: OK.

JANE 11

Jane: I had a dream last night that I'd like to work on. I'm at this carnival, and it's very noisy and it's very hectic. . . . And I'm going through the crowd and I'm bumping into people and they're bumping into me and I'm not having a good time. And I'm holding onto my little brother's hand, so he won't get lost. And we're going through the crowd, and he says he wants to go into—a—uh—this carnival ride where people get in these little seats and go through a tunnel. And—uh—

Fritz: Back to the "and" bit. You use "and, and, and," as if you are afraid to let events stand for themselves.

J: Yeah. So, we don't have any money—we don't have any money to get into the ride. I take a watch off my wrist, I give it to my brother, and I ask him to ask the ticket man if he'll take the watch for both of us. He comes back and tells me the ticket man won't take the watch, so we're gonna sneak in.

F: Let's start the whole dream all over. This time you're not dreaming it; your brother is dreaming it.

J: (*More boisterous*) Well, we're at this carnival and it's real fun except my sister's got hold of my hand. She's constricting me at the wrist so she won't lose me. She's got me—she's holding me very tightly on my wrist, and I wanna—I want her to let go of me. I don't really care if I get lost. But she does, so I let her hold onto my wrist. There's a ride I wanna go on. I don't care if she goes with me or not, but I know she won't let me go unless she can go too, unless she can be with me. She doesn't . . . she doesn't wanna be by herself . . . We don't have any money to get on—to get on the ride, and she gives me her watch. I'm really happy that—that we have a way of getting in. I go up to the ticket man and it doesn't work, but I really wanna go on the ride.

F: Say this again.

J: I really wanna go on the ride. /F: Again./

I really wanna go on the ride. /F: Again./

(*Louder*) I really wanna go on the ride!

F: I don't believe you.

J: Ohh . . . *I* don't, my brother does. (*Laughs*) Umm. I really want to go on that ride, Jane. I really want to go . . . Whether you go with me or not, I wanna go. It's *fun*. So gimme your watch . . . So she gives me her watch. The ticket man says no. Jane! We're gonna sneak in. She doesn't want to. Well, then I'm going to sneak in. Ohh. You don't want to go without me, so you'll sneak in, too. OK. So we'll sneak in. Now instead of you taking *my* hand, I'm gonna take your hand, 'cause I'm gonna help you sneak in. So hold on, and go under the gate, I'm very small, I'm very young—

F: Interrupt it, now. Close your eyes, experience your hands.

J: Hm. My right hand's stiff, very stiff. It's pointing. My left hand is shaking and it's—it's open. It's—um—both my hands are shaking. Both hands are shaking. And my knees and my ankles feel stiff. And I don't feel a heaviness in my chest like I usually do. But I feel heavy in the chair, and my right hand is pointing. And now—

F: I noticed that when you pulled, the right hand is the brother, the left hand is Jane—

J: Hm . . . I forgot where I was. I'm Jane. Oh, we're gonna—yeah—I'm gonna sneak in. So I'm very scared, but I'm more afraid of losing him than of sneaking in and getting caught, so I take his hand and—I take his hand—

F: Wait a moment. What's your brother's name?

J: Paul.

F: *Paul* is still dreaming the dream.

J: Oh. OK. So take my hand. I know how afraid you are of doing things like this, but I also know that you're *so* afraid that I'll get lost, so I can get you to sneak in with me, 'cause I want to sneak in to this ride. And I love to have fun, and I'm gonna have fun whether you're afraid of it or not. So we go—we go under the railing, and we go between people's legs, in and out, past the ticket man—

F: I don't believe you. You are not in the dream. Your voice goes Ahhhh-hhrrrrr . . .

J: My legs are aching and my upper leg's kind of. . . . I have Jane by the hand. We're going—we're going (*voice becomes more expressive*) We're going between the legs of all the people and we're—we're crawling, and (*Bright, happy*) I like it, I like doing this, and she's afraid. (*Sigh*) And we're gonna—we're gonna go up to the door, and we're gonna go through the door, and she's *pulling* me, and I'm *pulling* her. I'm trying to pull her through, and she won't come with me. So I grab her wrist like she had my wrist and I pull her and I'm littler than her, but I can pull her through, and she's on her hands and knees and I'm pulling her along. And we go through—we go through the door, and I hop on the ride, and I leave her standing there, and the little clod goes in the door—she doesn't—she loses me. Once I got in there, I could go on the ride . . .

F: Now say good-bye to Jane.

J: Good-bye, Jane!. . . I'm—I didn't want to say good-bye to her. I'd rather have fun. . . . Jane's standing back there looking like a jerk. She's standing there with her legs shaking, and I don't give a shit. I really don't give a shit. It's easy to say good-bye to her. *(Laughs)* She's standing there like some fool, and she's calling me, she's calling my name. She looks frantic, she looks like she's in a panic. *(Disinterested)* But I'd rather have fun. She'll be all right.

F: OK. Now change roles again. Be Jane again.

J: The dream is very long.

F: There is so much already there.

J: Be Jane again. OK. I'm at the carnival with my brother and we're going through—I really *don't* think I want to be here, and—

F: Tell us. Tell us your position . . .

J: What I just said?

F: Your whole position. The situation is open, right? Very clear. There is your brother, and there is you. You want to hold onto him; he wants to be free.

J: Well I think—I think he's younger than me, and he *is* younger than me and I don't want him—to do what—what I did. I wanna *(Quietly and hesitantly)* protect him or something. I hold onto him. I think I—I think I keep trying to do what my mother can't do. . . . It's insane. It's really insane. . . . I talk to him. I tell him. Paul, stop taking drugs, and stop roaming around. *(Cries)* Stop trying to be so free, because you're gonna regret it. When you're twenty, you'll regret it.

　　Now I want to take his side. He'd say, how can you tell me not to do exactly what you do?—what you did when you were sixteen and seventeen. How can you say that? That's not fair. I *like* what I'm doing. Leave me alone! You're—you're really a bitch. You're just like my mother, you're such a bitch. How can you be such a bitch when you already did this? . . . *(Sighs)*

　　I . . . I'm trying to take care of you. I'm trying to take care of you, and I know I can't—*(Cries)* I know I have to let go of you, but I keep trying in my dreams, to hold onto you, and to keep you safe, because it's so dangerous what you're doing! . . . You're gonna get all fucked up. *(Cries)*

　　But you're not all fucked up! So look at you! You've changed, you've really changed. You don't lie any more. Much. *(Laughter)* You don't take drugs any more, like you used to. I'll change that. I just have to do what I have to do. You don't trust me, do you? You're like my mother, you don't trust me. You don't think I'm strong.

F: OK. Jane, I think you can work this out on your own. I want to do something else right now. I want to start with the beginning. Always look at the beginning of the dream. Notice where a dream is taking place, whether you are in a car, whether the dream is taking place in a motel, or nature, or in an apartment building. This always gives you immediately the impression of the existential background. Now you start your dream out, "Life is a carnival." Now give us a speech about life as a carnival.

J: Life—life is a carnival. You go on this trip, and you get off. You go on that trip, and you get off. And then you bump into all kinds of people, you bump into *all kinds* of people, and some of them you look at, and some of them you don't look at, and some of them irritate you, and really bump you, and others don't, others are kind to you. And you win things at the carnival. You win presents . . . And some rides—most all the rides, the trips, are scary. But they're fun. They're fun and they're scary. It's very crowded, and there are lots of people—lots and lots of faces. . . . And in the dream, I'm—I'm holding onto somebody in the carnival, and he wants to go on all the trips.

JANE III

Jane: The dream I started on, the last time I worked, I never finished it, and I think the last part is as important as the first part. Where I left off, I was in the Tunnel of Love—

Fritz: What are you picking on? *(Jane has been scratching her leg.)*

J: Hmm. *(Clears throat)* . . . I'm just sitting here, for a minute, so I can really be here. It's hard to stay with this feeling, and talk at the same time. . . . Now I'm in the intermediate zone, and I'm—I'm thinking about two things: Should I work on the dream, or should I work on the picking thing, because that's something I do a lot. I pick my face, and . . . I'll go back to the dream. I'm in the Tunnel of Love, and my brother's gone in the—somewhere—and to the left of me, there's a big room and it's painted the color of—the color that my schoolrooms used to be painted, kind of a drab green, and to the left of me there are bleachers. I look over and there are all people sitting there. It looks as though they are waiting to get on the ride. There's a big crowd around one person, Raymond [her fiancé]. He's talking to them and he's explaining something to them and they're all listening to him. And he's moving his finger like this, and making gestures. I'm surprised to see him. I go up to him, and it's very obvious that he doesn't want to talk to me. He's interested in being with all these people, entertaining all these people. So I tell him that I'll wait for him. I sit three—three bleachers up and look down, and watch this going on. I get irritated and I'm—pissed off, so I say, "Raymond, I'm leaving. I'm not gonna wait for you any more." I walk outside the door—I stand outside the door for awhile—I get anxious. I can feel anxious in my dream. I feel anxious now, because I don't really want to be out here. I want to be inside, with Raymond. So I'm going inside. I go back through the door—

F: Are you telling us a dream, or are you doing a job?

J: Am I telling a dream—

F: Or are you doing a job?

J: I'm telling a dream, but it's still—I'm not telling a dream.

F: Hm. Definitely not.

J: I'm doing a job.

F: I gave you only the two alternatives.

J: I can't say that I'm really aware of what I'm doing. Except physically. I'm aware of what's happening physically to me but—I don't really know what I'm doing. I'm not asking you to tell me what I'm doing . . . just saying I don't know.

F: I noticed one thing: When you come up to the hot seat, you stop playing the silly goose.

J: Hm. I get frightened, when I'm up here.

F: You get dead.

J: Whew . . . If I close my eyes and go into my body, I know I'm not dead. If I open my eyes and "do that job," then I'm dead. . . . I'm in the intermediate zone now, I'm wondering whether or not I'm dead. I notice that my legs are cold and my feet are cold. My hands are cold. I feel—I feel strange. . . . I'm in the middle, now. I'm—I'm neither with my body nor with the group. I notice that my attention is concentrated on that little matchbox on the floor.

F: OK. Have an encounter with the matchbox.

J: Right now, I'm taking a break from looking at you, 'cause it's—it's a—'cause I don't know what's going on. and I don't know what I'm doing. I don't even know if I'm telling the truth.

F: What does the matchbox answer?

J: I don't care if you tell the truth or not. It doesn't matter to me. I'm just a matchbox.

F: Let's try this for size. Tell us, "I'm just a matchbox."

J: I'm just a matchbox. And I feel silly saying that. I feel, kind of dumb, being a matchbox.

F: Uhhm.

J: A little bit useful, but not very useful. There's a million like me. And you can look at me, and you can like me, and then when I'm all used up, you can throw me away. I never liked being a matchbox. . . . I don't—I don't know if that's the truth, when I say I don't know what I'm doing. I know there's one part of me that knows what I'm doing. And I feel suspended, I feel—steady. I don't feel relaxed. Now I'm trying to understand why in the two seconds it takes me to move from the group to the hot seat, my whole—my whole *persona* changes. . . . Maybe because of—I want to talk to the Jane in *that* chair.

She would be saying, (*With authority*) well, you know where you're at. You're playing dumb. You're playing stupid. You're doing this, and you're doing that, and you're sucking people in, and you're—(*Louder*) not telling the truth! and you're stuck, and dead . . .

And when I'm here, I immediately—the Jane here would say, (*Small, quivering voice*) well, that's—I feel on the defensive in this chair right now. I feel defensive. I feel like for some reason I have to defend myself. And I know it's not true. . . . So who's picking on you? It's *that* Jane over there that's picking on me.

F: Yah.

J: She's saying . . . She's saying (*Briskly*) now when you get in the chair, you have to be in the here and now, you have to do it *right*, you have to be turned on, you have to know everything—

F: "You have to do your job."

J: You have to do your job, and you have to do it *right*. And you have to— On top of all that, you have to become totally self-actualized, and you have to get rid of all your hang-ups, and along with that—it's not—it's not mandatory that you do this, but it's nice if you can be entertaining along the way, while you're doing all that. Try to spice it up a little bit, so that people won't get bored and go to sleep, because that makes you anxious. And you have to *know* why you're in the chair. You can't just go here and not know why you're there. You have to know *everything*, Jane.

You really make it hard for me. You really make it hard. You're really putting a lot of demands on me. . . . I don't know everything. And that's hard to say. I don't know everything, and on top of that, I don't know what I'm doing half the time. . . . I don't know—I don't know if that's the truth or not. I don't even know if that's a lie.

F: So be your top-dog again.

J: Is that—

F: Your top dog. That's the famous top dog. The righteous top dog. This is where your power is.

J: Yeah. Well—uh—I'm your top dog. You can't live without me. I'm the one that—I keep you noticed, Jane. I keep you noticed. If it weren't for me, nobody would notice you. So you'd better be a little more grateful that I exist.

Well, I don't want to be noticed, *you* do. You want to be noticed. I don't want to be noticed. I don't want . . . I don't really want to be noticed, as much as you do.

F: I would like you to attack the righteous side of that top dog.

J: Attack—the righteous side.

F: The top dog is always righteous. Top dog *knows* what you've got to do, has all the right to criticize, and so on. The top dog nags, picks, puts you on the defensive.

J: Y e a h . . . You're a bitch! You're like my mother. You know what's good for me. You—you make life *hard* for me. You tell me to do things. You tell me to be—*real*. You tell me to be self-actualized. You tell me to—uh, tell the truth.

F: Now please don't change what your hands are doing, but tell us what's going on in your hands.

J: My left hand . . .

F: Let them talk to each other.

J: My left hand. I'm shaking, and I'm in a fist, straining forward, and [*Voice begins to break*] that's kind of—the fist is very tight, pushing—pushing my fingernails into my hand. It doesn't feel good, but I do it all the time. I feel tight.

F: And the right hand?

J: I'm holding you back around the wrist.

F: Tell it why you hold back.

J: If I let go you're—then you're gonna hit something. I don't know what you're gonna hit, but I have to—I have to hold you back 'cause you can't do that. Can't go around hitting things.

F: Now hit your top dog.

J: *(Short harsh yell)* Aaaarkh! Aarkkh!

F: Now talk to your top dog. "Stop nagging—"

J: *(Loud, pained)* Leave me alone! /F: Yah, again./ Leave me alone! / F: Again./ *(Screaming it and crying)* Leave me alone! /F: Again./ *(She screams it, a real blast.)* LEAVE ME ALONE! I DON'T HAVE TO DO WHAT YOU SAY! *(Still crying)* I don't have to be that good! . . . I don't have to be in this chair! I don't *have* to. You make me. You make me come here! *(Screams)* Aarkkh! You make me pick my face, *(Crying)* that's what *you* do. *(Screams and cries)* Aaarkkh! I'd like to kill you.

F: Say this again.

J: I'd like to kill you. /F: Again./
I'd like to *kill* you.

F: Can you squash it in your left hand?

J: It's as big as me . . . I'm strangling it.

F: OK. Say this, "I'm strangling—"

J: *(Quietly)* I'm gonna strangle you . . . take your neck. Grrrummn. *(Fritz gives her a pillow which she strangles while making noises.)* Arrghh. Unghhh. How do you like that! *(Sounds of choked-off cries and screams)*

F: Make more noises.

J: Hrugghhh! Aachh! Arrgrughhh! *(She continues to pound pillow, cry and scream.)*

F: OK. Relax, close your eyes . . . *(Long silence)* *(Softly)* OK. Come back to us. Are you ready? . . . Now be that top dog again. . . .

J: *(Faintly)* You shouldn't have done that. I'm gonna punish you for that . . . I'm gonna punish you for that, Jane. You'll be sorry you did that. Better watch out.

F: Now talk like this to each one of us. . . . Be vindictive with each one of us. Pick out something we have done. . . . Start with me. As this top dog, for what are you going to punish me?

J: I'm gonna punish you for making me feel so stupid.

F: How are you going to punish me?

J: *(Promptly)* By being stupid . . . Even stupider than I am.

F: OK. Do this some more.

J: Raymond, I'm gonna punish you for being so dumb. I'll make you feel like an ass. . . . I'll make you think I'm smarter than you are, and you'll feel dumber and I'll feel smart. . . . I'm really scared. I shouldn't be doing this. *(Cries)* It isn't nice.

F: Say this to him. Turn it around, "You should not—"

J: You sh—you shouldn't—you shouldn't—you shouldn't be doing—hooo—you should be doing—you shouldn't be so dumb. You shouldn't play so dumb. Because it isn't nice.

F: You're doing a job again.

J: Yeah, I know. I don't wanna do it. *(Crying)* I—I know how I punish you. *(Sigh)* I'll punish you by being helpless.

Raymond: What are you punishing me for?

J: I'll punish you for loving me. That's what I'll punish you for. I'll make it *hard* for you to love me. I won't let you know if I'm coming or going.

F: "How can you be so low as to love somebody like me?" Yah?

J: I do that.

F: I know. How can you love a matchbox? . . .

J: Fergus, I'm gonna punish you for being so slow—in your body, but so quick in your mind. The way I'm gonna do that—I'm gonna excite you, try to excite you, and it's the truth. I'll punish you for being sexually inhibited. I'll make you think I'm very sexy. I'll make you feel bad around me . . . And I'll punish you for pretending to know more than you do.

F: What do you experience when you are meting out the punishment?

J: *(More alert, alive)* It's a very strange experience. I don't know that I've ever had it before, for such a long time. It's kind of—it's a feeling I used to get when I—When I got back at my brothers for being mean to me. I'd just grit my teeth and think of the *worst* thing I could do—and kind of enjoy it.

F: Yah. This is my impression; you didn't enjoy this here.

J: Mm.

F: OK. Go back and be the top dog again, and *enjoy* punishing Jane—pick on her, torture her.

J: You're the only one I enjoy punishing . . . When you're too loud—when you're too loud, I'll punish you for being too loud. *(No sound of enjoyment)* When you're not loud enough, I'll tell you that you're too inhibited. When you dance too much—when you dance too much, I'll tell you that you're trying to sexually arouse people. When you don't dance enough, I'll tell you that you're dead.

F: Can you tell Jane, "I'm driving you crazy"?

J: *(Cries)* I'm driving you crazy. /F: Again./
I'm driving you crazy. /F: Again./
I'm driving you *crazy* . . . I used to drive everybody else crazy, and now I'm driving you crazy . . . *(Voice drops, becomes very faint)* But it's for your own good. That's what my mother would say. "For your own good." I'll

make you feel *guilty* when you've done bad things, so you won't do it again. And I'll—I'll pat you on the back when you do something good, so you'll remember to do it again. And I'll keep you out of the moment. I'll—I'll keep you planning—and I'll keep you programmed, and I won't let you live—in the moment. I won't let you enjoy your life.

F: I would like you to use this: "I am relentless."

J: I—I *am* relentless. /F: Again./
I am relentless. I'll do anything—especially if somebody dares me to do something. Then I've gotta tell you to do it, Jane, so you can prove it, so you can prove yourself. You've *gotta* prove yourself—in this world.

F: Let's try this. "You've got a job to do."

J: (*Laughs*) You've gotta job to do. You're gonna quit fuckin' around, and—you've been doin' nothin' for a long time—

F: Yah. Now, don't change your posture. The right arm goes to the left and the left arm goes to the right. Say the same thing again and stay aware of this.

J: You've been doing nothing for a long time. You gotta do something, Jane. You've gotta *be* something . . . You've gotta make people proud of you. You've got to grow up, you have to be a woman, and you gotta keep everything that's bad about you hidden away so nobody can see it, so they'll think you're perfect, just perfect . . . You have to lie. I make you lie.

F: Now take Jane's place again.

J: You're—you're (*Cries*) you are driving me crazy. You're picking on me. I'd really like to strangle you—uh—then you'll punish me more. You'll come back—and give me hell for that. So, why don't you just go away? I won't—I won't cross you up any more. Just go away and leave me alone—and I'm not begging you!! Just go away! /F: Again./
Just go away! /F: Again./
Go away! /F: Change seats./
You'll be just a half if I go away! You'll be half a person if I leave. Then you'll really be fucked up. You can't send me away, you'll have to figure out something to do with me, you'll have to use me. Well then—then I—I would change your mind about a lot of things if I had to.

F: Ah!

J: And tell you that there's nothing I could do that's bad . . . I mean, if you'd leave me alone, I wouldn't do anything bad . . .

F: OK. Take another rest.

J: (*Closes eyes*). . . I can't rest.

F: So come back to us. Tell us about your restlessness.

J: I keep wondering what to do with that. When I had my eyes closed, I was saying, "Tell her to just relax."

F: OK. Play *her* top dog, now.

J: Just relax.

F: Make her the underdog and you're the top dog.

J: And you don't have to do anything, you don't have to prove anything. *(Cries)* You're only twenty years old! You don't have to be the queen . . .

 She says, OK. I understand that. I know that. I'm just in a *hurry*. I'm in a *big* hurry. We've got so many things to do—and now, I know, when I'm in a hurry you can't be now, you can't—when I'm in a hurry, you can't stay in the minute you're in. You have to keep—you have to keep hurrying, and the days slip by and you think you're losing time, or something. I'm *much* too hard on you. I have to—I have to leave you alone.

F: Well, I would like to interfere. Let your top dog say, "I'll be a bit more patient with you."

J: Uh. I'll be—I'll be a bit more patient with you.

F: Say this again.

J: *(Softly)* It's very hard for me to be patient. You know that. You know how impatient I am. But I'll—I'll try to be a bit more patient with you. "I'll try"—I'll *be* a bit more patient with you. As I say that, I'm stomping my foot, and shaking my head.

F: OK. Say, "I *won't* be patient with you—"

J: *(Easily)* I *won't* be patient with you, Jane! I won't be patient with you./F: Again./

 I won't be patient with you. /F: Again./

 I won't be patient with you.

F: Now say this to us . . . Pick a few.

J: Jan, I won't be patient with you. Claire, I won't be patient with you . . . Dick, I won't be patient with you. Muriel, I won't be patient with you. Ginny, I won't be patient with you . . . And June, I won't be patient with you, either.

F: OK. How do you feel, now?

J: OK.

F: You understand, top dog and underdog are not yet together. But at least the conflict is clear, in the open, maybe a *little* bit less violent.

J: I felt, when I worked before, on the dream, and the dream thing, that I worked this out. I felt *good*. I keep—I keep—it keeps—I keep going back to it.

F: Yah. This is the famous self-torture game.

J: I do it so *well*.

F: Everybody does it. You don't do it better than the rest of us. Everybody thinks, "I am the worst."

Editors' Introduction

Arnold Lazarus is one of the most innovative people in contemporary psychotherapy. After making multiple contributions in behavior therapy, Lazarus went on to develop and research his own system of multimodal therapy which, in a relatively short time, has amassed a considerable number of adherents.

The multimodal therapy procedures described in Lazarus's chapter in Current Psychotherapies *are illustrated quite clearly in the following case of "George," an agoraphobic patient who had been previously treated without success by numerous therapists. The reader may find it helpful to speculate about how George would have been treated by the proponents of each of the other systems discussed in this book.*

THE CASE OF GEORGE

Arnold A. Lazarus

George was 32 years old when he first consulted me. A sallow, ungainly, over-weight man, with reddish brown hair that he nervously pushed from his fore-head from time to time, George slouched in the chair and conveyed an aura of helplessness and hopelessness. His tattered sneakers, baggy corduroy pants and faded shirt helped to round out the picture of a most unhappy individual. The man made virtually no eye contact. His cousin, one of my colleagues, described him as "a basket case, an emotional cripple." His mother, with whom he lived, accompanied him to the first session and explained that "George is very nervous and has always been delicate." As family systems theorists would express it, mother and son were "enmeshed."

George complained of multiple fears, generalized anxiety, panic attacks, obsessions and compulsions, and many somatic difficulties, adding "I guess I'm a bit of a hypochondriac." He was agoraphobic and would not leave the house unless accompanied by his mother. He had "panic attacks" when he attempted to do so. He had specific phobias of illness and death, as well as compulsive washing and cleaning rituals related to germ phobias. He traced the beginning of his major fears to age 17, when he had completed high school and was about to leave for college. "But come to think of it," he added, "I've sort of been afraid all my life."

Excerpt from Arnold A. Lazarus, *The Practice of Multimodal Therapy* (pp. 19–31), published by McGraw-Hill, Inc. in 1981. Reprinted by permission of the author.

George was the only child of an alcoholic and abusive father and an exceedingly overprotective mother. As he was growing up, he felt alienated from his father and assumed the role of his mother's protector, often interceding when his father became nasty to her. His mother frequently said, "I don't know what I'd do without you." At age 17 he was in a quandary. He wished to go to college, but how could he abandon his mother? The eruption of his pervasive feelings of anxiety led his mother to collude with him. He was "too sick to leave home." Thus, the stage was set for a paradoxical relationship in which he functioned as his mother's protector while nurturing an infantile dependency on her. He managed to take courses in a community college near his home and almost earned a B.A. degree. It was about this time that he developed his agoraphobia.

When George was 20 his father died of a coronary thrombosis. His mother's widowed sister moved into the home, and George now assumed the role of a "double protector." He was the "man of the house" who looked after his aunt and mother, even though he never left the house without his mother. He began complaining of numerous physical ailments and, together with his mother, made the rounds of various specialists who subjected him to extensive medical tests and examinations. When he was 21, his internist referred him to a psychoanalyst.

George was analyzed several times a week for over six years, at which point he concluded that he was not being helped. He was as fearful, phobic, compulsive, and hypochondriacal as ever. His family situation remained unaltered; he had no friends, no independence, no mobility. He stayed at home, watched television, played cards with his aunt, went grocery shopping with his mother, and spent many hours preoccupied with bathroom rituals. He then consulted a "behavior therapist." George liked this therapist and together they embarked on a course of *in vivo* desensitization, thought-stopping, and progressive relaxation training. After two months George was able to go to and from the supermarket without his mother. On one of his excursions, he had what he called "a panic attack." (Careful questioning revealed that he did not suffer from a classic panic disorder but would generate high levels of anxiety.) Thereafter, he retreated back into the home, and terminated behavior therapy. Over the next few years his situation deteriorated. Frequent nightmares of dying added to his burdens. His compulsions increased in number, as did his psychosomatic complaints. He became prone to temper outbursts directed at his mother. By the time George was referred to me, he had received—in addition to his six years of psychoanalysis and his brief exposure to behavior therapy—drug therapy, electroconvulsive therapy, primal therapy, transactional analysis, transcendental meditation, and existential therapy. He still continued to suffer from anxiety, panic, withdrawal, hypochondriasis, agoraphobia, other phobias, nightmares, temper tantrums, bathroom rituals and obsessive-compulsive habits.

AN INDICTMENT OF THE FIELD?

Before discussing the specifics of the multimodal approach that was employed with this client, let us first ask: What is happening here? Is this a "resistant patient" who doesn't want to get better and who will fight desperately to maintain his *status quo*? Is he a "therapist killer" who will continue making the rounds of various therapists and therapies to "defeat" them and add more and more therapists and systems to his collection of "trophies"? Is he a "therapist shopper" whose *modus vivendi* now requires him to "be in therapy"?

Significantly, in his search for help, the client avoided the lunatic fringe. He consulted only reputable internists, psychiatrists, a most highly respected psychoanalyst, and licensed clinical psychologists. Why then did he experience no relief from his suffering? How can his first therapist justify charging approximately $50,000 while prescribing more and more of the same over a period of six years, without *any* evidence of results? Since it is claimed that primal therapy is the only cure, which renders all other psychologic theories obsolete and invalid, we are entitled to ask why George was not cured by primal therapy. Similarly, did he just happen to see a poorly trained transactional analyst, a half-baked existentialist, an unqualified behavior therapist, and so forth?

Some theorists and therapists stress commonalities among divergent therapeutic approaches. They seek similarities and point out where different systems and methods overlap. But to ignore differences is to overlook significant factors that may account for critical variance. Multimodal therapy obviously has much in common with many other psychotherapeutic approaches. Is there anything unique about it? Do multimodal therapists do anything that differs from what other psychotherapists do?

PROCEEDING MULTIMODALLY: HOW AND WHERE TO INTERVENE

By the time George consulted me, his morale was low. He was anxious, depressed and skeptical about embarking on yet another futile endeavor. Since his cousin, whom he respected, had recommended me so highly, he was willing to give me a try. Clearly, the challenge was to achieve his compliance and establish a liaison that would succeed where so many others had failed.

It requires considerable skill to motivate patients, to augment compliance, and to diminish resistance. In the psychotherapeutic arena, innumerable clinicians have stressed the need to "talk the patient's language," and to establish a level of rapport that transforms a respectful "working alliance" into a truly cooperative venture. The importance of achieving and maintaining flexibility and versatility has been widely recognized, and it is well known that the manner in which specific techniques are explained and presented to clients will determine whether or not they are put to good use. Nevertheless, despite a vigilant lookout for individual and personalistic entry points, if the therapist's personality and approach do not mesh with the client's fundamental expectancies, compliance is unlikely to occur. In these cases, it seems best to refer the client to a more compatible resource rather than try to "work through" the differences.

Although the points discussed in the foregoing paragraph all fall under the rubric of "common sense," they are often violated in clinical practice. Too many therapists are apt to approach patients in a stylized manner that may appeal to some and alienate others. Following Gordon Paul's admonition to determine, as precisely as possible, who or what is best for each individual, the major question was how to gain George's cooperation and compliance, especially in view of his many treatment failures.

To smoke out possible oppositional tendencies, I asked him if he could visualize himself cooperating with me. "What happens," I asked, "if I say to you that there is a new rhythmic breathing exercise that I want to teach you in order to diminish certain feelings of anxiety? Can you picture yourself allowing me to teach it to you and then can you see yourself applying it, or do you see yourself opposing me?" George said that he would probably be cooperative. I immediately stressed that "probably" was not good enough and asked if I could depend on a 100 percent level of cooperation for four sessions. "By that time I will know if you will work with me or against me," I said.

I asked George to complete the Multimodal Life History Questionnaire and bring it to his second session. Thereafter, the modality profile shown in Box 10.1 was drawn up.

This cursory profile lists some of George's main problems and provided a flexible "blueprint" for establishing treatment goals and evaluating progress. After examining the profile and rereading his Multimodal Life History Questionnaire, it seemed best to start with his biological modality. I shared my reasoning with George by pointing out that he was obviously physically unfit, overweight, and that he spent most of his time sitting around the house and got very little exercise. I stressed the mind-body connection and pointed out that an immediate objective was to have him attain a higher level of physical fitness. I emphasized that someone who is in top physical shape was less likely to feel anxious, or suffer from psychosomatic afflictions and low self-confidence. We discussed the role of good nutrition and I underscored how George's current eating habits could have contributed to his emotional problems. He was informed: "Step number one in your therapy therefore is going to have to be a vigorous physical training regimen. I also want you to put yourself in the hands of a qualified nutritionist." When asked how he felt about the idea, George said, "It makes sense."

I insisted that he undergo a medical checkup including a stress electrocardiogram. "I want to be sure there are no physical defects," I said, "because I am going to push you like a coach or a trainer getting an athlete or a fighter ready for a big event." It was evident from his responses on the Multimodal Life History Questionnaire that George very much wanted someone to "take charge." There are those therapists who would see this as a reason to maintain distance to avoid fostering his dependency. I regard this as a common

BOX 10.1 **George's Modality Profile**

Behavior	Avoidance
	Playing sick role
	Absence of mobility or involvement
	Bathroom rituals and other obsessive-compulsive acts
Affect	Fear
	Panic
	Anxiety
	Impetuous anger
	Discouraged/depressed
Sensation	Dizziness, palpatations
	Tremors
	Aches/pains
	etc.
Imagery	Poor self-image
	Feuding parents
	Teasing from sadistic teacher
Cognition	Other people see me as odd and peculiar.
	No woman would ever want to get close to me.
	Contamination notions
	Musts and shoulds
Interpersonal	Timid, inept, hermit-like
Drugs/Biology	Regularly takes Valium 10 mg t.i.d.
	Eats junk foods
	Flabby, unfit, overweight

error. If we are to gain compliance, it is usually necessary to respond in ways that match the client's expectancies. I was willing to take charge *initially* in order to mobilize adaptive behaviors.

For George, the image of an athlete being trained to win the "big event" had metaphorical overtones that matched his needs and perceptions. On the Multimodal Life History Questionnaire, in response to the question, "How do you think a therapist should interact with his or her clients?" George had stated that an effective therapist would be like a hard-driving Army sergeant who is very demanding, acts tough with his men, but who, deep down, has a soft spot for them. (His father had been "an Army man" but was a *bad sergeant*—irresponsible and abusive without the redeeming virtue of basic compassion.) Upon inquiry, I learned that the least effective therapists were those who played a warm, avuncular role with him, and who were unconditionally supportive and empathic. It was obvious that if I was to gain George's cooperation, I would have to "come on strong," or my "multimodal therapy" would be as ineffective as his previous treatments.

The medical examinations revealed slightly elevated levels of cholesterol and triglycerides, and mild hypertension which reinforced the need for a change in his dietary and exercise habits. He joined his local YMCA and, while his mother knitted in the lobby, George started walking and then jogging around the track, and gradually added swimming and bodybuilding exercises to his regimen. Cognitive relabeling was deliberately emphasized. Instead of viewing heart palpitations with alarm and terror, his new association was to be in terms of cardiac output, collateral circulation, and cardiovascular activity.

Concurrently with his physical training and nutritional changes, he and I embarked on a systematic program of *exercises in coping imagery*. One of my fundamental assumptions is that before people are capable of doing certain things in reality, they first need to rehearse them in imagery. If people cannot picture themselves performing an act, they will probably not be able to do it in real life. George had to cultivate pictures of himself moving about, dealing with people, having gainful employment, developing and maintaining friendships, dining in a restaurant, being at a party, making love to a woman, and, of course, leaving his mother to her own devices.

We constructed a hierarchy of situations, starting with some simple desensitization images (walking half a block from his home and gradually increasing the distance until he could visualize himself driving to the supermarket without his mother, driving to the YMCA alone, and so forth), and then I added imaginary social situations (picnics, cocktail parties, formal dinners, etc.). I had recommended group therapy as an adjunct to his individual therapy, but he remained opposed to this idea and I decided not to insist, as I was already requiring a great deal from him.

Within a few weeks George started looking trimmer and his jogging time and distance had increased. He still complained of endless pains, aches, and imaginary afflictions. I consistently ignored these to avoid reinforcing his hypochondriacal tendencies. At times, I resorted to my "tough sergeant" position and said: "The next time I hear anything about your aches and pains, I will insist that you run around the track three times carrying 20-lb. dumbbells!"

It was emphasized that he would invariably have "anxiety attacks" from time to time, and that this would not mean that he or his therapy were failing. Rather, it was necessary to find a method of containing, checking, and eliminating these attacks. In multimodal assessment, we use a method known as *tracking*. This consists of identifying the modality firing order, or sequence, that usually precedes negative affective reactions. George began to see that his anxiety attacks usually followed an S-I-C-B-C sequence. First, he would become aware of some minor *sensation* (a slightly rapid heartbeat, some facial tension), which would produce frightening *images* (fleeting scenes of operating rooms and intravenous drips), whereupon his *cognitions* would signal "danger!" and add a "what if" to the equation (generally "what if I become catastrophically ill?"), whereupon he would retreat *behaviorally* and intensify the vicious circle by dwelling on further *cognitions* ("something must be dreadfully wrong with me"). Having identified the order of events, effective measures could be prescribed. As soon as George experienced a negative sensation he was instructed to use differential relaxation plus the breathing techniques he had been taught. He was then to switch to various success and coping images, while subvocally chanting, "Keep cool, keep calm, and cut the crap!" He was told: "Instead of retreating, withdrawing, and running away, hang in there and use your sequential antidotes." (In therapy, "talking a client's language" often adds up to tracking his or her modality firing order—identifying sequential proclivities—and intervening in the relevant modalities. An A-B-S-C sequence calls for a different treatment from a B-C-S-A or a C-S-A-B sequence, and so forth. *Tracking* is an important feature of multimodal assessment and therapy.)

George's cognitive modality was addressed first by stressing the unfortunate consequences of living by categorical imperatives (what Karen Horney called "the tyranny of the should," a point that Albert Ellis has elaborated on to offset absolutistic thinking). We also devoted several hours to general discussions such as the virtues of "long-range hedonism" and his entitlements as a human being. A variety of techniques were employed including self-monitoring, imaginal and in vivo desensitization, thought-stopping, mental imagery exercises, role playing, assertiveness training, and the empty chair technique (mainly to complete "unfinished business" with his late father).

George's bathroom rituals called for response-prevention (or response attenuation) since outcome data suggest that compulsive habits typically do not respond to other methods. Consequently, we agreed that instead of his spending four hours in the bathroom performing his rituals, George would reduce this time by half or forfeit watching his favorite TV shows for an entire week. Thereafter, bathroom time was systematically reduced from two hours to less than 45 minutes. (When the going got tough, George typically suggested that it might be better for us to explore the meanings behind his symptoms. I would react, using my "tough army sergeant stance" by pointing out that he had devoted six years of his life to exploring meanings and dynamics to no avail.)

In addition to our individual sessions, I also had family therapy sessions with George and his mother, and on two occasions, I worked with George, his mother, and his aunt. The two women, especially his mother, seemed to have vested interests in infantalizing George and in maintaining his dependence. Significantly, when George managed to come to his sessions without his mother (after therapy had been ongoing for about a year) her attitude toward me and the therapy became extremely antagonistic. She refused to have any further family meetings; nor would she meet with me individually. She went out of her way to persuade her son to terminate therapy.

One of George's major anxieties revolved around the theme of being alone in a strange city and becoming ill. I suggested that if this occurred he could go to the nearest hospital emergency room and see the physician on duty. I wanted George to realize that the world is full of benevolent others, better trained and more capable than his mother of ministering to him. Accordingly, I presented the following image: "Imagine that you are all alone in Chicago. You become ill and are admitted to a hospital. . . . Now imagine the scene in the hospital. . . . The doctors are standing around your bed, talking to each other, helping you, curing you. . . ." At this point the client started hyperventilating, sobbing, retching and panicking.

This image had elicited a "forgotten memory" that evoked a full-blown abreaction. When he finally calmed down, George recounted vivid memories of an event that took place when he was 7 years old. He was in a hospital after a tonsillectomy and was coming out of the anesthetic and could barely make out some people hovering around his bed. His mother was talking to someone about his frail and sickly make-up. "I hope he lives to see 21!" she declared. I asked him why his mother labelled him "frail and sickly," and he replied that perhaps it was because he was prone to infections and high fevers as a child, which is why the doctor had recommended a tonsillectomy. But his mother's alleged postoperative commentary about the delicate state of his health—"I hope he lives to see 21!"—had left an indelible impression.

As we explored the repercussions of his mother's appraisals at subsequent sessions, it seemed probable that George's somatic and psychosomatic tendencies were related to her attitudes. His mother's alleged pronouncement as he was coming out of the anesthesia seemed to play a central etiological role. He had been (a) in a semiconscious, perhaps highly suggestible, postoperative (traumatic) condition, when (b) an authority (his mother) proclaimed him to be frail and sickly, which, in turn, (c) centered on self-deficiency as a focal guiding concept. There could be little doubt that these messages had influenced the development of his symptoms.

Regardless of the accuracy of this brief analysis, George was obviously upset by these real or imagined events, and something had to be done to alleviate his distress. My initial entry point was to emphasize that *benevolent intent* on his mother's part lay behind all her actions, but that we were concerned with the consequences. Since in multimodal therapy, we try to cover the entire BASIC I.D. whenever feasible, the "antidotes" listed in Box 10.2 were prescribed.

As these recommendations were discussed and applied, other feelings and associations emerged. For example, George raised his ongoing fears about death, and he discussed his ambivalence, particularly his antagonistic feelings, toward his mother. (Incidentally, his preoccupation with death seemed to abate after a most fatuous discussion. George was born in 1942. I asked him where he had been in 1941. He answered, "I wasn't born until 1942." I then said, "Oh, so you weren't alive in 1941. . . . In other words, if you were not alive in 1941 or 1931 or 1921, it means that you were dead during those years. Tell me George, was 1941 or 1906 or 1873 a particularly bad year for you? Do you remember suffering and being dreadfully unhappy in 1920? So when you die, it will be back to 1941 or 1901 or 1899 for you. What's the big deal?")

BOX 10.2 **Multimodal Recommendations for George**

Behavior	Several times a day, close your eyes, relax, and repeat to yourself "I am not frail and sickly. I never was frail and sickly."
Affect	Try to generate anger or indignation in place of anxiety.
Sensation	Use "directed muscular activity"—pound a pillow to assist with anger arousal.
Imagery	Picture yourself going back in a "time machine" so that you, at age 32, can appear "out of the future" to reassure yourself, at age 7, in that hospital bed. That little boy (you in the past) senses something special about that 32-year-old man (you at present) reassuring the child that he is not frail and sickly.
Cognition	Understand that your mother was projecting her own hypochondriacal and anxious feelings. There was no "objective reality" to her remarks.
Interpersonal	Discuss your recollection of this event with your mother. Be confrontative, but do not attack or blame.
Biology/Drugs	Keep working at improving physical fitness, and ask your doctor to gradually phase out the Valium.

One of the coping images that called for repeated rehearsal and role playing was the scene in which George pictured his mother begging him not to leave home, not to desert her. By the time these issues were receiving attention, therapy had been continuing for about 15 months. Behaviorally, George had made impressive gains. He was willing and able to travel alone, and his numerous fears, avoidance, compulsions, and generalized anxiety had diminished significantly. Nevertheless, George became discouraged by setbacks from time to time. I found that he remained unresponsive to reassurance, morale-building, and empathic encouragement, but tended to snap out of his depression when I used paradoxical statements. For instance, I would say: "Well, as everybody knows, you are frail and sickly, weak, defective, about to fall apart, living on borrowed time, inferior, contaminated, deficient. . . ." He would invariably laugh, utter some expletive, and therapy would proceed in a positive direction.

After twenty months of therapy, despite the improvements already mentioned, George was still living with his mother and her sister; he had not looked for gainful employment; and he had not gone out on a date. (What remained of the father's life insurance policy and his army pension, plus the mother's and aunt's social security checks were the family's sole means of financial support.) Getting George to move out of his mother's home, to find a job, and to start socializing with women proved extremely difficult. One of my many tactics was the use of "coercive persuasion." I painted an ugly verbal picture of him as a bewildered, nervous, and incompetent recluse who would lapse into his pervasively neurotic ways if he refused to risk taking three essential steps: (a) gaining employment, (b) leaving home, and (c) dating women. His mother did not make the task easy. She played on George's sense of obligation and managed to ignite his residual doubts and fears on several occasions. I was more persuasive and George prevailed. He moved into an apartment, obtained a job with a company that was willing to give him managerial training, started dating one of the secretaries, and finally lost his virginity at age 34.

Our meetings had tapered off at this stage and we met once every 6 or 7 weeks for "booster" sessions. George suffered needless discouragement following minor episodes of anxiety, but was soon back on track. A year later, he had changed his job (he was earning a good salary plus commission from selling life insurance), had moved to a better apartment, was enjoying "plenty of sex," had become an excellent squash player, and was taking up horseback riding. On the negative side, he remained somewhat phobic—he avoided crowded places and insisted on having the aisle seat in a theatre. George still seemed overconcerned about his health, and while he looked remarkably trim and fit, seemed to be overly invested in health foods and jogging.

At a four-year follow-up George's progress had been maintained. He was water-skiing and had made two trips to Acapulco. He was thinking about "settling down and getting married." He had won an award as "insurance salesman of the year" and, during the follow-up interview, had the audacity to attempt to sell me life insurance! He was in training for the New York marathon and was "trying out vegetarianism." While he still reported some discomfort in crowded places, he claimed to be less claustrophobic. Interestingly, his mother's view of the treatment outcome was that her son had been corrupted. He overheard her telling someone that he used to be "such a good boy," but by the time an "awful psychologist" got through with him, he started running around with women and had picked up other bad behaviors. As for his relationship with his mother, he said: "We get along just fine because she has learned to keep away from certain subjects."

About three years later, I received a wedding invitation with a cursory note to the effect that he had moved to the midwest to assume a "high-powered" managerial position.

DISCUSSION

It seems evident that certain constructive objectives were achieved. Some might argue, however, that these benefits may have come about with or without multimodal therapy. Others may even claim that positive gains had occurred in spite of therapy. When I first presented this case at a professional meeting shortly before George and I had terminated therapy, a psychoanalyst claimed that the treatment was "superficial" and predicted that George had an inability to form mature attachments, and that this deficit would lead him to become seriously depressed within three to five years. But the client had undergone six years of psychoanalytic therapy with no discernible improvement!

Perhaps this client needed six years of psychoanalysis, plus behavior therapy, plus drug therapy, electroconvulsive therapy, primal therapy, transactional analysis, transcendental meditation, and existentialism—all of which merely primed him to respond to whatever brand of therapy happened to be number nine. Would he have done as well if he had not received any previous treatment? How long would it have taken to achieve the noted improvements if he had initially received multimodal therapy? Had his previous therapy rendered George more accessible to multimodal therapy? On the contrary, I believe that more "unlearning" was required to correct impressions that he had acquired from previous therapists, because similar cases who received no previous treatment have tended to respond rapidly to multimodal methods.

Reaching people whose excesses and deficits across the BASIC I.D. are rigid, encrusted, and pervasive requires hard work, sensitivity, wisdom, and talent. In most instances, the patient-therapist relationship provides the soil that enables the specific techniques to take root. I believe that the case of George exemplifies the way in which the "right" relationship blended with the "correct" techniques to produce a salubrious result.

Editors' Introduction

With family therapy there is the same dilemma we faced with behavior therapy: dozens of good teaching cases are available, but it is virtually impossible to select a single case that will adequately illustrate the multiple and variegated techniques used by most family therapists. Ultimately we elected to use a strategic therapy case to serve as an exemplar of family therapy.

We feel fortunate to have been able to locate the following case by Peggy Papp. It demonstrates the effective treatment of the family of a young anorectic woman and demonstrates the use of a "Greek Chorus"—a group of observing therapists who remain behind a one-way mirror. The Greek Chorus is always available to consult with the therapist, and the group will periodically make recommendations about treatment. Family therapists, more than any other group, have used such procedures to good advantage.

THE DAUGHTER
WHO SAID NO

Peggy Papp

This case illustrates the step-by-step process of putting concepts into practice over time. It describes the treatment of a 23-year-old anorectic daughter and her family who present the classical pattern of an anorectic family: a high degree of enmeshment, covert alliances between the generations, subverted conflict, and power struggles fought with guilt and martyrdom.

The parents, in rigidly symmetrical positions, are in constant conflict and divert this conflict through Rachel, the anorectic daughter, hence isolating her from her siblings and the world of her peers. The therapeutic dilemma centers around what will happen to Rachel and the various members of her family if she gives up her symptom and becomes a full-blown woman. The consultation group is used to debate this dilemma, and the sibling subsystem is enlisted to free Rachel from her involvement in the parental generation.

Twenty sessions were held over the period of one year with a one-, two- and three-year follow-up. All sessions were videotaped and observed behind a one-way mirror.

For the purpose of clarity, the case is broken down into stages according to the following outline.

Excerpt from Peggy Papp, *The Process of Change* (pp. 67–120), copyright 1982 by Guilford Publications, Inc. Reprinted by permission of the publisher.

Stage I: *Forming a hypothesis*
    Step 1: Gathering information
    Step 2: Connecting the symptom with the family system
Stage II: *Setting the terms for therapy*
    Step 1: Defining the therapeutic dilemma
    Step 2: Setting the terms for change
Stage III: *Putting the therapeutic contract into operation*
    Step 1: Involving father in the therapeutic dilemma
    Step 2: Dramatizing the therapeutic dilemma
Stage IV: *Coping with the forces of change*
    Step 1: Defining change within the therapeutic contract
Stage V: *Coping with the fallout from change*
    Step 1: Defining resistance within the therapeutic framework
    Step 2: Shifting the definition of the problem
    Step 3: Prescribing enmeshment
Stage VI: *Enlisting the sibling subsystem*
    Step 1: Forming a coalition with the sisters
    Step 2: Differentiating from the sisters
Stage VII: *Saying no to therapy*
    Step 1: Pushing the prescription to the breaking point
    Step 2: Escalating the therapeutic triangle
    Step 3: Opposing the group
    Step 4: Supporting autonomy
Stage VIII: *Solidifying change*
    Step 1: Anticipating and rehearsing a regression
    Step 2: Redefining the marital relationship
Stage IX: *Prescribing a farewell ritual*
Follow-up

STAGE I
FORMING A HYPOTHESIS

Step 1: Gathering Information

The information I obtained from the first session is summarized here since information gathering tends to make tedious reading. Rachel, 23, requested therapy for herself, and her sisters, Clare, 31, and Sandy, 26; her mother agreed to participate in therapy, but her father emphatically refused. Having been pushed into various kinds of therapy by his wife for the last five years, he told Rachel in no uncertain terms she would have to solve her problem herself.

I agreed to see the family without him, believing I could involve him later. Some therapists will not see the family unless everyone is present for the first session. Since my way of dealing with resistance is indirect rather than direct, my decisions are based on an evaluation of each case. In this situation it seemed important to go along with father's resistance since it was obviously a reaction to his wife's pressure. Also, the intensity of his feelings was a good indication he could be involved at a later date.

Only mother and Rachel appeared for the first interview as Sandy was in the hospital having her first baby and Clare refused to come after a fight with Rachel.

Rachel appeared frail and flat-chested, but animated, with huge dark eyes and a thin face. She was exceptionally articulate, expressing herself in colorful language and sometimes adding a comic delivery. Her mother, a large, handsome, robust woman with short, white hair, stylishly cut, possessed the style and flair of a seasoned actress. With the exuberance of Lady Bountiful she embraced family therapy, saying she "believed" family members should help one another and she would do anything to help Rachel. She tempered each criticism of her with "there's really nothing wrong with you, you're a wonderful child, but—."

Rachel had begun dieting four years ago during her second year at college. Since that time she had slowly but steadily lost weight until she finally weighed 89 pounds. She had not menstruated for a year and a half. During the last three years she had made several attempts to leave home but failed, each time feeling depressed, isolated, lonely, and coming back home. She now had an interim job as a secretary but was dissatisfied with it. Although living at home, she was talking about moving into an apartment of her own.

The primary concern of Rachel and her mother was not her weight loss or her diet, but the psychological implications, which they saw in terms of Rachel's intrapsychic problems. Rachel's previous individual therapy of one year had focused on the classical individual symptoms of anorexia—high expectations, over-achievement, perfectionistic attitudes, obsessions, and control over the body—but had not connected these in any way with the family system.

The mother was interested in our helping Rachel with her high expectations of herself, describing her as being "obsessively and rigidly perfectionistic." She also stated Rachel had been a rebellious child all her life. "I have been worried about Rachel since she learned to say no. It has been no and no and no and no and no and no and no ever since then. She has not wanted to adopt any of our standards, and I question her judgment." She gave as an example of this Rachel's not wanting to join B'nai B'rith or date Jewish boys, and her tendency to pick a boy up off the street and make a date with him. Rachel accused her mother of matchmaking. "I feel like it's mating season. I'm in heat and it's time to find a male for me quick before I'm not eligible anymore. I don't enjoy that." Mother then mentioned drugs, and Rachel admitted she had experimented in college with pot, speed, LSD, and mescaline and ended with, "I don't regret anything."

Mother had kept everything away from father over the years to protect Rachel and to avoid a conflict. When asked what he would have done had he known about these things, she stated "I don't know. I wasn't going to give him a chance! The girls have accused me of being manipulative and maybe I am but I have to be." She spoke of the many disagreements between her and her husband, describing a longstanding conflict because of her closeness with her parents.

At the end of the session, after consultation with the team, I told Rachel and her mother we felt we did not have enough information at this point to make any suggestions and would like to delay our comments until we had met with other members of the family. Rachel agreed to try and get Clare to come to the next session but Sandy was still recuperating from the birth of her baby.

In the following session, Clare, a thin, attractive woman, fashionably dressed, was more than happy to give her impressions of Rachel and other family members. She described Rachel as being "very difficult" and her family as being one in which it was difficult to become independent, as her mother was controlling and "throws guilt around a lot." Both she and Rachel had rebelled against her mother's control, but Sandy "is the model daughter, model sister, model grandchild and, now having had a baby, will be the model mother. She never displeases anyone. She is the buffer, the peacemaker."

Both Rachel and Clare spoke of their being afraid of their father when they were growing up. He was very conservative and strict about dates, two-piece bathing suits, boyfriends, hours, and so on. The mother, more lenient, took this opportunity to say that she was also afraid of his wrath and stated pathetically, "Thank God he never hit me." She compared him unfavorably with her own father and started to cry. "I tried very hard to get my family to help me, and my father would talk to my husband in a gentle manner and say how precious a wife is, how nothing really was as precious as a wife, and really she's the only one who is most important in life. But my husband would become antagonistic toward such conversations." She went into individual therapy at the recommendation of her doctor when she developed stomach trouble, and her doctor put pressure on her husband to go with her. Both blamed him for her physical problems.

Rachel and Clare defended their father and accused their mother of being overly close to her family and rubbing the father's nose in it. Rachel then spoke of her father and her as being the "underdogs in the family. We're ostracized by the rest of them." Rachel had given me the first clue as to how she fit into the power struggle between her parents: She identified with the father's underdog position. I now wanted to know the function of this identification: how it was used in the ongoing day-to-day battle between the parents and how the sisters responded to it. The following dialogue was included to demonstrate how these questions were explored.

Peggy: So you feel you're the bad guy and your father is the bad guy in the family. In what way do you feel you can bring comfort to your father?
Rachel: Because I can understand his viewpoint.
Clare: If there are two bad guys, then you both share the burden?
Rachel: There's company.
Peggy: How do you go about giving him company?

Rachel: We have a lot of common interests, we both like cars and nature and the Bronx Zoo, and we have a good time. We go across the country together.

Peggy: What do you think his life would be like if you weren't around?

Rachel: I don't know—I guess he'd survive.

Peggy: Do you think he'd be lonely?

Rachel: Maybe, sometimes—I'm nice company for him.

Peggy: Then who would there be around to really understand him?

Rachel: *(Long pause.)* I don't know.

Peggy: You don't think your mother could understand him?

Rachel: She will never ever. I shouldn't say that, but as far as I can see, it'll be a very tough thing for my mother to ever understand how my father feels about her family. She will never ever see how he feels about her.

Mother: But who do I think of when I want somebody to make nice to me? I go right back to the womb. On Tuesday I spent the day with my mom and dad and it was a good day. It was a hard day. I took them shopping. They're very old.

Peggy: Do you feel they're the only ones who nurture you?

Mother: *(Nodding.)* Who really take care of me. I don't want anyone here to feel bad, but Sandy also takes care of me.

Rachel: But you demand too much. You're very hard to give to when you demand.

Peggy: Let's see then. When you feel ganged up on by Rachel and your husband, you then go for nurturing to your parents. And who does your husband go to?

Mother: There's always been a young man in his life who treats him like God. Now it's Roy.

Peggy: You're saying that he always finds someone who is like a son to him?

Mother: Yes, Roy is like a son.

Peggy: Was he disappointed he didn't have a son?

Mother: *(Whispers.)* Very.

Peggy: You whispered that "very." You don't want the girls to hear that?

Mother: *(Emphatically.)* Very displeased that he didn't have a son.

Peggy: Do you think they don't know that?

Rachel: I'm daddy's son.

Peggy: In what way have you been his son?

Rachel: Just—my interest in things which aren't typically feminine. I'm not scared of bugs, little things like that. Cars. Daddy asked me to cook hamburgers on the barbecue pit because I can handle it. *(She imitates a boy.)*

Peggy: What's that like for you to be his son?

Rachel: I kinda like it. *(She laughs and acts like a boy again.)* I don't mind, but I don't think he thinks of me as a boy.

Peggy: Do you think of yourself as a boy?

Rachel: No. I was saying that I felt so independent on this move. It always bugs me to depend on people.

Peggy: What do you think it's going to be like for him, your moving out?
Rachel: I think it's going to be all right for him. Already they're talking about switching homes with me.
Peggy: Do you think he's going to miss you?
Rachel: Maybe. He said he was going to miss some things but not others.
Peggy: Well do you think your mother's going to be able to take care of his loneliness?
Rachel: Not unless she starts to look at him from a more objective point of view.
Peggy: Do you think you can teach her?
Rachel: I try, I really try. Then she accuses me of ganging up on her.
Clare: (Defending mother.) Daddy's not nice all the time, either.

Step 2: Connecting the Symptom with the Family System

After this exchange, the therapist left the session to have a consultation with the group. We formed a hypothesis based on answering the following questions:

What function does the symptom serve in the system? We speculated that Rachel was starving herself in order to remain a son to her father and fill up the emptiness in his life that she perceived was left by her mother. By not eating, she kept herself looking like a boy, prevented herself from maturing into womanhood, and implicitly promised to remain the guardian of her parents' marriage. The symptom served to keep her at home where she could continue to serve as her father's ally in his battle with her mother and to give her mother a reason for remaining close to her family. By identifying with her father as the underdog in the family, she formed a coalition with him in the service of fighting against her mother's control. The symptom also served the function of freeing the other sisters to establish independent lives outside the family, since Rachel had accepted the responsibility of mediating the parents' marriage.

How does the family function to stabilize the symptom? When mother and father became involved in a power struggle that they could not resolve, mother moved closer to her parents and compared father unfavorably to her own father. Father retaliated by siding with Rachel against his wife, and Rachel joined him to get back at her mother. She became involved in masculine activities to please her father, knowing he felt alienated in a family of women. She cannot give up the symptom as long as she believes she is needed to be a son to him. The power struggle between mother and Rachel has taken many forms over the years, including Rachel's taking drugs, quitting jobs, leaving school, dating non-Jewish boys, and disassociating herself from the family religious beliefs, as well as her present symptom of self-starvation.

What is the central theme around which the problem is organized? The central theme in this family seems to be control—who is going to control the beliefs and values of the others. This is a conventional family that places high value on conformity, respectability, achievement, duty, and family loyalty. Mother is less concerned about some of Rachel's other activities than she is about her not accepting the tenets of the Jewish faith. She complains that her husband rejects her father's value of a wife as being something "precious."

Since we have not yet seen father and Sandy, we are unable at this point to obtain a complete picture of the way each individual operates to maintain control around these central issues.

What will be the consequences of change? If Rachel stopped being a son to her father, she would have to abandon him to what she perceives to be an unloving wife, and she would also be robbed of her major weapon against mother. If she left home, mother and father would have to face their conflicts alone and would probably create a triangle involving Sandy or Clare. Mother might move even closer to her own parents and father closer to his surrogate son, Roy. This would widen the breach between the parents. If father agreed to come for therapy in order to try and resolve these issues, he would lose a major battle with his wife regarding the value of therapy.

Rachel would have to confront the outside world and its relationships rather than centering her life on the family. This would mean her taking responsibility for becoming an adult woman sexually, professionally, and socially.

What is the therapeutic dilemma? The family must decide between Rachel continuing to be symptomatic or facing the above consequences.

STAGE II
SETTING THE TERMS FOR THERAPY

Step 1: Defining the Therapeutic Dilemma

Our first intervention consisted of setting the terms for the therapeutic contest that was to follow by defining the problem as a family dilemma. The family had defined the problem as an individual one—Rachel's rebelliousness, her obsessions, rigid expectations, and self-starvation all were seen as being disconnected from the family. In defining the problem as a dilemma, we connected the symptom with the system.

Peggy entered the session with the following message:

Peggy: (*Sighs.*) We are stuck.

Mother: So are we.

Peggy: We are in a bind and I don't know what to do about it except just be very honest and open and tell you what we're stuck with. Rachel, we are very hesitant to help you in the way we were planning therapy to take, which would be to help you think and feel more like a woman, to gain weight, to have curves, to menstruate, to go out with boys, and to just be yourself. Because, you see, we are concerned about what will happen to your father, that he will become more isolated in a family of women, that he will turn more to his surrogate son, Roy, leaving your mother more alone, so that she will turn more to her own family. We are worried this will create an irreparable distance between the two of them.

Clare: It's a vicious cycle, isn't it?

Peggy: And, you see, we are concerned about all the members of your family, and when one person in the family changes, that changes the relationship of everybody.

Rachel: *(Long pause.)* I don't think I want to sacrifice myself for my parents. I don't think I care that much. I want to help myself right now.

Peggy: *(Still posing the dilemma.)* I can understand how you feel. I just want to make sure you are aware of the effect it will have. . . . Well, think about these things and decide what you want to do.

Clare: *(Suddenly becoming aware of the implication of the terms I have set.)* I want to say that I got very angry about what the group said. That you decided to change your tack. I think that is wrong. *(She bursts into tears.)* I'm worried about Rachel and that's not the thing to do for her.

Peggy: You feel that we should help her—?

Clare: Yes, that's terrible! How can you say because it will affect other members of the family—what should she do—starve herself?

Peggy: *(Puzzling over the dilemma.)* Well, you know, I think that has to be Rachel's decision and all we can do is—.

Clare: But you function in that decision. You are here to help her.

Peggy: Well, you see, Rachel is so close to her family that—.

Clare: I think that's terrible! *(She strides across the room and grabs a Kleenex.)* I obviously don't understand what's behind it. I think it's awful.

Peggy: We feel responsible—we feel obligated to let you know what we think the consequences of change will be and to prepare you for them.

There was a knock on the door and the group summoned me out for a brief consultation.

Step 2: Setting the Terms for Change

Rachel and Clare had reacted against the therapist's homeostatic position and were pressing for change. We decided to use this as an opportunity to bargain with them over the conditions of change and set the price as Rachel's agreement to turn the burden of her parents' unhappiness over to me. We were aware that the father might not agree to do this since he was boycotting therapy. However, it was our way of dramatizing the connection between Rachel's problem and her parents' unhappiness.

Peggy: *(Entering the session.)* The group wanted to let you know that they heard what you said and that they take it very seriously, and perhaps there is a way I can help you. *(Turning to Rachel.)* If you would be willing for me to see your parents together and for me to take on the responsibility of what will happen to them if you change, then perhaps you could begin to eat. Could you allow me to take on that responsibility rather than your shouldering it?

Rachel agreed to do this and mother was more than willing to have her husband brought into therapy.

Peggy: My group feels that then it would be safe for you to become a woman. And I will handle the consequences of that with your father and mother.

I informed them I would call father and ask him to attend the next session. To summarize the terms of therapy:

1. We defined Rachel's symptom as her remaining at home and failing to become a woman in order to stabilize the relationship between her parents.

2. We defined the relationship between her parents as not being able to tolerate her absence.

3. We defined the therapeutic dilemma as having to choose between helping Rachel to become a woman and preserving the stability of her parents' relationship.

4. We defined the solution and therefore the terms for change as Rachel's agreeing to pass the responsibility for preserving her parents' relationship to us. This set up the following situation: If the parents allowed us to help them with their relationship, thus releasing Rachel, she would be relieved of her burden and able to leave home. If they did not, we would ask someone else in the family to take on the burden, or else pass it back to Rachel. By making a hot potato of the parents' unhappiness and passing it around to various members of the family, we would dramatize the therapeutic dilemma.

STAGE III
PUTTING THE THERAPEUTIC
CONTRACT INTO OPERATION

Step 1: Involving Father in the Therapeutic Dilemma

After this session I telephoned Sam, the father, and told him I respected his wish not to be involved in family therapy but since his wife had probably given me a one-sided view of the family situation, I would like to get his impressions over the telephone. He was more than willing to share these and spent the next half hour talking about how his wife put too many expectations on Rachel at too early an age, pushed her to leave home and go away to college at 16, and how he had nothing to say about it because his wife controlled the children and paid no attention to his opinions. He ended the conversation by saying he would be willing to come in for a session if it would help Rachel. I told him I would let him know when I thought it would be helpful, not wanting to seem overly eager about his becoming involved.

A week later Rachel moved away from home into her own apartment and I asked the father to come in for a session. He agreed, but only if Rachel and his wife were present, as he didn't want to be in a session with four women. His terms were accepted, and I began by informing him that we had discovered that Rachel was reluctant to leave home for fear he might be lonely if left alone with his wife. He initially scoffed at this idea, but as I began to discuss the family dinners in which Rachel sided with him against mother and her family, he validated the hypothesis. He admitted that he and Rachel had a lot in common. "We identify in certain ways, we understand each other." Rachel agreed with this.

Peggy: What else do you understand about each other?

Father then described a family dinner held with his wife's family at which he sat next to Rachel for comfort and mother had commented, "Like Robin Hood and his men, they gang up and snicker."

Peggy: What will happen at these dinners when Rachel is not there anymore? I worry about what will happen to your father when you're not there. He will be losing an ally.
Rachel: He won't assimilate.
Father: I don't understand what's going on. I don't think she's worried about me in every situation. Do you think about me when there's a party?
Rachel: Of course I'm concerned about you. It makes me feel bad when you're both unhappy.
Peggy: How do you know when either of them is unhappy? What are the signals?
Rachel: When I speak to mother I hear about things that aren't happy in her life, and vice versa. I don't think either of you should keep me out of it, though. You shouldn't try to hide it.
Peggy: Do you think you can be helpful to them?
Rachel: I could be—I don't think they think I care.
Mother: I don't think she doesn't care about us. She cares desperately. She's been very helpful, she picks up my spirits, talks to me when I'm feeling down.
Peggy: I guess you're not only worried about what will happen to your father when you're not there, but to your mother also.

Rachel agreed with this, and mother and father began to quarrel about their respective needs and sensitivities.

Peggy: (*Again using parental conflict as an opportunity to define why Rachel cannot leave home.*) What will happen when Rachel is not there?
Father: She's not there now.
Peggy: What is happening?
Father: We're having a bad time the last few months.
Peggy: Maybe you'd better go back home, Rachel.
Rachel: I'm not going home.
Mother: I don't want her home. We can straighten out our lives better without her there.
Peggy: Can you? Can you do it?

Father: But if she wanted to be home—I don't think we would—I don't—right, Helen?

Peggy: *(To Rachel.)* It's a tremendous temptation, isn't it?

Rachel: No. I don't really want to go back there. I don't.

Mother: I'm glad.

Peggy: I don't know. How are the two of you going to make it on your own?

Mother and Father: *(Together.)* I don't know.

Rachel: Do you think it's going to go on like this forever?

Father said again that it was no concern of hers, but Rachel kept insisting it was and that they try and work it out.

Rachel: I'd like it if you could both be happy.

Father: How could we do that?

Rachel: I don't know, but you're certainly not trying.

At this point I explained to father that during a previous session the group had counseled me not to help Rachel unless she agreed to release the responsibility of their unhappiness to me. I asked if he would be willing for me to take on that responsibility and he refused my offer. Mother then put pressure on father.

Mother: You see how Sam calls the shots? When you say you won't come here to help us, I'm at your mercy.

Father: I didn't want to start in the beginning. I've been through this and it didn't help.

Peggy: Yes, you told me that.

Mother: What bothers you? Do you feel vulnerable? Do you feel it is an undue expenditure? What is more important—an undue expenditure or our happiness?

Father: Why do I have to be put in the position of choosing on the basis of what is important?

Mother: There we are!

Father: So it's therapy or nothing?

Mother: Of course. It's not important—we're not important.

Peggy: You may be able to work it out without therapy, but what concerns me is are you going to be able to work it out without Rachel?

Mother: We should be able to go hang ourselves and have it not affect Rachel.

Peggy: But how are you going to keep Rachel out of it?

The parents argued and Rachel tried to mediate. The therapist took a break to have a consultation with the group.

Step 2: Dramatizing the Therapeutic Dilemma

The group agreed that if I continued to pressure father to come into therapy I would be siding with mother and he would resist more and more. We decided the group should support his autonomy and recommended that the burden of the parents' unhappiness should be passed to Sandy. Since Sandy was considered a superhuman being and this was a superhuman job, she seemed the appropriate person. I read the following message:

> The group, not having met Sam before, is impressed with his ability to take care of himself. Somehow, the family mythology had led us to believe otherwise. We trust mother has the strength to do the same. As for Rachel, she has carried the burden of her parents' unhappiness long enough and should now pass the burden to Sandy.

All three burst into laughter. Father asked if I had met Sandy, and I replied, "No, but I'm looking forward to it." Rachel said they were just talking about what a super person she was, and I replied, "Then we've chosen the right person for the job."

Father offered to keep coming to the sessions on the basis of helping Rachel but not to work on his relationship with his wife. Sandy accompanied the family to the following session.

STAGE IV
COPING WITH THE FORCES OF CHANGE

Step 1: Defining Change Within the Therapeutic Contract

Rachel began the session by reporting a sudden and unexpected change. She had started menstruating for the first time in a year and a half and gained several pounds. Following through on my definition of the problem, I gave father credit for convincing Rachel he could manage his life without her.

Rachel: I have to tell you something exciting that's happened. I got my period. It's very exciting.
Peggy: You did?
Rachel: Yes, at my sister's surprise party. (*Much laughter.*)
Peggy: Is this the first time?
Rachel: In a year and a half. I stopped expecting it.
Peggy: You've decided to become a woman?
Rachel: (*Laughingly.*) I'm considering it.
Peggy: You'd better think this over carefully.
Rachel: I know it's a big step.
Peggy: (*To the parents.*) Well, how do the two of you feel about what's happening to her?
Father: Very much relieved that she's on her own path. Things are becoming more normal—not altogether, but approaching it.
Peggy: You're not afraid you're going to lose your companion?
Father: No, I'm praying for it. (*Laughter.*) I was pleased that Rachel is approaching normalcy. She also said she gained three pounds. She is very happy about it. Didn't seem to worry about the three pounds.

Peggy: I think you did a very good job.

Father: I did?

Peggy: Yes, I think you did a very good job. Last time you were here you convinced Rachel you could manage your life without her, that you would be okay, that even if your marriage wasn't the greatest or if you didn't stay together that—.

Father: Well, we didn't tell these kids that yet. *(Referring to the other sisters.)*

Peggy: Well, but you told that to Rachel and I think you did an excellent job in assuring her you're going to be okay and that it's okay for her to become an independent woman.

Father: And in the last two weeks things are even better between Helen and me.

Sandy was informed of our having designated her to relieve Rachel of the burden of the parents' unhappiness. Everyone reacted with amusement. Sandy refused, saying she had a new baby and besides the parents seemed to be handling their own burden now.

STAGE V
COPING WITH THE FALLOUT
FROM CHANGE

Step 1: Defining Resistance Within the Therapeutic Framework

Neither Rachel nor her family were prepared for this amount of change and Rachel suffered a relapse. We immediately realized our mistake in not anticipating the consequences of change and predicting a relapse to lessen the chance of its occurrence. The family used the Jewish holidays as a way of recreating the family turmoil, with Rachel at the center. By refusing to go to synagogue on Passover, she created a minor crisis. Mother reacted in her characteristic fashion by provoking guilt, father tentatively supported Rachel, and Rachel became depressed to keep attention focused on her. She tearfully complained about her apartment, her job, the classes she was taking, and ended with: "There's nothing good about my life right now."

The whole family became involved in trying to analyze Rachel's depression and giving her helpful advice about how to pull herself out of it. Father brought up the inflammatory subject of Rachel not having gone to temple on Passover and asked if her depression was related to her feeling guilty. She denied this, and father stated: "That's good." Mother vehemently disagreed with him. During the following exchange they spoke simultaneously.

Mother: I don't think that's good, that's my problem. I see it as bad that Rachel, who loves us and whom we love, can do something to make us feel badly continuously and continuously—.

Father: That's something for us to get used to—.

Mother: When it would be good if she would do something to make us feel good.

Father: Helen—no—that's—(*Indecipherable.*)
Rachel: How can you expect me to do something I don't believe?
Father: Helen, that's something—(*Indecipherable.*)
Mother: But you do believe. You've told me you believe.
Father: Helen, she believes in a different way.
Rachel: But I don't. I believe in my fashion. I don't believe in keeping kosher, I don't believe in going to temple, I don't believe in dating Jewish boys, I don't believe that!
Mother: All right. And I believe, Rachel, that it is a sign of not quite loving us enough! I see it as a very selfish kind of act. You have no consideration. She's liable to do exactly what she wants to do because she doesn't want to please us. She's very rebellious.

Mother then went into a long harangue, giving a history of Rachel's rebelliousness. She ended up talking about how important the Jewish tradition was to her.

Mother: I've cried about the continuation of our Jewish tradition.
Rachel: I'm sorry, Mommy; you can cry and cry, but I'm not going to become more Jewish because you cry.
Mother: Therefore, then I don't think that you love us very much.
Rachel: Well, Mommy, if that's your criteria, then I really can't help you.
Mother: Okay, these are my feelings. That's my criteria. Yes.
Peggy: If she really loved you enough, she'd believe what you believe?
Mother: No, dear, no; because I know she believes. She's told me she believes. She believes in God. She says the most important prayer in our religion every night of her life, which I don't do.
Rachel: Why not? Don't you love me?
Mother: Rachel, stop shouting at me.
Peggy: You didn't answer her.
Mother: Why don't I say that prayer? Have you ever asked me to join you in that prayer?
Rachel: No, it's a private prayer. You're supposed to say it by yourself.
Mother: So why are you shouting at me?
Rachel: Why don't you say that prayer? You love me?

Mother accused Rachel of being sarcastic. I asked father if he felt the same way as mother about Rachel's not going to temple. He said he would like her to attend but didn't feel as intensely as his wife. I then asked Clare and Sandy if they had a problem becoming independent in this family, and both answered in the affirmative, describing the pressure and guilt that were applied to them throughout their lives. Asked how they dealt with this, Clare replied she didn't let her parents know about half of what she was doing, and Sandy said she always did what she wanted to do. Both parents were attacked for their rigidity, and the session ended with everyone quarrelling over who was most to blame.

The group was not present during this session and the family was told they would receive a message from them after they had seen the tape. In a consultation with the team, I defined the relapse as a systems problem rather than an individual one and sent the following message:

> It is the conviction of the group that Rachel has wisely decided she has not yet finished her job of diverting her parents from their unhappiness. Since Sandy and Clare have refused to accept this job, she should return home until it is completed.

It was then agreed that at the next session I would take a more lenient position regarding this message, encouraging Rachel's independence in opposition to an adamant position from the group, thus intensifying the triangle between therapist, family, and group.

Step 2: Shifting the Definition of the Problem

In the following session, Rachel adamantly refused to return home and the parents insisted they did not need her anymore to solve their marital problem. Rachel reacted to this exclusion by complaining about every aspect of her life—her job, her apartment, her boss, her feelings of isolation and loneliness. As she enumerated her complaints, the family, following their characteristic pattern, gave her "helpful" advice replete with platitudes about how to pull herself up by her own bootstraps.

We saw Rachel's litany of complaints as a reaction to giving up her important job of repairing her parent's marriage and decided to ask the family to allow her to mourn her leave taking rather than trying to cheer her up. This was impossible for them to do.

Peggy: The group has observed that Rachel's unhappiness seems to be a reproach to you and you're not allowing her to be unhappy. Rachel, they want to say that it's very important that you are unhappy and that your family allow you to be. How can you get them to allow you to be unhappy?

Rachel: I'll just have to keep away from them, I guess.

Father: Then we would worry about her.

Mother: I worry about my children, especially when they're alone.

Peggy: This is supposed to be a happy family, so it's difficult for you to allow anyone in the family to feel unhappy.

Mother: Are you speaking about a facade, Peggy?

Peggy: All families are supposed to be happy. This is a very close family, so it is very important for you to feel that everyone's happy. And when anyone is unhappy *(Mother sobs.)*, it's really hard, isn't it? How can you get mother to allow you to be unhappy?

Rachel: I don't know. I can't reassure her.

Mother: *(Sobbing.)* I worry about you every day.

Clare then jumped in to say she never told her mother her problems because she didn't want this kind of reaction. Mother and Clare became involved in a heated argument. Mother stated she couldn't help crying over her children's problems. I then focused the issue between the parents.

Peggy: Do you also cry over Sam's unhappiness?
Mother: Yes, a little bit. I do. He doesn't even know it.
Father: I don't believe it. I really don't believe it.
Mother: So I don't tell him.
Father: I don't believe it. *(The parents begin to argue.)*
Peggy: When do you cry over his unhappiness?
Mother: When I see that he is unhappy in his business, that he's unhappy with his partners, if I see he's unhappy in community situations, when he's hurting himself and feeling terrible about it. When I see he's unhappy in relation to Clare's husband and himself, when I see he's unhappy about his mother and sick brother-in-law, my heart hurts—and it's very hard for me to let him know it bothers me, and so I do it in my own little corner.
Peggy: *(Sympathetically.)* You cry over him without letting him know?
Mother: Cry tears? No. For my children I cry tears.

Step 3: Prescribing Enmeshment

The group discussed the futility of persuading mother to allow any of her children to be unhappy. Worrying over her children was an important life job. Rachel knew this and kept her mother involved with her by continually giving her something to worry about.

Rather than trying to diffuse this intense involvement, we decided to prescribe the family's enmeshment—but in a way that would involve father in the transaction. We added a task that shifted some of mother's involvement with her children toward her husband. Our purpose in doing this was to test the parents' readiness to bridge the gap in their relationship left by Rachel's departure.

Peggy: It is the group's conviction that I am asking the impossible by asking a mother with a heart as tender as Helen's to allow her children to suffer. *(As an aside, I say, "There are a lot of Jewish mothers out there." Mother waves in recognition.)* It is equally impossible for Rachel to break her mother's heart. We, therefore, recommend that Rachel call every day and tell her mother about her unhappiness. Mother should then share this with Sam, who should then comfort her. *(Mother cries, father reacts negatively.)*
Father: I don't want that kind of scene. I don't want her to call every day and make Helen unhappy and I don't want her to confide in me. I don't see anybody getting better from a thing like that.
Peggy: You won't do that for your wife and Rachel?
Father: *(Laughs.)* It's like a prescription.
Peggy: That's exactly what it is—a doctor's prescription.
Father: That's terrible, that's very bitter tasting.

Mother: Why is it so hard to comfort me?

Father: Helen, the whole idea doesn't—.

Mother: Why, honey? The only thing that's changed is the comfort, because she does call every day and unburden herself and I do listen.

Father: *(Surprised.)* You do call every day?

Mother: And I don't share it with you because I get the . . . *(She indicates with her thumb a downward movement.)* The only difference would be you would put your arm around me. *(She caresses him.)*

Clare: It would be nice if you were on mummy's side a little bit.

Father: I'm not not on her side.

Peggy: *(Earnestly.)* Sam, this is very important. Can you do that for Rachel—and for your wife?

Father: Sure I can do it.

Rachel did call her mother every day as requested, but mother became bored with her complaints, stopped trying to cheer her up and give her advice, and finally told her she would have to solve her problems herself

After this session, the parents took a month vacation, cutting the bond with Rachel more decisively. Threatened by this separation, Rachel moved back to their home where she felt isolated and lonely without her old job of mediator. She fell into a morose state and complained endlessly about her feelings of unhappiness and failure.

There is a myth in our profession that if parents get together and free the child from the position of mediator, the child will automatically spring forth mature, well adjusted, and symptom-free. This rarely happens since the child's social development has been retarded through his/her preoccupation with the parents' problems. The child usually goes through a period of feeling a loss of identity as he/she relinquishes this very important family position.

Our next task was to help Rachel find a different position for herself. But this could not be done in the same way the family had tried, through encouragement and helpful advice, since she only rebelled against this. We decided instead to use her rebellious streak in the service of change and to define her unhappiness and failure as her way of differentiating herself from her family, which placed such a high premium on happiness and success. We decided to enlist her sisters in helping her to accomplish this task. Rachel had never felt supported by them in her attempts to establish her autonomy, as the sisters often took the side of the parents in haranguing and pushing her. The support she received from them in this new alliance proved to be enormously beneficial.

STAGE VI
ENLISTING THE SIBLING SUBSYSTEM

Step 1: Forming a Coalition with the Sisters

The sisters were more than happy to continue to meet without the parents and quickly joined me in my position that Rachel needed to keep rebelling in order to establish her independence. In the following session, I continually reframed Rachel's complaints within this framework.

Rachel: I feel sapped at this point.
Peggy: Well, your parents certainly wouldn't approve of that.
Rachel: No. I have to keep going.
Peggy: That's right, and by being completely sapped you're saying no to them, which takes a lot of guts.
Sandy: *(Wistfully.)* That's really true.
Rachel: But I have no self-respect.
Peggy: Do your parents want you to have self-respect?
Rachel: I think so.
Peggy: And you're saying you don't have self-respect. You say your parents want you to be happy and you're saying, "I'm unhappy."
Rachel: My parents want me to gain weight.
Peggy: And you're staying thin.
Rachel: I've gained five pounds and I'm very upset about it.
Peggy: I can understand that because you feel you're losing ground with them, that you're doing something they'd like you to do, which makes you feel a nonperson.
Rachel: I should move to Kalamazoo, get the hell out of New York, and not even think of pleasing my parents.
Sandy: *(Now in full support.)* Listen to what Peggy is saying. You are living your life to displease them.
Rachel: I want to please myself.
Peggy: Well, you are because you're displeasing them. The most important thing in your life right now is to say no to your parents, and you've found many ways of doing that.
Rachel: I want to please me.
Peggy: Well, you are because you're displeasing them.

The session ended with the group suggesting that Rachel enlist the sisters' help in the planned rebellion, saying it was too much of a burden for her to think up these elaborate schemes herself. The sisters eagerly agreed, with Sandy stating that it would be good training for her.

Step 2: Differentiating from the Sisters

We failed to anticipate that Rachel would sense her sisters' help at pressuring her to change, since it was being given within the context of therapy. Before forming an alliance with them, she made it clear that she had to first rebel against their expectations of her progress in therapy. She did this by remaining depressed and making veiled suicide threats. I defined these threats as her way of differentiating herself from her sisters' expectations.

Clare: I feel angry. What Rachel is doing is hostility, talking about killing herself. Besides the fact I love her, I'm angry at her for doing it to me.

Rachel: Then maybe I'll just make believe things are okay.

Clare: Why can't I say what I feel?

Rachel: Maybe I have to work it out away from my family. There are too many expectations and pressures.

Clare: Who puts expectations on you?

Rachel: You all do. You all expect me to deal with my problems in a certain way.

Peggy: *(Supporting her attempt to differentiate from her sisters.)* I think that's true. You do expect her to deal with her problems in a particular way and Rachel is saying no to all of you. Not only no to her parents but to her sisters.

Rachel: I don't think so—maybe if I were getting pleasure out of it, I could think so.

Peggy: I know you're not getting pleasure out of it, that's not the purpose.

Rachel: What is the purpose?

Peggy: The purpose is to establish who you are, and that you are the one who says no to expectations.

Clare: You really calm down when we get upset, don't you?

Sandy: I noticed that last time. As soon as we get upset, you sit back. Maybe this is what you want. Maybe we have to prove we're so concerned, or maybe you want to shake us up.

Rachel: I'm not doing it to be dramatic.

Clare: Look at you. Five minutes ago you were crying and saying how miserable you were.

Rachel: *(Coolly.)* It doesn't take that much to make me go one way or the other. I don't know what it takes.

Clare: *(Heatedly.)* Bullshit! *(They argue.)*

Peggy: *(Defining this again as Rachel's way of rebelling against her sisters.)* I can understand why you're feeling better now, because you've just said no to your sisters and their expectations of you. I think you need to just keep doing that, Rachel, and to find other ways of doing it.

Rachel: I really don't get this whole thing.

I then enlisted the sisters in trying to think of more constructive ways for Rachel to rebel and asked about some of the ways they had successfully rebelled. Clare listed her rebellious acts as going out with married men, dating non-Jewish boys, letting her parents know when she was having sex, not joining B'nai B'rith, and so on. Rachel joined in listing her accomplishments, such as going without a bra, wearing pantyhose without panties, raising her voice in public. Sandy suddenly burst out with, "I enjoy talking about these things. It makes me feel good." The tense atmosphere changed to one of camaraderie and laughter as they banded together in discussing acts of "disloyalty."

Some questions might be raised as to the advisability of encouraging sisters to band together to form a coalition against parental control. The fact that the sisters were all adults rather than young children who are financially, physically, and emotionally dependent on their parents was a determining factor in this intervention. We would refrain from doing this with younger children with whom obedience to parental control is age appropriate.

Rachel's rebellious acts had always been accompanied by enormous guilt, and she therefore failed in each endeavor to become independent. By bringing her rebelliousness out into the open, planning it, condoning it, and scheduling it with the help of her sisters, we stripped off its more toxic aspects. Note that she then chose to rebel in relatively benign ways rather than those destructive to her health and well-being.

The parents returned from their vacation, and I telephoned to let them know we had not forgotten about them but had found the sessions with the sisters so helpful to Rachel we wanted to continue them for a while longer. I assured them they would be involved later on.

In the following sessions, I pushed the sibling alliance further and suggested Sandy teach Rachel how to become self-indulgent since Rachel emulated her father by being rigidly self-denying and frugal. Sandy coached her by instructing her to buy things she would never think of buying, such as expensive perfume, luxurious underwear, silk suits; jewelry, expensive cosmetics, and so on. I warned Rachel against indulging in food, however, and cautioned her against gaining too much weight. I set the limit at what Sandy weighed, nine pounds heavier, and thus,while seeming to restrain her, I actually encouraged her to gain. As they continued to discuss different modes of self-indulgence, some of the suggestions became outrageous, and I joined them in their frivolity and laughter.

The group interrupted to restrain me and to point out that the kind of rebellion I was suggesting was too enjoyable. I agreed with them that it was too soon to stop pushing the unhappiness prescription and I returned with the following message:

Peggy: *(Looking contrite.)* I have been reprimanded by my group.

Sandy: *(With dismay.)* Again, Peggy? You're doing badly.

Peggy: Yes, but I can see their point. They feel I got swept away in talking about things that would make Rachel happy, like being self-indulgent, buying expensive perfume, underwear, indulging in sex, because, Rachel, that would make you happy. And your parents would know you were happy.

Sandy: That makes sense to me. Does it to you, Rachel?

Rachel: It doesn't make sense to me. How does it make sense to you?

Sandy: Because if you're happy, Mummy will do what she did to me. She'll make you want to puke. She'll make more fuss over that than she does over you now. If you're unhappy on your job, you can quit, and that will make them unhappy. As the job goes on, you make a list of all the things that you can complain about, so even if you have some happy moments, don't talk about those. Go home and tell them about all the lousy things that happened to you today, and make their evening miserable, and that will make you miserable too.

Peggy: Good, good, very good.

At the end of the session the sisters gave the first indication of how they saw me in relation to the group. Although I had consistently told Rachel she must remain unhappy, they perceived me as being on Rachel's side. They picked up the second level of the paradoxical message.

Sandy: You have children, don't you Peggy?
Peggy: Yes. I have a son, 17, and a daughter, 21.
Sandy: Is your daughter why you keep on wanting Rachel to be happy? Do you identify a little? The group keeps reprimanding you for being too soft-hearted.
Peggy: I don't know. I'll think about that. It's hard for me to tell Rachel to be unhappy. *(To Rachel.)* Do you know that? *(I reach out a hand and touch her.)* It's hard for me to tell you to be unhappy— but I know they're right. When I think about it and I'm objective, I know that's what you must do.
Sandy: I guess that's what's good about having a group. They keep you objective.
Peggy: That's right.

STAGE VII
SAYING NO TO THERAPY

Step 1: Pushing the Prescription to the Breaking Point

This next session was the most crucial session in therapy, marking the turning point of a lasting change. Before Rachel could become a truly independent woman, she had to be able to say no to therapy and to the absurd task we had given her of keeping herself miserable. She had been conscientiously trying to follow it, but she was becoming more and more dissatisfied with living with her parents and remaining unhappy. During this session, I pushed the prescription to the point where Rachel said no to therapy.

Peggy: *(To Rachel.)* Well, Rachel, are you being unhappy, covering up what is pleasurable? How well are you doing that?
Rachel: I'm trying to cover up whatever's pleasurable.
Peggy: Good. How well are you doing in that?
Rachel: I'm trying to say no to all my mother's suggestions, and I hate it there. *(She cries.)*
Peggy: You're supposed to hate it there. Of course you hate it there.
Rachel: I feel so out of it there, I really can't stand it.
Peggy: You're going to be unhappy as long as you're at home.
Rachel: So why do I have to be there? I don't want to be there. I have this chance to sublease this apartment and I think I'm going to do it, if it works out.

Sandy: They're telling you to do something and if you're planning to rent an apartment in April you're just not listening again. And just like mother's going to have to be unhappy for a while until things get better, maybe you're going to have to be unhappy for a while.

Rachel: Why can't I get out of there? I want out.

Sandy: Well, you can't. So it's just too bad.

Rachel moans and groans and ends up looking imploringly at me with big, wet eyes, asking, "Why can't I sublease the place for just six months?"

Peggy: The harder it is for you now, the better.

Rachel: I don't understand it, and I can't go on like this.

Peggy: You won't understand it right now.

The sisters supported me and Rachel argued, finally screaming, "I can't stand it, and why do I have to force myself to be there?"

Peggy: *(Kindly but firmly, like a doctor administering medicine.)* For the time being, the worse it is, the better it will be. The worse it is now and the more unhappy you are, the better it is. So have your sisters been helping you with that?

Rachel: With being unhappy? No.

Sandy: We were supposed to—if she felt guilty doing something, she would call us.

Clare: She hasn't been calling me.

Peggy: How come you haven't been calling your sisters?

Rachel: Sometimes I don't feel like it because I'm frustrated and I don't like this. I feel like evaluating the situation and how to make things better, and instead I'm told to make things worse, and I can't stand that. I can't go against my instincts any longer.

Peggy: For the time being, Rachel, you have to make things worse.

Rachel: Well, I can't, Peggy. I want to go out and get a better job and I want to make myself happy. I can't make myself get a bad job and I can't make myself more unhappy.

Sandy: Is it necessary for her to stay with her present job to make her more unhappy?

Peggy: She should make herself unhappy in every way possible.

Sandy: Why?

Peggy: Because only in that way is she going to be able to find herself.

Clare: She is making my parents so dissatisfied with her they both stood there and smiled at me like dummies, they were so happy to see me. They never did this before. I looked so good in comparison with Rachel.

Peggy: Don't you appreciate what she's doing for you?

Clare: Yes. I felt I didn't deserve it.

Peggy: She's giving you a gift.

Clare: I guess so, so I shouldn't be mad. I feel guilty when I get mad at Rachel. This is my baby sister.

Peggy: No. Anything you can do to help Rachel be unhappy is fine.

Clare: Rachel is so self-involved right now.

Peggy: But she needs to be self-involved in her unhappiness. She should be totally preoccupied with it.

Rachel: *(Crying.)* I can't deal with people on that basis. This totally isolates me from the entire world. It's a ridiculous request to make. How am I supposed to relate to friends when I'm unhappy? Who the hell wants to be with me?

Peggy: *(Sympathetically.)* I know this is hard.

Rachel: This is crazy! Not hard—crazy! This means you're asking me to exist alone, to lock myself in my parents' basement and exist alone, because no one is going to want to be with me and I don't want to be with myself when I'm like this. It doesn't give me any reason for doing anything—any purpose for wanting to exist. It's making my existence so much more miserable.

Step 2: Escalating the Therapeutic Triangle

Peggy: Let me talk to my group a minute. Maybe they will allow you to do something that will relieve you a little bit. You seem to get into trouble, though, every time I relent . . .

The group decided not to relent but to take a position of consternation in relation to Rachel's rumbling of rebelliousness.

Peggy: The group says it sounds like you're not only saying no to your mother but you're getting ready to say no to me, and they are quite appalled. Are you saying no to me?

Rachel: *(Hesitates, and then blurts out.)* Yes, I am. *(Changes her mind.)* Not to you, to the group. *(She is not quite brave enough to risk alienating me, but she feels it's safe to take a position against the group since she knows I have sometimes disagreed with them.)* I'm fed up. I don't know what to do. My human instincts tell me to do something to make things happier, and you people are telling me to be unhappy, and I don't know how to relate to other people on that basis.

Peggy: *(Acting puzzled.)* That was the way you were relating to them for quite a while. Can't you just go back to that? Or stay there?

Rachel: No, I can't. I can't sit around and complain.

Peggy: But you have been doing that, so it's hard for me to understand what would be intolerable about it now, since you were doing that for quite a while. What's different about it now?

Rachel: Because I see it differently now. I see the world is not interested in me and my problems and it's not appropriate,

I dismissed myself to talk to the group, thinking it might be time for me to take a position in favor of change. It is decided I should first explore what Rachel would do if she were allowed to change.

Rachel: I don't know. All I know is I've really been trying the past few weeks to do what you told me to do and really work at it between sessions, and Peggy, I can't stand it! And I can't stand living with my parents. I'm regressing.

Peggy: *(Pursuing the question of change.)* What would happen if you said no to them and me? What would you do?

Rachel: I'd try to do what the rest of the world does—break away from home, become an adult, get a job, find my own place to live, find my own circle of friends.

Peggy: *(Challenging her to prove herself.)* But that's just what we're afraid of, Rachel. You know the consequences of that. You know what's happened every time you've attempted to do that. The results have been disastrous for you. You've felt you couldn't do it, felt like a failure, something has always gone wrong, you've felt lonely, isolated, that you were going crazy, the noises bothered you—it was a disaster, and we're trying to save you from that.

The group called me out and we decided it was time for me to side with Rachel against the group and push for change. When given her freedom to go forward, Rachel hesitated. The medicine I had been prescribing, despite its bad taste, was a comfort to her, giving her a sense of security. The sisters also registered some apprehension as to Rachel's ability to assume responsibility for her own happiness.

Step 3: Opposing the Group

I entered the room and asked Rachel to support my opposition to the group.

Peggy: Rachel, you want to help me say no to the group? I just had a big fight with them. I can't budge them. Let's you and me say no to the group.

Rachel: *(Tearfully.)* I was afraid when you went out there I was going to hear my sentence for the week.

Peggy: Are you ready to say no to them with me?

Rachel: What do they say?

Peggy: They're adamant. I cannot budge them. They say absolutely you should stay at home. You should be unhappy, should not make your life any better, should stay miserable, isolated, complain, not look for a job.

Rachel: Forget that. Forget that right there.

Peggy: *(Extending her hand.)* Thanks, thanks. I told them you had suffered enough, been unhappy enough, said no to Mother enough, and enough is enough. And you have the right, if you feel you can do something different, to try. And I want to say, "Go ahead."

Rachel: With what?

Peggy: With whatever you want to do. Whatever you want to do to make yourself happy, and we will know whether or not I'm right or the group is right.

Rachel now had a choice of siding with me by changing or letting the group win a victory by remaining the same.

Rachel: How about saying no to my parents?

Peggy: I think you've had enough of that.

Clare: Can't she say no when she wants to say no?

Peggy: Oh, that's fine; if you want to say no or if you want to say yes, feel free at this point to do whatever you want to do.

Rachel: *(Stunned at this sudden shift and not knowing how to respond.)* Are you sincere?

Peggy: I am.

Rachel: *(Apprehensively.)* What do they feel I'm going to gain from doing things their way? Because, Peggy, the only thing is that when I'm unsure and don't know what I'm doing I can say, "Well, my therapist told me to do this, so it must be what I'm supposed to do." So I just don't know.

Clare: You're taking all the supports away from Rachel by saying do whatever you want to do.

Peggy: You mean you feel the group is right?

Clare: I would say it's all right to say, "Do whatever you want to do" in certain directions, but I think you're pulling all the props out from under her by putting all the responsibility on Rachel. I feel she's not ready.

Peggy: What do you think, Sandy?

Sandy: I'm a little bit afraid for her.

Peggy: Do you think the group's right, too?

Sandy: I think they are too extreme.

Peggy: Maybe I just had a reaction against them.

Sandy: I think gradually. I look back on her life as being too much at one time and see her doing the same thing again. She'll have too many demands on her and expectations will be too great.

Peggy: Actually, then, the two of you are taking a position between me and the group.

Rachel: I'm also taking a position between the two.

Step 4: Supporting Autonomy

I then took the position that Rachel had the right to decide on her own how fast she should change.

Peggy: I think you're right. My position is extreme. I lost my head and got angry. I admire the fact that you were able to say no to the group and also to me just now, and to stop me from going too far. I think your judgment will guide you now as to how much pleasure and progress you allow yourself.

Her task had been changed from being unhappy and saying no to deciding on how rapidly to say yes. Thus, she was placed in charge of her own change.

STAGE VIII
SOLIDIFYING CHANGE

Step 1: Anticipating and Rehearsing a Regression

Having defied the therapists, Rachel took a giant step toward independence and in the following session described her new life. The group reminded me to schedule a regression in order to solidify change.

Clare and Sandy arrived for the session without Rachel, who was late for the first time having gone for a job interview. Sandy burst out with: "She's so happy. She's always happy. I've been under pressure lately, I've had a lot on my mind, and there's Rachel off being so happy, and I'm saying to myself, 'Goddammit, enough of this already with the smile.'"

Peggy: That must be quite an adjustment for you.
Clare: Even my mother and father commented on how happy Rachel is. I'm giving my parents problems now, so it takes the pressure off Rachel.
Peggy: That's terrific. What kind of problems?

Rachel entered, elegantly dressed and looking radiant.

Rachel: *(Glowingly.)* I'm having such a good time, Peggy. I can't believe it. I bought myself this silk suit. *(Proudly shows off an elegant and stylish suit.)* A hundred and fourteen bucks. I want to start being really good to myself.
Peggy: *(Cautiously.)* I'm afraid to be too enthusiastic because of my group.
Rachel: I'm afraid to be too enthusiastic too. I'm so happy I began to be afraid it wouldn't last. I don't want to be devastated. I haven't been this happy in years.
Peggy: What's making you so happy?

Rachel spoke excitedly about her new life. She was working on a magazine, getting published, meeting famous people, and doing something for the first time in her life that she really enjoyed. She had a chance to sublet an apartment for six months and was thinking about taking it. She felt she was making less frantic decisions, but looked apprehensively toward the mirror as she said, "I know the group won't like my moving." I said maybe they would change their minds now. She spoke about a new interesting man she was dating who looked like Woody Allen. I asked if her parents would approve of him and she said she was afraid they would. She discussed her problem of saying no to men for fear of hurting their feelings, and I asked her sisters to help her with this since they had had more experience. As I joined them in a humorous and intimate conversation, the group interrupted with a knock on the door and called me out to say they would like to take a position counter to the merriment and begin instead to worry about a regression. Passover was coming up and would probably create tension and conflict as it had last year. Also, Rachel was planning to move again and we could anticipate a recurrence of the former problems.

Peggy: The group is critical of me again. They feel we're having too good a time. *(The sisters boo.)* They are worried about what is going to happen on Passover or if you attempt to move again.

Rachel said she had already told her mother that she was not going to go to Seder on Passover. I asked her to anticipate her parents' reactions so she could be prepared for the worst. How might they draw her back into the fight between them? How could she deal with her guilt? How would she keep from siding with one against the other? What would happen to father at the dinners when she wasn't there to side with him against mother's family? Rachel replied, "I'll just have to give up that quest to please him." We went over all the possibilities carefully and Rachel said she was confident she could handle them.

Before the session ended I came back with one last warning from the group against premature optimism.

Peggy: The group is not as optimistic as we are. They anticipate you will get depressed again, and this will probably occur around Passover or if you move. They recommend, therefore, that you deliberately allow yourself to get depressed on those two occasions.
Rachel: What if I'm not?
Peggy: Try to feel that way. Try to go back to the way you were feeling or— *(Loud groans and laughter from everyone.)* You don't have to go all the way back.
Rachel: You don't know what you're asking. I want to be able to deal with these times.
Peggy: Then practice them.
Rachel: Okay.

We decided it was time now to involve the parents again as we anticipated they would have a reaction to the new Rachel.

The whole family was convened for this session. Rachel looked stunning with a new hairstyle, new clothes, new makeup, and a radiant expression on her face. She began the interview with:

Rachel: I'm great. I've never been greater.
Peggy: Tell me about it.
Rachel: Number one—I'm in love.
Peggy: In love? Not with a man? *(Laughter.)*
Rachel: Yes, with a man—with a really nice man.
Peggy: Jewish?
Rachel: *(Chagrined.)* Yes. That's his only drawback, but he didn't want a Jewish woman either, so we decided we'd overlook it. We don't have those attributes we were trying to avoid.
Peggy: Well, at least it's equal.
Father: Maybe you'll both convert. *(Much laughter.)*
Rachel: He's the one who looks like Woody Allen. Things are working out nicely. He's very kind and sensitive. Lots of fun. He loves me, and

I'm living in Manhattan doing publicity work and I have a lot of promising job prospects.

Both parents expressed their pleasure over the changes in Rachel and only once attempted to use her new romance as a focal point for an old argument between the two of them.

Step 2: Redefining the Marital Relationship

It was quite clear now that the parents would never have a tranquil relationship but would probably go on fighting for the rest of their days. The important thing was that Rachel was no longer involved in their battles. She managed to stay out of this one and I described the parents' relationship as a profound and lasting bond between two stalwart, equally matched opponents who had strong and differing points of view and felt free to express them on every subject. Since it was their way of making love, they certainly didn't need any interference from anyone outside. Father, surprisingly, agreed, saying, "After all is said and done, we are meant for each other." And mother conceded that there must be something they enjoyed about fighting since they were always doing it.

An appointment was made for one month later, and I stated this would give us time to see if Rachel could stay out of her parents' love making. If she felt her parents needed a third party, she should call one of her sisters and ask them to be the third member. The sisters vociferously declined.

STAGE IX
PRESCRIBING A FAREWELL RITUAL

In a presession discussion we decided that if Rachel had managed to maintain her gains, we would ceremonialize her leave taking by prescribing a farewell ritual.

The family reported things *were* going well and the parents declared it was a relief to have Rachel out of the home as it was more peaceful. The session was spent giving the family credit for the changes that had been made, anticipating future trouble spots, and making some suggestions as to how to avoid them. The session ended with my suggesting they plan a farewell party to celebrate Rachel's becoming a woman and leaving home, and that father should propose a toast to send her on her way. They responded positively and Sandy suggested they have a broomstick for Rachel to jump over, as in Jewish weddings, symbolizing the beginning of a new life.

FOLLOW-UP

A one-, two-, and three-year follow-up revealed Rachel still in good spirits, living alone in her own apartment and loving it, excited about her new career, and dating several different men. The parents were still making love in their characteristic way, but the three sisters were staying out of it.

Editors' Introduction

This case illustrates an eclectic approach and one way in which meditation can be used as a tool in psychotherapy. Deane Shapiro teaches meditation, a technique often associated with Asian approaches to personal growth, in the context of a behavioral approach to therapy that also addresses client insight and the importance of interpersonal relationships in understanding this client's depression and insomnia.

Shapiro uses the case to point out the parallels between meditation and hypnosis, another technique used in many different schools of psychotherapy. While Shapiro presents meditation to this particular client in the context of self-management, transpersonal and humanistic psychologists are likely to frame the experience in terms of personal growth and transcendence. Although the theoretical explanations for the efficacy of the technique may vary across orientations, instruction in the actual practice of meditation is fairly consistent across practitioners.

This case describes a common clinical scenario: a motivated client who presents with multiple concerns including the desire to minimize or eliminate the use of psychotropic medication. The client's problems include insomnia, a lack of assertion skills, excessive self-criticism, poor stress management skills, and vocational problems. The sense of mastery associated with the development of skill in meditation appears to have generalized and had a positive influence on many of these concerns. The case reminds us that few clients, few problems, and few approaches to therapy are as tidy as our theories suggest.

MEDITATION AND PSYCHOTHERAPY: A CASE STUDY

Deane H. Shapiro, Jr.

THE ORIENTATION OF THE THERAPIST

I remember being asked my religious orientation in a religious studies class at Stanford. I wrote: a Jewish existentialist with Zen Buddhist inclinations. My clinical orientation is similarly complex. It is behavioral, insofar as that implies belief in the importance of carefully evaluating the efficacy of my clinical work (rather than adherence to a specific body of techniques). It is also behavioral in that it involves an emphasis on action-oriented therapy, a setting of goals with the client, the collection of data, working on change—behavioral or cognitive—i.e. new ways of acting, thinking, feeling about the world and oneself. It is insight-oriented insofar as that means that a client's understanding of his/her behavior, thoughts, actions, habit patterns is important, rather than *a priori* assuming historical insight into psychosexual stages is needed. It is relationship oriented—I believe trust, empathy, and understanding provide a critical context for therapeutic change. However, I do not believe, in general, that relationship is sufficient, and do not believe it should be the focus of therapy, except as it facilitates changes the client is trying to make outside of the therapeutic context. Finally, it is religious, spiritual, transpersonal, insofar as this means I am committed to my own personal growth and work, believe in working toward developing myself toward the farther reaches of my potential, desire to find a core connection between myself and others, and have experienced feelings of unity and oneness with nature, myself, and others. It does not mean I believe all clients should experience this; that there is only one path to its experience; or that it is an *a priori*, true reality, but rather one which I believe to be true, part of my path of heart: a belief system that, for now, *works* to nourish and sustain me.

Thus my orientation is really a combination of personal, clinical, and religious elements. Interestingly, at the risk of being an overly "general" armchair philosopher, it appears to me that for many, there is a large overlap between the psychological and religious. Scientists and psychotherapists have, for many in our culture, become a type of guru: priests of a technological and secular age.

To label my orientation, we could say I am an applied pragmatic behaviorist who believes in relationship, insight, and spiritual growth, all with appropriate reservations!

THE THERAPIST'S BELIEF IN THE EFFICACY OF THE STRATEGY

I believe meditation to be a useful self-regulation strategy for certain clients with certain clinical problems. I do not believe meditation to be any more (or less) effective than other self-regulation strategies for a client who wishes some type of stress-management strategy. My decision to use it (rather than other strategies) would depend upon the client's belief system, values, and expectations. Further, I do not feel a particular need to call a cognitive focusing strategy "meditation" if a client has a resistance to that term either because of prior religious training, or dislike of its "mystical" association. I am also not convinced, at the level of actual behavior, how different meditation is from other cognitive strategies. As Ted Barber noted,

> The overlap between self-hypnosis and meditation is tremendous. In fact, it seems to me that the variability within self-hypnosis and meditation is almost as large as the variability between these procedures. There seems to me to be so many parallels that it appears possible to at least conceptualize self-hypnosis as one type of meditation, or vice versa, meditation as one type of self-hypnosis.

It should be noted, however, that for me we are talking here only about meditation as a self-regulation strategy, and its use for clients who wish some form of training for a stress-related problem.

THE CLIENT AND PRESENTING PROBLEM

James Sidney, an Australian male in his mid-thirties, was a short, rather unassuming individual, with a kind and sensitive face. When he introduced himself to me, he shook my hand, but didn't directly make eye contact. Although he had a pronounced accent, his speech was clear and lucid, but his voice was often so soft that I could not hear his words. When we sat down, he said, "I have a problem with insomnia, and wondered if you could teach me meditation." He said he knew of my clinical interest in meditation, and on the recommendation of a mutual colleague on the East Coast, presented himself to me to learn an approach to meditation that was not immersed in "cultic" paraphernalia: incense, pictures of gurus, candles, etc.

I told him that yes, I would be glad to teach him meditation and work with him on the issue of insomnia. As one way of doing this, I told him it would be helpful for me to get to know him a bit better and to learn what he had heard about and expected from meditation.

Clinical Note

I have three goals in obtaining this information. First, before teaching a technique to a client, it is important to gather information about the client's expectations, hopes, motivation for learning a particular technique. Second, I interact with this information in a way which attempts to build a trusting relationship between us. I believes this relationship provides an important context for the teaching of technique and skill training. Without the trust, the teaching of any technique, whether meditation or a behavioral strategy, is more difficult. Third, I want to obtain some initial background information about the client, as well as a broader profile of what other issues may currently be going on in this client's life that may be relevant to therapy.

Overview of Therapy Duration

This client was seen for ten months. The first six months we met once a week; the next two months, once every other week, and then I saw him twice at three-week intervals. There was a six-month, written follow-up. The sessions were face to face in the office and involved homework assignments and data collection outside the office.

CLIENT EXPECTATIONS

The client noted he had heard and read in the newspaper about the scientific experiments showing meditation's effectiveness for stress and felt it would be helpful for him. He said that he was not particularly interested in the "spiritual mumbo-jumbo" that went along with the technique. He noted that although raised a Catholic. he had had no formal religious affiliation for several years. "I consider myself more interested in down-to-earth human concerns than metaphysical issues."

CLIENT BACKGROUND

The client noted he used to sleep about eight or nine hours a night, but that a couple of years ago, for no reason he was aware of, he began to wake up during the night. He began to awaken with increasing frequency per night during the next six months, and finally decided to go into therapy. He noted that he was in therapy for the next six months, and that the therapy focused almost exclusively on trying to understand his dreams. The therapist indicated that the sleep disturbance was only a "symptom." After six months of dream analysis and no improvement, and even some deterioration in sleep, he left therapy. The therapist told him he was not giving the process long enough, and was only leaving now out of fear of confronting the really deep, true material.

The client then began taking Valium (5–10 mg. nightly) and had been doing so for the year prior to our first meeting. He came in now because the insomnia problem seemed quite bad, he felt tired and tense at night from fear of not going to sleep; and during the day from lack of sleep. He also had read and been told that it was not good for him to continue to use Valium every night.

Over the next few therapy sessions, I learned the following information. In addition to the issue of insomnia (Concern Number 1), he was quite shy and unassertive. He noted that he had almost no contact with either his own or the opposite sex. Further, it was hard for him to be assertive, particularly with his family. He had two brothers, and both parents were living. He felt quite pushed around, "bullied" by the older brother, and ignored and not attended to by the father. The mother was somewhat distant and he had never really felt too close to her. The issue of shyness and assertiveness became Concern Number 2. The client also noted he was quite self-critical, frequently noting in the session how poorly he did almost everything (Concern Number 3); felt stress a high proportion of the time during the day (Concern Number 4), and finally that he was an administrative assistant in business, currently out of work and having difficulty finding a new job, partly because of a poor recommendation from his previous employer (Concern Number 5).

CLIENT MOTIVATION

The client felt his general weariness and stress from lack of sleep had reached "crisis proportions" and something needed to be done. He noted he was quite willing to learn and practice the technique of meditation.

The client initially appeared highly motivated to me and this was borne out in the course of therapy. Initial concurrent evidence of this motivation and ability to adhere to self-regulation practice was a special diet he was put on by his physician for a phosphorous imbalance. He had to be extremely careful about his eating behavior and monitor closely his intake. He followed this diet meticulously.

During therapy he maintained accurate and complete records of the home-work assignments of areas monitored, practiced meditation exactly as instructed, and put a great deal of personal effort and energy into each problem we worked on.

BASELINE DATA

Because of the behavioral part of my orientation, I felt it important to have the client gather data (i.e., monitor) in diary and/or chart form, on each of the areas of concern: i.e., the frequency, nature, duration of the target behav-iors. This baseline data for each of the areas of concern is discussed below.

Concern Number One: Sleep Behavior

As noted, the client stated that he used to sleep seven to eight hours a night, believed he currently was getting only three to four hours of sleep per night, if that; and felt he needed at least six to seven hours. To assess current sleep patterns we monitored length of night, amount of time asleep, number of times awoke, length of time awake, and whether or not he took Valium that night.

From a two-week baseline we found that this client on an average was sleeping a mean of 5.8 hours, was waking about 4.14 times, and was up 1.53 hours (i.e., twenty-seven minutes per time). The kinds of things that awoke him were: (a) anticipation of a noisy neighbor coming in; (b) actual noise from a neighbor (e.g., jogging upstairs, loud music); (c) a bad dream; (d) no actual incident. We also noted that Saturday nights were particu-larly difficult, partly because of the general noise in his apartment complex. During each week of the two-week baseline, the client took Valium on six of seven nights.

Concern Number Two: Companionship/Assertiveness Skills

The client was asked to monitor the amount of his social interactions not related to job searching. The first week, he noted that his only companionship was a hitch-hiker to whom he had given a ride. The next week, it was his brother on the phone, the one he felt nagged him too much—about his health, about not having a job. When asked how he responded, he said he didn't say anything to the brother about the nagging. We discussed the client's fear of being pushed around, being taken advantage of and used both by his family and by potential acquaintances.

The client also noted that he really didn't want to have people back to his apartment because others might think it was sterile and unattractive, "just because it is neat, clean, and totally bare." He said he didn't feel any need to fix it up and artificially put "his stamp on it." He also noted that he seemed to have a response of ignoring (or pretending to ignore) insults or put-downs of other people and then all of a sudden to "snap" (his word) and become ag-gressive and verbally angry.

Concern Number Three:
Positive and Negative Self-Thoughts

The first week of monitoring positive and negative thoughts, the client noted that his thoughts were primarily negative and that every time he had a positive thought (e.g., my piano playing sounds good), he followed it with a negative statement (e.g., who cares?).

Concern Number Four:
Stress/Relaxation Experiences

A fourth area of monitoring was stress—times when he felt stress (antecedents, behaviors, consequences). He felt he was always pushing himself—what's going to happen next; how will I cope with tomorrow? Stress for him included physical symptoms of tight jaws, back, and shoulders. Mentally, he would block everyone out and ignore them. Stress frequently occurred for him when he felt there was too much to do with too little time. We also looked at times when he felt relaxed: when he was walking alone and sometimes when reading.

Concern Number Five: Job

The final area of monitoring was to look at behaviors he engaged in that led him toward finding a new job and how that process felt to him.

INTERVENTIONS

Thus, after the first few weeks, a more complete picture of this person began to emerge, and we began to work together to set goals in each of the areas of concern and develop appropriate intervention strategies to help him meet these goals.

Meditation

In structuring a treatment intervention, I try to relate the client's concern to the research literature, to see what interventions have and have not been effective with this type of problem. To my knowledge there is only one study in the clinical literature on meditation and insomnia (Concern Number One). Although there are methodological problems with the study (measuring sleep onset and sleep duration), meditation was shown to be as effective as progressive relaxation in treating insomnia, and both were more effective than a non-treatment control. Further, as there are problems with drug dependence and as the client requested to learn meditation, it seemed to be the treatment of choice for the sleep problem. Further, it was hoped, with appropriate cueing and practice, that the relaxation aspect of meditation would generalize to other high-stress times in this client's life (Concern Number Four: Stress).

Clinical Note: Client Background Information

Before actually teaching meditation, the therapist should have made a careful assessment of the client's feelings, hopes, and expectations. Why did the client come into therapy? What is his/her concern? Is the client willing to take responsibility for that concern? How committed is the client (i.e., how motivated to change)? What is the client's vision of what might (can) happen if he or she does try to change? Does the client fear failure? Why? What are ways the client might sabotage his or her own efforts to change? Does the client fear success? Why? What are the client's reactions to "meditation"? Is there a fear of it, e.g., as mystical? Why? Does the client fear being controlled or losing control? Is there an attraction to meditation? Why? Is the client motivated by the idea of learning to yield and let go of thoughts? A cognitive avoidance? Or a hope for growth? Is the client willing to trust him or herself with an essentially non-analytical technique?

After this assessment, the therapist should determine whether meditation is indicated or contraindicated.

Characteristics of This Client That May Be Helpful for Meditation

First, the client requested meditation. Second, the research literature suggests its effectiveness for insomnia and stress management. Third, the client's anxiety was primarily cognitive. The client was highly motivated and once he made a decision would stick to it and therefore would probably score high in internal locus of control, and also fit a personality profile of inward-directed, relatively neutral affect (one which correlates with success in meditation).

Potential Contraindications

The client seemed shy and of low affect. Meditation as a sole strategy might merely reinforce that behavior pattern. Further the client was a "perfectionist" and might apply these same standards to the technique, perhaps being too self-critical.

If an individual has negative association to the term "meditation," I feel no need to try to convince the client that it is an effective strategy and that the client should change his or her beliefs. Rather, as noted earlier, I would rather change the label—e.g., calling it a relaxation technique, a cognitive (attention) focusing strategy, etc.*

---

*Earlier, before I would screen clients for their reactions to meditation, I had an interesting experience teaching meditation as part of a relaxation group in a psychiatric ward at the V.A. Hospital. A patient leaped up and ran out of the room shouting, "You're trying to steal my mind with Eastern witchcraft."

Assuming the client does want to learn meditation, what do I then tell them in terms of outcome results and practice?

Clinical Note: "Demand" Characteristics Outcome Results and Practice

Because I believe it therapeutically beneficial to create positive expectancies, I often find it useful to share in lay terms these results. In this particular case I noted, "I think your choice of meditation for dealing with insomnia and general stress is a good one, for it has in fact been found to be effective for these types of concerns."

However, I also feel it important to state that meditation is not a magical panacea, and that the effects from meditation are a result of practice. I ask if the client is willing to give it a chance to work. "Normally, you should begin to feel a significant reduction in stress and anxiety within four to ten weeks. Are you willing to practice the technique on a regular basis for at least that period of time?" If the answer is yes, I spend some time talking about, planning when, and visualizing where the person might have an opportunity to practice on a daily basis. If the answer is equivocal, I spend some tune on this issue, again stressing the importance of practice and talking with the client about how much effort they are willing to expend to deal with their concern. Before teaching a strategy, I do try to get some form of commitment from the client.

Relationship Issues

By this time there should also be at least the initial development of trust and rapport between the therapist and client. As noted, the therapist should be aware that techniques appear to be more effective if offered within a context of trust and support. Because exploring one's self, with any strategy, can be frightening, the therapist's gentleness and encouragement in this process are crucial.

Selection of a Meditation Technique

The research literature on this point is not yet very helpful. For example, we do not yet know whether individuals with certain strong perceptual representational systems (e.g., visual, auditory, tactile, etc.) would be better off with an object of meditation which either is or is not in that same representational system (e.g., should an "auditory" person utilize a mantra or a mandala?). The biofeedback literature indicates that relaxation is facilitated if the feedback is in the non-preferred mode: i.e., biofeedback is more effective for an auditory person receiving visual feedback than for an auditory person receiving auditory feedback. However, Davidson and Schwartz suggest that an object of concentration in the same mode as the problem is preferred. If a person has too many thoughts, he or she should attend to a verbal focus such as a mantra, koan, etc. Further, there is some question about whether individuals would be better off learning concentrative versus mindfulness meditation, or both; and if both, in which sequence. The classical literature says first concentration, then mindfulness.

Instructions

This client was initially instructed in breath meditation, including counting one through ten, and asked to practice twice a day, twenty minutes each session. Why breath meditation? There is no empirically valid rationale for choosing this particular meditation technique over any other. Personally, it is the one I was taught in the Orient, and clinically, it is the one with which I am most experienced. At this point, there seems no clear-cut reason not to utilize the meditation technique with which a clinician feels most comfortable.

I generally spend part of two or three sessions instructing clients and having them practice the technique in the office. There are particular signs of "correct" practice I look for, and particular areas of the "teaching" that I believe important to emphasize.

One question often raised is when, in relation to the therapy session, should the person meditate? Carrington and Ephron have described having individuals meditate right before a treatment session so that whatever material may surface would be available for that therapeutic session. I have a meditation room next to my office where individuals can meditate prior to the session, for reasons similar to Carrington and Ephron's, as well as after the session, as a way of attempting to make sure that anything which is dealt with in the therapy session, which may be painful, might just be observed for a certain period of time during the meditation session without undue analysis. Meditation sessions before and after, even though brief, seem to serve also as a helpful transition, both preceding therapy and following therapy before returning to the "real world."

Why a Tape?

In addition to the verbal instructions and practice in the office, I also often give clients a tape to utilize at home. The tape follows the instructions in the office and provides a time frame of twenty minutes. I do this as a way of facilitating practice at home. There are two potential advantages to the tape. (1) The tape repeats the office instructions, and thus provides clients an opportunity to re-check in case they feel they have forgotten or are not practicing correctly. This helps avoid the statement the following week of "I didn't remember exactly how to do it so thought I would wait till our next appointment." (2) The tape is structured with a successive approximation to silence. The first part contains dialogue of instruction followed by a thirty-second silence, then re-instructions to keep focused on breathing, followed by a ninety-second silence; then briefer re-instructions, followed by a ten-minute silence. Many people find this gradual approach to silence more comforting than just abruptly sitting down and counting breaths. Some people, how-ever, find the instructions a disruptive, external intrusion. Therefore, in my instruction to the use of the tape. I note that some people find the tape helpful to facilitate their practice, by keeping them from having to worry about time boundaries, etc. I ask them to try it and if they find it helpful initially, to continue to use it. I note, however, that once they feel comfortable they can practice on their own schedule and time, using the tape only as a checkup when and if they feel it appropriate.

James's Experiences During Meditation

A general description follows of the issues that occurred during the nine months of meditation practice and how they were dealt with.

First Month

After the first week of practice, James noted tension in his face that he had not realized was there and also how hard it was for him to be attentive and re-laxed. In the morning he felt his heart beat slowly and heavily, but not in the evening—then he got restless. He noted that the tape kept him sitting. This points out one of the potential initial issues in working with a client in med-itation: that initially a certain discipline is necessary. Generally, he said, by the end of the tape, even though he was not aware of the process by which it happened, he felt more relaxed and refreshed. He noted, "It's easier with the tape than without it." Without it, he said, he felt too time-conscious.

Several times in the first month he noted that he felt "energetic" during meditation—a positive contrast to the lethargy he often felt during the day. The nature of the thoughts that occurred were generally of a "planning ahead" nature, such as people he had talked to or he was planning to talk to. Nice images included flowers, trees, mountains, birds. Sometimes he said he felt sad, lonely, and withdrawn.

Clinical Note

The above comments raise several important issues. First, what should you instruct a client to do with thoughts—either positive ones or aversive ones? I agree with the recommendation of Glueck and Stroebel that when ideas that seem important to the therapeutic session come up during meditation, the meditator is to treat them like any other thought and return to the meditation focus or "anchor."

In other words, the client is instructed to merely observe the thought, no-tice any feelings associated with it, watch it and when he or she is ready, to return the focus to the breathing. In the therapy session, we then would spend time discussing issues or insights resulting from meditation. For example, the client's strong awareness of his/her feelings of loneliness became part of the incentive and motivation for him to decide to risk practicing social skills. The positive images gave us helpful information about useful competing responses to the aversive, fearful images in the evening of not being able to fall asleep.

It should be noted that Easterners say we should let go of thoughts when we meditate. They criticize the Western approach of thinking about thoughts and say that many Westerners believe they are meditating when in fact they are only performing therapy on themselves. My feeling is that a balance is needed. During meditation I believe, as noted, that it is best to let thoughts go. In meditation as a clinical self-regulation strategy, we can learn to see what issues come into awareness, feel how salient they are (i.e., how attached we are to them); watch them with equanimity, and then let them go. However, I believe that after meditation, in therapy, the talking about, discussing, analyzing the issues, antecedents, consequences, etc., is important to facilitate change. The East would say let it all go. The West would say analyze it when it comes up. I think. sequentially, both approaches are possible and useful.

A second important issue is the "anxiety about anxiety" that often can occur when people initially meditate. They become aware of how tense they are (e.g., face tension for this client), how restless they are, and how inattentive their minds are. Here the therapist's reassurance that "this is part of the process" is important.

Third, it should be noted that there is a certain discipline needed for the practice of meditation. For this client the tape helped, i.e., kept him sitting, so that by the end he felt more relaxed.

Next Four Months

These were generally positive sessions for the client in which he experimented with a variety of cognitive strategies—self instructions, imagery, etc. The client noted that the best way for him to let go of thoughts was an image of a window in his mind's eye. He meditated on one side of the window in the room (in his mind); outside the window was a pasture with cows. He opened the window and let the thoughts fly out to pasture to graze with the cows, or let the thoughts "drift away" like kites without a string.

He also said he generally looked forward to the meditation practice, felt it refreshing, that it gave some structure to his days, and to him, a sense of competence. He learned about his thought process, realizing which thoughts he felt were more important (i.e., he was more attached to) because these thoughts had a higher emotional charge and it was harder to let them go.

Sixth to Ninth Month

At the start of the sixth month of meditation he said he was attaining deeper levels of meditation; that he liked it, in general, and yet he was noticing more thoughts and he felt he was more distracted than when he had initially begun. After six months of meditating, we shifted from counting one through ten to just counting one after each out-breath. He said he did not like this as much as there was too little structure, and so we returned to counting one through ten. He noticed, however, that there was still a constant stream of thought and he was becoming angry at himself for this, feeling a failure every time a thought occurred.

We discussed the importance of acceptance. I re-emphasized that "if thoughts come, that's okay, if they do not, that's okay, too." I tried to get the client to view meditation as a process of acceptance of what is and help him become aware of how he was bringing "old" behavior patterns to the practice, and applying "perfectionist" (goal-oriented, accomplishment-oriented) standards to meditation. We explained how this could, in fact, just be a way of setting himself up for failure. The image he liked was one which recognized the discipline it takes to practice meditation while trying to stay calm: "A fighter who meditates acceptingly." After two more months, he noted that he was fighting the meditation less and becoming more accepting of where he was with the process. He still noted that at times he felt inundated by his mind: "I can only turn it off . . . so seldom, it feels keyed-up, planning, worrying, finding chores to do." During the positive times he said his hands felt warm and good. They turned into furry, soft, heavy paws.

At this point I suggested he choose his own length of meditation. If he felt distracted and not able to meditate well, not to force it. It was all right to just stop after a few minutes. Again, it was a process of acceptance, not a goal of "reaching the end of the tape." He found this helpful, and sometimes he meditated more, sometimes less, "Not to fight it, to give up if thoughts get away from me."

Clinical Note

It is important to note the issue of balance involved here. Initially, I believe a certain discipline is necessary to give a self-control strategy like meditation a chance. However, we need to be careful that the discipline does not turn into a compulsive rigidity: "I must practice twenty minutes or I'm a failure," etc. The therapist needs to be sensitive to when to encourage the discipline, and when to encourage the letting go of "rigid" standards, e.g., you "should," "it is 'better' if you can practice twenty minutes twice a day." Further, as noted, the therapist can utilize this information to explore with clients their psychological patterns and styles as an aid to therapeutic learning.

Non-Meditation Interventions, by Concern Areas

Let us now turn to each of the five specific concerns of this client and note how other interventions, in addition to meditation, were utilized to help him accomplish his goals.

Concern Number One: Insomnia

The client's general insomnia-related goals, on coming into therapy, were to lose his dread of going to sleep at night, increase sleep to at least six to seven hours per night, stop taking Valium, and as a by-product, feel more relaxed and rested during the working day.

After the two-week baseline, the client realized he was getting much more sleep than he had thought. This self-observation in and of itself, therefore, became an intervention, and helped the client to feel more confident about his sleep problems. A second intervention was my telling the client, "When you are lying in bed, either initially or after awakening, you should remember that resting quietly is as good as sleeping. So don't worry about being awake. Just let yourself lie there and relax." The client noted that it really helped him to say this statement. (This cognitive restructuring was a strategy taught to me by my father when I was a child!) As the client noted, "I am practicing relaxing and meditating, and I'm getting pretty good at it. I'm not dreading going to sleep as much. It's good to know I'm getting an adequate amount of sleep."

In addition to the regular meditation practice twice a day, the client used the focused breathing and counting as a general relaxation strategy while lying in bed beginning to go to sleep. Besides meditation, the baseline observation, and the cognitive restructuring strategy, this client also used humming, listening to an ocean record, and pep-talks (self-instructions) to deal with the anxiety and fear associated with sleep and the racing future-planning thoughts that would keep him tense and lying awake.

Another sleep-related issue the client had which we monitored during the initial few weeks was the amount of Valium that he took. The first two weeks he went one night each week without it; the third week, two nights; the fourth week, three nights. The fourth week of three nights without Valium was quite difficult for the client and in the following few weeks he resumed taking it every night. However, since the client was sleeping between five and six hours per night and felt comfortable with this, the sleep issue faded into the background and, with only minor spot checking (weeks six through ten, week fourteen), we turned to the other areas of concern.

At week twenty-one, we returned to the sleep issue, particularly in relation to Valium consumption. The client was feeling quite confident about his sleep patterns and wanted to work on stopping the Valium. We decided to take a "successive approximation approach," beginning by not taking it two nights of the week.

While going off Valium he gave himself the following self-instructions, "I am practicing relaxing, meditating, so I'm getting pretty good at this. I am not taking that much Valium anyway; don't force it; let it go. If I can't get to sleep right away, it's not a big thing. Practice and be gentle on yourself as you try something new."

Weeks twenty-one through thirty-one involved working on decreasing the number of evenings in which Valium was taken. He gradually tapered off Valium, until in the last two weeks, he took it only twice.

This felt like a comfortable level to the client—to take it if he needed it, or felt in trouble, but to first practice the strategies mentioned above.

Interestingly, the sleep data revealed that often the client slept as well with or without Valium. These data charts helped him realize that in many ways the Valium was merely a "psychological" aid, one which in fact did not seem to help him on a regular basis—many nights he would sleep better (i.e., more sleep time, less awakenings, less time up per awakening) without Valium than with it. However, we agreed that sometimes, when needed, there was certainly no problem with taking it.

In summary, for this client in the area of concern about sleep, the following observations are in order. The actual amount of sleep per night, on the average, did not change throughout the course of therapy, ranging from a low of $\bar{x} = 4.8$ hours in week twenty-six, to a high of $\bar{x} = 6.28$ hours in week five. If anything, there is a slight, though non-significant downward trend in the data, indicating slightly less sleep per week. However, the client reported feeling quite pleased about this area of concern, noting that his fear of going to sleep had lessened, his ability to stay relaxed when he woke up during the night improved, and he was able to substantially reduce his Valium intake.

Concern Number Two: Assertive-Companionship

After several sessions of not dealing directly with this issue because it was too anxiety provoking, we began to talk about companionship and meeting other people. The client got in touch with the "dread" of meeting other people, the fear of being taken advantage of, the fear of getting into hassles with other people, and not wanting to snap, and yet not wanting to be passive either. Yet, he acknowledged that he did have a desire to meet new people. Therefore, we made lists of places where there would be the opportunity of meeting new people. He refused to go to bars, so we came up with the YMCA, a dance-movement class, and a singing and music appreciation class. After exploring several options, he did join a music appreciation class. There he noted that he had a "freedom reflex," i.e., if somebody approached him, his "gut response" was to hide, to feel trapped, and to abruptly end the conversation.

Over the course of the music class, he was able to approach and initiate conversation with several people of both sexes. In addition, he was able to stand up in front of the group and sing, a risk-taking behavior he had not believed possible.

Another issue he raised was his feeling that all the people he seemed to meet were merely acquaintances (superficial). He also realized how lonely, depressed, and withdrawn he felt and decided it was worth the risk to try to meet other people.

Our goals for companionship were twofold: 1) to increase the number of people (quantity) from the baseline of zero to three or four, and 2) a later goal was added of increasing the depth of intimate experience.

We made weekly tasks, beginning with inviting one acquaintance to lunch. We made a list of current acquaintances—there were three—and several times in the office we role-played asking each of them out to lunch. After three months he had gone out with each several times and felt comfortable about it. However, he felt the conversations were still too superficial, so we began, at least "loosely," to operationalize what was meant by a "more intimate conversation."

It should be noted that at the same time I agreed to work cooperatively with this client on the goal of developing "deeper" relationships I also requested that we spend part of our sessions acknowledging the enormous progress that had been made over baseline in even asking people to lunch!

The client felt, by the end of therapy, that he was able to improve the depth of sharing with two of his "acquaintances," and felt genuine intimacy was occurring with greater frequency in their conversations.

Toward the end of the therapy session he noted that in general he felt more natural being with people, although he still had a gut feeling that he did not contact people very well and the would not really be interested in getting to know him. He admitted that although he could do it, he still did not enjoy taking the initiative and felt it an enormous strain on him. The reason he was willing to take the risk is that he balanced strain against the fear and the dislike of the isolation. He also noted that he did feel *more* confident and more able to non-defensively take criticism than before.

Finally, on the issue of assertiveness, he confronted his parents and expressed his feelings of hurt and not feeling cared for; and was able to ask his brother tactfully not to nag him about his health problems, his job, or lack thereof, and to explore other areas to communicate about. Although he noted relapses, a falling back into "my old docile, trying-to-please self," he generally was able to behave much more assertively, both with his family, and at work, to "not be afraid to say what *I* feel."

Concern Number Three: Positive and Negative Self-Statements

This was a theme that ran throughout this client's life. His critical, perfectionistic standards got in his way whether trying to learn to meditate, meet new people, or perform a job correctly. Here we worked on increasing positive self-thoughts, in particular, and on "sprucing up" his appearance and environment.

He agreed to "fix up the apartment" for himself—a candle, a couple of green plants, flowers, a Sierra Club calendar. He also decided to take more pride in his appearance: new clothes, getting his hair cut stylishly, grooming himself. He noted, "I am beginning to feel more confident more often although it is so hard for me to justify 'pampering' myself. Am I really worth it?" We worked on catching the "critical" self and using these statements as cues for positive ones. We made a list of the positive qualities he had: intelligence, sense of humor, thoughtfulness, musical ability, a good sense of rhythm. Homework for a while was at least one positive thought per day more than the number of critical thoughts.

He also realized a need to be gentler on himself—not to be always pushing for meeting new people. Sometimes it was all right to feel comfortable being alone, a self-retreat or a self-nurturance; to walk, to swing, to play the piano, or to read. Or, as we discussed earlier with meditation, not needing to have a *perfectly* "empty" mind.

Concern Number Four: Stress/Relaxation

First, we worked on generalizing the relaxation from formal meditation to other times throughout the day. We did this by recognizing antecedents to stress, and also by using the behavior of stress as a cue for relaxation (focused breathing, coping self-instructions, and imagery).

Concern Number Five: Job

He did get a job in May after eight months of conscientious searching. It included several different simultaneous demands: phoning, typing, filing. His perfectionist side rebelled. We worked on generalizing the "accepting" attitude of meditation, and stress-management strategies of focused breathing, coping self-instructions, etc. At work he found it easier to set limits on what he could accomplish by being more assertive with others and more accepting of his own limits. He found that people did not reject him when he did set the limits.

DID MEDITATION AND THERAPY WORK EFFECTIVELY FOR THIS CLIENT?

The client noted at the end of therapy that he was smiling more, seeing more colors in the world, holding his head higher, hearing the wind, taking the time to look at things. A six-month follow-up revealed that the client still felt good about his sleeping patterns; used Valium only infrequently (once every two or three weeks); continued to see the friends he had made on a weekly or more frequent basis; practiced meditation at least once, and generally twice a day; and felt much less stress throughout the day.

Why?

He attributed this success both to meditation and to his excitement at working on the companionship area. Yet I could also, with a certain justification, add the issue of dealing assertively with his familial relationship, increased pride in his appearance, and finding a job. Meditation did seem a useful and powerful therapeutic tool for this client. However, we must recognize it as one technique among many. On an applied clinical and empirical level, we do not really know much more than that.

The client learned the skill of being able to observe thoughts, watch them with relative equanimity and eventually let them go. In this way, high-affect issues were diffused. This is a mechanism involved in many therapeutic approaches. For example, the task of the therapist, as Freud noted in his *Studies in Hysteria*, is to help the patient assume objectivity to his own dilemma. This was done by making the patient into an intellectual collaborator, and by showing the patient that he had nothing to fear by revealing the true memories. And Rogers noted that by fulfilling certain conditions of interpersonal warmth and acceptance, the therapist creates an interpersonal situation in which material may come into the client's awareness and in which "the client can see his own attitudes, confusions, ambivalences and perceptions accurately expressed by another, but stripped away of their complications of emotion. This allows the client to see himself objectively, to see that these feelings are accepted and are acceptable, and paves the way for acceptance into the self of all these clients. The therapist helps the client to see that the client is a person who is competent to direct himself and who can experience all of himself without guilt." From a behavioral perspective, classical systematic desensitization involves having a person observe, in a relaxed way, issues that normally cause distress. This results in extinction of the maladaptive affective charge associated with the fear or phobia.

Similarly, meditation helped give this client a perceptual clarity on events in his life, and with a lessened affect. This may have allowed him to face so many aspects of himself as quickly as he did. Emphasis on meditation therapy is on detachment (objective assessment) and not a manipulation of the environment. This increased equanimity may have helped in the decrease of negative thoughts (Concern Three); the reduction of stress (Concern Four); and the ability to deal more calmly and acceptingly with the number of job-related inputs. This affect-reduction and acceptance might have also been helpful in giving the client the inner strength to be more assertive with others. Further meditation in many ways seemed to help give this client a sense of mastery and control, a sense of increased self-esteem at his success. It also afforded him a "portable" relaxation technique to help him cope with his "generalized anxiety," and a technique he could use any place at any time.

But I believe meditation was only part of the reason for the therapeutic success. Another part was that the client, feeling more confident, was willing to have his affect *raised* and to take risks. He was willing to be assertive with his family, take the initiative to invite people to lunch or to talk with them. The social-skill and assertive-skill training also seemed a critical element in this case. Further, the baseline data and goal-setting seemed to help with his perfectionist style. It showed him the progress he had made so that he was literally forced to acknowledge improvement, even though his preference would have been to ignore (forget) improvement and only focus on the next mountain. Finally, the client himself was very highly motivated, the therapeutic relationship was an accepting one, and the therapist seemed to be both trusted and respected.

SUMMARY CLINICAL NOTES

In this case there were several areas of concern, individual strands of this person's life. They were not all tackled simultaneously. Sometimes more time in a session would be spent on one issue, sometimes another. However, all of the areas of concern together were important in the fabric of this person's life, and to have had the focus of therapy exclusively on only one would, I feel, have done a therapeutic injustice to this individual.

The following points, illustrated by the case of James, need to be kept in mind when using meditation as a self-regulation strategy with a client.

The client initially presented a problem area of insomnia and requested meditation; however, meditation was not offered as a technique until the context of his life was better understood and his reasons (expectations) for wanting to learn it were made clear. Clinicians need to gather such contextual information to insure that they understand the full scope of the problem and that there are not reasons why meditation might be contraindicated. Second, meditation was not taught as a unimodal strategy for insomnia, but one technique among many. Third, meditation was taught within a therapeutic context of trust. Fourth, additional techniques, which seemed useful for other areas of this person's life (ranging from assertiveness training to role-playing social skills) were also utilized. I do not believe that meditation alone would have been sufficiently therapeutic for this client. Clinicians need to be careful in matching therapeutic interventions individually and as appropriate to the presenting concerns. Finally, careful evaluation and assessment seem important to determine whether the technique-therapy is having its desired effect. If not, why not? What changes can be made? The above comments are standard operating procedures for all good therapists. If meditation is to be considered as a therapeutic treatment, the same guidelines apply.

INDEX

Acting *as if*, 45
Addiction to therapy, 146, 185
Adler, Alfred, 23, 24, 26, 41
Adlerian psychology, explanation of, 23–24, 47
Adlerian psychotherapy, 22–47
  confrontation and, 40
  dream analysis in, 45–46
  forming a relationship in, 25–27
  modifying convictions of patient in, 32–46
  use of Life Style Assessment, 27–29, 32
Affective disparity, 8
Agoraphobia, 25, 183, 188, 191
Alcohol problems, 24, 82, 84, 184
Alfred Adler Institute of Chicago, 24
Alternative therapy, 121–22
Analytical psychotherapy, 49–55
  dealing with hatred of patient, 53
  dream analysis in, 49–51
  intimacy with patient in, 54–55
Antithetical modes of apperception, 34
Anxiety, 146, 148–49, 152, 183, 188, 191
Assertiveness difficulties, 228, 229, 238–39
Aversive scenes, 112–114
Awareness of experience, 57–60

Barber, Ted, 226
Barlow, David, 106
BASIC I.D., 187, 190–91
Beck, Aaron, 118
Behavior therapy, 106–16, 184
  assessment, 109–11
  behavior analysis, 109–11
  treatment program, 111–14
  results of, 114–15
Borderline personality disorder, 2–20
Boyer, L. Bryce, 2, 22

Carrington, Patricia, 233
Change
  coping with, 206–09
  modifying convictions and, 24, 32–46
  resistance to, 207–09
  setting terms for, 202–03
  solidifying, 220–222
Closure, 122
Coercive persuasion, 192. *See also* Propaganda
Cognitive relabeling, 188
Cognitive therapy, 118–35
  questioning, 121, 122–23

broadening patient perspective, 121, 123–25
alternative therapy, 121–22, 125–29, 133–35
obtaining accurate data, 122
closure, 122, 129–33
Compulsive behaviors, 183, 189, 191
Conflicting therapies, receiving, 193
Confrontation in the therapeutic relationship, 40
Connecting symptom with family system, 200–01
Control issues, 26–27, 38–39
Convictions, modifying, 32–46
Cooperation of patient, gaining, 186
Countertransference, 51, 61, 136–60
Covert sensitization, 106–16
Current Psychotherapies, 106, 136

Data
importance of gathering, 229
obtaining accurate, 121, 122
Davidson, Richard J., 232
Death
acceptance of, 14
fear of, 148–49, 154–55, 190
of a parent, 153–54, 184
Defining the problem, 25–27
Dependency, 133–34
Didactic strategy, 128
Dream analysis
in Adlerian psychotherapy, 45–46
in analytical psychotherapy, 49–51
in contemporary psychoanalysis, 11, 12, 15, 19
in existential therapy, 151, 155
in Gestalt therapy, 163–81
in REBT, 95–96
Dreikurs, Rudolf, 24
Duration of therapy, 227

Ego-bolstering, 90
Ellis, Albert, 80, 118, 189
Empirical test, 135
Emptiness, psychological, 146
Enmeshment, 183, 195, 210–11
Ephron, Harmon, 233
Existential Psychotherapy (Yalom), 136
Existential psychotherapy, 136–60
dream analysis in, 151, 154, 155
patient assumption for responsibility in, 142–143
process versus content, 143
use of group therapy, 148, 150
termination of therapy, 157–60
Experiencing of the self, 57–60

Family therapy, 189, 194–222
Fear, 39–40, 83, 183, 191

of failure, 94
of rejection, 99–100
Flashbacks, 153
Freud, Sigmund, 241
Frigidity, 5, 53
Fusion, 7

Game of Probabilities," 46
Gestalt therapy, 162–81
Glueck, Bernard C., 234
Greek Chorus, 194
Grief, 156
Group therapy, 148–49, 163–65
Guilt, 43–44, 86, 89–90, 195, 198

Hatred, feelings of, 69–75
Homosexuality, 25, 38–39
Horney, Karen, 189
Human nature as positive force, 67–69
Hypothesis, forming a, 196–200

Imagery
coping, 188
use of, 42, 110
Individual Psychology, 23
Inferiority complex, 37, 41, 43
Information gathering stage, 196–200, 227
Insomnia, 228, 229, 230, 237–38
Irrational beliefs, disputing client's, 85–88, 90, 91–93, 95–97, 98–104, 118, 120–21, 128

Isolation, 146–47

Job related problems, 25, 228, 230, 240

Learning in therapy, 64
Life Style Assessment, 27, 28–32, 47
Lifestyle, investigating and interpreting client's, 24
Love's Executioner (Yalom), 136

Maniacci, Michael, 22
Martyr complex, 5, 29, 195
Masturbation, 3, 12, 18, 50, 153
May, Rollo, 136, 141
Meditation, 224–242
client expectations of, 227, 231
contraindications for, 231
effect of, 240–41
efficacy of, 226
other interventions to complement, 236–40
technique, selection of, 232–33
Modifying convictions, 32–46
Mosak, Harold, 22
Mother, controlling, 184, 192, 198
Motivation of patient, 185, 228–29
Motivation to change, 109

Multimodal therapy, 183–193
Multimodal Life History Questionnaire, 186
Multiple psychotherapy, 28

Neurosis, 26, 41–42
Nightmares, 5, 132, 154

Obesity, 136–60. *See also* Weight problems
Objectivity of therapist, 14
Obsessive-compulsive neurosis, 5

Panic attacks, 154, 184
Papp, Peggy, 194
Patient feedback about session, 134
Paul, Gordon, 186
Pedophilia, 106–16
Perfectionism, 83–84, 93, 197, 231, 236,
    239–40
Perls, Frederick S., 162
Person-centered therapy, 57–78
    affectual relationship, experiencing, 60–64
    awareness of experience in, 57–60
    becoming one's organism in, 76–78
    liking of one's self, 64–67
    positive nature of mankind, discovery of,
        67–75
Perspective, changing patient's, 121, 123–25,
    127
Phobias, 25, 183
Primary process thinking, 8, 12
Probabilities, suggesting for patient, 127
Process versus content, 143
Projective identification, 9, 10
Promiscuity, 6, 12, 29, 82
Propaganda, therapist's use of, 95
Psychoanalysis
    of borderline patient, 2–20
    disadvantages of, 91
    dream analysis in, 11, 12, 15, 19

"Question, The," 26
Questioning
    appropriate, 120
    dialogue, 103–04
    to obtain vital information, 121

Rank, Otto, 147, 157
Rational Emotive Behavior Therapy (REBT),
    80–107
    attacking client's irrational views, 85–88,
        90, 91–93, 95–97, 98–105
    dream analysis in, 97–98
    emphasis on value system of client, 92
    gathering background information, 82–84
    hypothesizing in, 88–89
    quick implementation of, 93
    propaganda, use of, 93–94
    versus other dynamic systems of
        psychology, 88

Rationalizations, 109
Rebellion, 197
Regression, 151, 220–22
Rehearsal, 191
Reinforcing client, 91, 129, 133
Rejection
    of children by mother, 6, 51–52
    fear of, 42
    of therapy, 215–219
Relationship with client
    forming a, 24, 25–27
    emotional, 14, 60–64, 140–41, 232
    fear of attack and, 9–10
    disdain for patient in, 51–52, 137–60
    anger in, 53, 150–51, 155
Repetitive teaching, 91
Resistance to changes brought about by
    therapy, 207–9
Responsibility, assumption of by patient, 142
Retrospective hypothesis–testing, 131–32
Rewarding client, 91
Rogers, Carl, 56, 90, 157, 241
Role playing, 191, 163–81

Schwartz, Gary, 232
Self, complete examination of, 72–75
Self-acceptance, 64–67
Sensory experience, therapy as, 76
Separation of client and therapist, 13, 15, 17,
    54
Sexual activities of parents, effect on
    children, 14, 16, 18–19
Sexual fantasies, 18, 152
Sexual identity, 152–53
Shapiro, Deane, 224
Sibling relationships, 211–15
Smith, Olive, 156
Social interest, 47
"Spitting in the soup," 40
Splitting, 9, 10, 12
Stress, 228, 230, 240
Stroebel, Charles, 234
Studies in Hysteria (Freud), 241
"Style of life," 23
Suicidal patient, 13, 119–35

Termination of therapy
    in analytical psychotherapy, 55
    in contemporary psychoanalysis, 19–20
    in existential psychotherapy, 158–60
    in family therapy, 222
    preset date for, 157
Theory and Practice of Group Psychotherapy
    (Yalom), 136
Therapeutic contract, 203–07
    change within, 206–07
Therapeutic dilemma
    defining, 201–02
    dramatizing, 205–06

Therapist
  emotional relationship with patient, 14,
    60–64, 140–41, 232
  fear of attack by patients, 9–10
  feeling of disdain for patient, 51–52,
    137–60
  orientation of, 225–26
  patient anger toward, 53, 150–51, 155
  wrong hypothesis of, 88–89
Therapy
  addiction to, 146, 185
  alternative, 121–22
  behavior, 106–16, 184
  group, 148–49
  as a sensory experience, 76
  setting terms for, 201–3
  as a visceral experience, 76–78
Tracking, 188–89
Transference, 53–55, 61

Unconditional acceptance, 100
Unconditional positive regard, 90

Value system of client, 90
Visceral experience, therapy as, 76–78

Weight problems, 25. *See also* Obesity

Yalom, Irvin, 136